HOSTING MEGA EVENTS IN ISLAND MICRO STATES
STATES
BARBADOS AND THE GOLF WORLD CUP

Wendy Sealy, PhD

DEDICATION

This book is dedicated to my family. My nephews, Jemarr, David and Derrick thanks for keeping my company on msn messenger when I was lonely. And last, but not least, I dedicate the completion of this project to my brothers Eyre and Terry Sealy, my mother Myrtle Sealy and my sisters-in-law Miranda and Jocelyn. To my mum, thank you for making the decision to send me to private schools. That decision has played a significant role in my academic and professional development. I really appreciate your prayers and support. To my deceased father, Martin Greaves, thank you for raising me to be the best that I can be. God bless you all.

ABOUT THIS BOOK

The hosting of major hallmark and mega events continues to be a contentious issue as we embark into the 21st century. This book will provide the reader with a trans-historical account of the emergent issues that have been the subject of much debate in this area. It will be particularly useful to scholars, students and industry professionals who wish to gain an introductory but pragmatic understanding of the complexities and caveats of this controversial industry.

The issues addressed in this book are of an organic nature and is based on research conducted on the island of Barbados in December of 2006. As some of the narratives contained herein are of a sensitive nature these could not have been published before. The book contains rich narratives in the linguistic style of the respondents that are insightful, controversial and at times humorous.

This book is organised into seven chapters. While the introduction provides a background to the purpose behind the investigation, the methodological issues are dealt with in chapter two. The philosophical underpinnings of this project and the eclectic data collection strategies are discussed in microscopic detail. This chapter will be particularly useful to scholars who are struggling to understand the basics of qualitative research methods, particularly ethnography and the engrained limitations.

Chapter three explores the different theoretical and multi-dimensional approaches to analysing the impacts of mega events as expounded by leading scholars and experts in this discipline. This chapter also discusses the many controversies involved with the staging of mega events from a media and image perspective. In this regard many of the caveats expounded by researchers concerning the media value of mega events are examined.

Chapter four provides the reader with an introduction to tourism in Barbados. The historical forces that shaped the Barbados society as well as the evolutionary trajectory of the tourism industry are examined. The chapter draws on the work conducted on island tourism by critically examining the views of diverse thinkers in the academic sphere. The chapter also provides the reader with a history of event tourism in Barbados and the Golf World Cup. This chapter will also provide an overview of the issues that are typically associated with the management of tourism in peripheral and insular areas.

Chapter five allows the international tourists' voices to be heard. It presents a discussion from the perspective of the international tourists which is presented in their own words with special attention being paid to the factors that influenced their decision to visit the island and their overall perception of the Golf World Cup event. Chapter six is concerned with the logic behind the hosting of the Golf World Cup as extrapolated from semi-structured interviews with tourism officials. This chapter will also address how the perception of Sandy Lane and the image of golf as an elitist sport influenced the participation of local residents. A major discovery in this research is the concept of social exclusion. An in-depth exposition of its nature in relation to this event will be expounded. Other issues identified during the fieldwork from a local perspective concerned the influence of sport stars on visitation; selective perception and the challenge of 'event saturation' on the destination. The final chapter contains recommendations for the marketing and management of event tourism in Barbados. Several themes are reviewed and recommendations are made for further research.

Those persons embarking on any form of qualitative research may find this book a useful tool on how to structure and report qualitative findings. It is hoped that the sharing of this information will motivate further investigation and will assist in the learning and teaching of event and tourism management in schools, colleges and universities.

TABLE OF CONTENTS

1 -CHAPTER ONE
INTRODUCTION, OBJECTIVES AND RATIONALE OF STUDY

1.1 INTRODUCTION AND AIMS

The growth in spectator sports has drawn increasing attention to the area of sport event tourism. High profile sport events are usually defined in the academic literature as 'mega events' (Delpy, 1998; Getz, 1997; Hall, 1992a). The term 'mega event' refers to events that, due to their scale and media interest, are capable of attracting a significant number of visitors, media coverage and economic benefits for the host destination (Koh and Jackson, 2006). In tourism organisations, events combined with strategic public relations programmes have become popular destination marketing tools (Coathup, 1999; Font, 1997; Laws, 1991; Ritchie, 1984).

Sport events in particular have become a major component of the destination marketing mix (Emery, 2002; Gibson, 1998; Hennessey, 1992; Ritchie, 1984). Bramwell (1997: 168) claims that these events are seen as significant tourist assets because they encourage increased general visitation to the host area. The attention that they receive in the media through news stories and advertising can constitute added exposure for the host location that fosters an interest to visit (Hede, 2005; Kim and Chalip, 2004; Ritchie, 1984). They can also attract participants and spectators, thus boosting the number of visitors to the host destination during the event and they provide an opportunity for locals to become involved through volunteering and as spectators.

The staging of sport events in Barbados has been attracting considerable debate on the island (Legacy Barbados, 2006; National Strategic Plan, 2005; Sustainable Tourism Policy, 2002) to the extent that the staging of high profile events has now become part of a national development strategy aimed at diversifying the tourism product in the light of the increasing competitiveness of the global tourism industry. The hosting of events has been identified as a major marketing tool for the island to entice visitors and to preserve the island's upmarket image.

The island of Barbados is located at the southern end of the archipelago that makes up the islands of the eastern Caribbean at 480 kilometres north of Guyana in South America, 160 kilometres east of

1

St. Vincent, and 965 kilometres south east of Puerto Rico, with a total land area of 430 square kilometres. In 2006 the estimated population stood at 270,000 individuals (Barbados Government Information Service, 2006) thereby making it one of the smallest, single, sovereign, microstates in the Caribbean at that time.

In 2006, Barbados hosted the World Golf Championships - Barbados World Cup (Golf World Cup), an annual event of the Professional Golfers Association (PGA). This event featured some of the world's top golfers who represented a total of 24 nations, including the host country. The 2006 Golf World Cup was sponsored by the Barbados Tourism Authority and generated significant press interest attracting around 200 journalists to the island with broadcasts in more than 140 countries by networks including ESPN and ABC in the United States and Sky Sports in the United Kingdom and Ireland. The Golf World Cup, which was initially projected to attract over 8000 foreign visitors, was played at one of the three golf courses at the Sandy Lane Resort in St. James, Barbados. It is the first PGA golf competition ever staged on the island and this is the first time that Barbados, despite having staged many events before, had staged a large scaled biddable, internationally owned event. Puerto Rico, a United States of America offshore territory, is the only other Caribbean island to have hosted the Golf World Cup in 1961 and 1994.

The staging of the 2006 Golf World Cup in Barbados provided an opportunity for an in-depth analysis of a major sporting event on the island. This study was therefore concerned with exploring the expectations and perceptions that specific stakeholder groups had of the Golf World Cup. The stakeholder groups that were the focus of this study included the international tourists visiting Barbados at the time of the Golf World Cup and local tourism stakeholders.

1.1.1 Aims and Objectives

The dearth of knowledge on the stakeholder perspective of mega events has inspired the aim of this study which is to identify the issues associated with the marketing and management of a mega event in Barbados through the exploration of stakeholders' perceptions and expectations. This study sought to identify these issues by exploring how individuals on the island of Barbados perceived the Golf World Cup. This study focuses on two distinct stakeholder groups: the international tourists and local tourism stakeholders and residents. A total of 85 research participants were interviewed across the two groups. Case study participants included senior managers of tourism and event organizations, public sector sports officials, hotel managers, local residents and international tourists visiting Barbados at the time of the Golf World Cup. To fulfil the aim of this study, this research needed to achieve the following objectives:

> To explore the perceptions and expectations held of the Golf World Cup by international tourists.

> To explore the perceptions and expectations held of the Golf World Cup by local tourism stakeholders and residents

> To establish a policy and research framework for the development of sport event tourism in Barbados.

A stakeholder can be regarded as anyone who has a legitimate interest in an organisation's activities and has the power to affect the organisation's performance. Tourism planners have recognised the value of the application of stakeholder theory to tourism planning (Buhalis, 2000; Masterman, 2004; Swarbrooke, 1999). No longer is stakeholder theory just an ethical business management tool but is a vital component of management and marketing strategies. Marketing and management strategies need to be modified depending on the stakeholder group targeted. Stakeholder groups are heterogeneous, context specific and hold vastly different missions and value platforms (Buhalis, 2000; Fredline, 2000). Stakeholders differ in how they approach tourism development and each group may have completely different goals and conflicting agendas, which can pose challenges for tourism planners. Getz (2000a) for instance, notes that event values differ among the various stakeholders - the sponsors, the community, organisers, the competitors and supporting agencies. He notes that failure or success means different things to different people.

The potential list of tourism stakeholders is endless, thereby creating the challenge of synergising each group's needs and expectations into event planning models (Buhalis, 2000). Swarbrooke (1999) identified eight stakeholder groups for sustainable tourism development - the host community, governmental bodies, the tourists, tourism industry operators, pressure groups, media, voluntary sector and commercial experts. He describes the host community groups as those employed in the industry directly, those not directly employed in the industry and local business people. Governmental bodies include, supra governmental organisations, national governments, regional councils and local government. Tourism industry operators have been grouped with tour operator businesses, visitor attractions, transport

3

operators, retail travel operators and the hospitality sector businesses. Media includes all aspects of the travel media and news agencies. Swarbrooke (1999) recognises the value of commercial consultants and academics under the heading of commercial experts while the voluntary sector includes non-governmental organisations in developing countries, and environmental charities. The value of the tourist as a stakeholder is recognised by Masterman (2004). For him, these stakeholders can be vital to an event's success since they travel and spend money at the event. This research also recognises the vast importance of the tourists to the success of any event, thus, the reason for including them in the stakeholder groups studied.

In the midst of such diversity it is no surprise that few researchers have explored stakeholder perceptions with regards to event tourism. As Godfrey (1998: 215) reinforces, "to date there is scant research on the views and opinions of those most likely to play the co-ordinating function of tourism management in destination communities". Predominantly, studies in event tourism have tended to focus on just one stakeholder group, mainly the host community residents, rather than the perceptions of various groups within a given context. There is, therefore, a lack of comparative work regarding different perceptions at various levels of the event industry.

1.2 BACKGROUND TO MEGA EVENTS

Although there is controversy in the literature as to exactly what constitutes a mega event, mega events are generally defined as "those events that are so large that they affect whole economies and reverberate in the global media" (Bowdin, McDonnell, Allen and O'Toole, 1999:16). Laws (1993: 97) defines mega events as significant tools for tourism promotion and describing them as "large events of world importance and high profile which have a major impact on the image of the host city"[1].

Roche (1994:7) notes that "mega-events are short-term events with long-term consequences". The benefits for the host destination are that the staging of mega-events, will result in the visitation of spectators and increased investment and other tourism benefits as a result of the related media exposure the host destination is afforded (Chalip, Green and Hill, 2003; Hede, 2005; Hede and Jado, 2005). The media provides destinations with the opportunity to create positive

---

[1]   See chapter 3 for a complete exposition on the definitional problems associated with mega events.

4

images that will act as an impetus to visitation for the event or in the future (Kim and Chalip, 2004; Light, 1996). However, some events also capitalize on the 'prestige' and 'glamour' factor to attract visitors to the destination and the actual event itself (Hall, 1992a; Laws, 1993).

The hosting of mega events is also gaining currency as they are perceived to produce net positive gains for the local community in terms of the 'psychic income' (Gibson, 1998; Waitt, 2003). These include the euphoria, community attachment, volunteering and civic pride that are the result of hosting the event. It is also argued that the physical structures that are developed to host the event can benefit the local community through increased participation in sport and they can be used for the hosting of future sporting or cultural events (Chalip, 1998; Essex and Chalkley, 1998). Furthermore, it is often stressed that local communities can benefit from other legacies such as city beautification and other infrastructural developments stimulated by the event (Masterman, 2004). Other socio-cultural outcomes could include unity within the host community and the chance to meet foreign visitors (Kim and Petrick, 2005).

However, other perspectives relay concerns about the contradictory effects of hosting mega events. One concern is that too much money is spent on preparing a location to host a major event in circumstances where the expected benefits may not be derived. There is an increasing body of literature about mega sport events failing to meet the expectations of host communities. Some opponents are of the view that mega events can result in increased debt for the host communities as well as other negative socio-cultural impacts (Higham, 1999; Kang and Perdue, 1994; Shapcott, 1998) including violation of human rights and general inconveniences caused by infrastructure development which discourages support for and participation in the event (Hall, 1992a; Higham, 1999). Researchers have also made reference to cases where tourism arrivals were not realised resulting in the under-utilisation of tourist related facilities and services (Jones, 2001; Pyo, Cook and Howell, 1991; Teigland, 1999). Thus, research into the impacts of mega events has pointed out significant gaps between forecast and actual outcomes, between economic and non-economic rewards, between the experience of mega-events in advanced and in developing societies (Gratton, Shibli and Coleman, 2006; Hall, 2006; Horne and Manzenreiter, 2006; Jones, 2001; Whitson and Horne, 2006). As a result, questions still remain about the trade-offs and opportunity costs of hosting mega events. Do such events ultimately deliver the benefits, tourism, social and otherwise,

5

that their proponents proclaim? How do visitors perceive the experience of mega events and what is the logic behind the decision to host? With the high cost of staging these events accruing to the host taxpayers, there is a need to understand how these stakeholders perceive mega events. What are their expectations and perceptions? Answers to these questions are essential in the marketing and management of mega sport events and these questions have influenced the direction that this study has taken.

1.3 LOCATING THIS STUDY

Mega sport events have received prominence in the tourism literature, having been studied from a variety of perspectives. The event management discipline has benefited mainly from work focussing on the economic impacts of mega sport events (Gelen, 2003; Gratton and Dobson, 1999; Jones, 2001; Kang and Purdue, 1994; Madden, 2002). Researchers such as Chalip (2002), Cashman (2003), Higham (1999), Shapcott (1998) and Waitt (2003), have all contributed to our knowledge of the social impacts of mega events while an understanding of the bidding implications and processes can be derived from the research of Emery (2002), Ingerson and Westerbeek (1999), Persson (2002) and Westerbeek, Turner and Ingerson (2002). Some work on mega sport events has also enhanced our understanding of the media and image impacts of these events. For instance, Ritchie and Smith (1991) conducted research on the impacts of the 1988 Calgary Olympics by examining the awareness that viewers had of the destination in the pre and post event stage whereas Kim and Morrison (2005) and Mossberg and Hallberg (1999) studied the impacts of the event media on the destination and product images of New Zealand and Korea respectively. Furthermore, Chalip, Green and Hill (2003) and Hede (2005) attempted to enhance our understanding of the direct impacts of mega sports media on respondents' intention to travel.

Despite the wealth of studies conducted on mega sport events, very few studies address the stakeholder perspective. Some work has focussed on the sport event visitor, but these are concerned more with spending patterns as an indicator of the economic impacts that these events have on the host economy (Burns and Mules 1989; Gibson, 1998). Furthermore, most of this work addresses methodological issues rather than opinions and expectations (Baade and Matheson, 2002; Gelan, 2003; Mazitelli, 1989; Mules and Faulkner, 1996). More significantly, no work could be identified that focussed on the local tourism officials, local residents' or the tourists' expectations and perceptions of mega events.

A major weakness of most mega event research is that the range of studies in this area is concerned with large-scale mega events such as the Olympic games, the Football World Cup or American football while ignoring smaller sport events of global significance like the Golf World Cup. More significantly, many studies on events tend to be based on sport events that are staged in large cities located on large continents with large domestic travel markets. No studies could therefore be found that gave insights into the stakeholder perspective of mega events on small islands like Barbados.

Getz (2000a) made the call for more context specific research in event tourism. Context specific research is particularly important where Barbados is concerned due to the nature of its tourism product. Tourism in microstates is conceptually and operationally different from tourism in continents or very large countries. For instance, unlike many major cities and large countries that have previously staged events, Barbados, due to its size, does not have a domestic tourism market and consequently the island is dependent on international markets for its tourists (Reid and Reid, 1994). Thus, unlike the United States or Japan, who both staged Football World Cups in the past, Barbados does not benefit from the economies of scale provided by large, domestic travel markets. Furthermore, the marketing of events for the international market is compounded by the other challenges of island tourism. Not only does size eliminate any dependence on domestic markets (Reid and Reid 1994) but the geographic isolation of islands means that tourism must be tied to sea and air transport modes, thereby making travel to islands expensive. Barbados is also particularly vulnerable due to its distance from its major tourist generating markets - the United States, Canada and United Kingdom. This means that visitors must invest considerable time and money to travel to this destination. This situation can be problematic since a major deterrent to travel to a mega event is the associated cost (Delpy, 1998).

Although the literature on events is blessed with a range of studies on the influence of festivals and carnivals on island tourism (Green, 2002; Nicholson and Pearce, 2001), at the time of doing this research no studies were identified that assessed how individuals in micro economies such as those in the Caribbean respond to mega sport events. Goldblatt (2000) drew attention to the mistake of evaluating events based on studies from other settings. They showed how hotels in the United States of America projected occupancy levels for the 1995 Football World Cup based upon studies of previous World Cups. The result was occupancy rates that fell below expectations. One-off events in particular may need more groundwork and detailed research due to the uncertainty of the target market (Shone and Parry, 2001). This is certainly the case with Barbados and the Golf World Cup. Although this event has been hosted all over the world, this is the first occasion that a golf tournament of this scale and prestige has been hosted in Barbados. Hence, drawing conclusions from the findings of previous studies may mislead decision-makers. So although previous studies in event tourism have looked at the relationship between sport events and the potential of luring visitors from overseas and domestic markets (Chalip, Green and Vander Velden, 1998; Kim and Chalip, 2004; Neirotti, Bosetti and Teed, 2001) it is recognised that all events must be analysed individually in the context of their host environment.

The research arena is further impoverished by the lack of studies in the area of golf event tourism. Research into golf tourism addresses mainly environmental and social issues. Stoddard (1990) for example discusses the environmental impacts of golf as more and more golf courses have been developed. He also scrutinises the socio-cultural impacts of golf that have re-enforced the social-exclusivity of the game. Customer focussed research in golf tourism tends to focus more on the 'active' (Standevan and De Knop, 1999) consumer of golf tourism which is the individual golfer who travels to play golf rather than to watch the game (Petrick, 2002; Petrick and Blackman, 2002). The literature contains very few studies dedicated to golf event tourism (Gauthier and Hansen, 1993; Hansen and Gauthier, 1994; Petrick, 2002). Trade journals and the popular press contribute much of the information pertaining to the golf industry and specifically to the professional tours (Hansen and Gauthier, 1993)[2]. Consequently, little attention has been paid to stakeholders' views of golf events. Thus, the voices of the stakeholders need to be heard. Identifying these viewpoints is crucial to the further development, marketing and planning of such events on the island of Barbados. Hence, the approach adopted in the study is eclectic in nature as it used a variety of methods to consider the viewpoints of a variety of individuals, during a specific event, within a specific time and at a specific place.

---

[2]   Also see the National Golf Foundation website at

http://www.ngf.org/cgi/home.asp

1.4 RATIONALE FOR THIS STUDY

Although authorities may plan events with the best intentions, part of an event's success lies in its capacity to stimulate international travel to the host destination (Kim and Chalip, 2004), hence an understanding of the international visitor is vital to the success of any sport event. The presence of the foreign visitor is important since it is through the foreign visitor that Barbados earns the foreign exchange required to service external debt and to purchase imports required to maintain the high standard of living experienced on the island (Lewis, 2002). Therefore, the success of the Golf World Cup was based on its effectiveness as an attractive 'pull' agent, particularly for international visitors. A 'pull' agent refers to those qualities that the destination possesses that act as a 'lure' for the potential visitor (Dann, 1977). These may include natural beauty, historical landmarks, friendly people or culture. The event's ability to attract visitors who will not only attend the event but will participate in other tourism activities is vital to its overall success.

Local stakeholders are just as important as international visitors in the staging of events since commentators (Getz, 1991a, 1997; Hall, 1992a, 1989a; Ritchie, 1984) on mega events stress the importance of their 'buy in' to the idea due to the investment in public funds ordinarily required to finance these events. They stress that events cannot be successful without local support and participation. Events are designed to provide something of value for the stakeholders whether it is entertainment, education, economic or social benefits or other benefits. Relationships are crucial with all stakeholders including the suppliers and local residents. However, according to Masterman (2004) many event organisers do not undertake stakeholder oriented research, believing in their own ability to know what their stakeholders want. This is partially due to evidence that suggests that many events tend to be politically motivated affairs. In the light of this, the decision to stage, or not to stage an event is often influenced by the political agendas of the authorities (Hall, 1989a).

Roche (1994) highlighted the view that prestige projects are usually the product of influential elites or a particular powerful individual. Consequently, many events go ahead as a response to urgent problems and without much, if any, evaluation of alternative cost benefit projections or community consultation or the relevant consumer research. As a result, many events can fail to meet the expectations of the stakeholders. Thus, in order to ensure the success

9

of future events there is a need to build a foundation of knowledge regarding mega events in Barbados.

Understanding how individuals perceive mega events is important to ensure appropriate and effective marketing and management strategies for event tourism (Turco, Swart, Bob and Moodley, 2003). The identification of the most highly perceived benefits provides insights for promotional strategies aimed at both local and foreign visitors (Masterman, 2004). The perception of benefits and expectations creates benchmarks for future events. This view is also echoed in the work of Gibson (1998) who calls for a more in-depth understanding of the expectations of sport tourists. Gibson criticised the body of studies in this area calling for the need to move from description to theoretically grounded explanation in the area of event tourism. If events are to be successful there must be an understanding of the expectations and perceptions that people have of them. Without this understanding it is not clear how these events should be designed, managed and marketed. By understanding how mega events are perceived by the stakeholders can place the event destination at a considerable advantage in that the marketers can direct strategies aimed at manipulating the elements and attributes that are most likely to influence support.

Commentators investigating the event tourism phenomenon are advocating the need for more explanatory research through the use of a variety of methods (Gibson, 1998; Getz, 1998; Masterman, 2004). Gibson, for instance, highlighted the importance of the use of multiple methods such as interviews, observations and ethnographies in researching event tourism. These methods help the researcher to obtain the thick descriptions and in-depth analysis required in order to better comprehend the perceptions and expectations of all stakeholders. The underlying basis of understanding any phenomenon is appreciation for how the actors construct and interact with their social world. Altheide and Johnson (1994) claim that the social world should therefore be individually constructed and interpreted. As Sparks (1992) suggests, social realities are multiple and exist in people's minds. In order to untangle and understand these realities, a qualitative approach through participant observation and semi-structured interviews provided the depth of information that permitted a detailed exploration of the issues in a way that would not have been possible with other forms of research (see Wickens, 2002). A full exposition of all methodological considerations is expounded in chapter two.

2 -CHAPTER TWO
RESEARCHING GOLF EVENTS -
METHODOLOGICAL PHILOSOPHY

2.1 INTRODUCTION

This chapter addresses the complexities of golf event research by providing an overview of the methodological, theoretical and practical issues that underpinned the data collection methods employed in this study. Firstly, the debate concerning the two research paradigms is addressed, including their relative strengths and limitations. Secondly, an exposition of the data collection procedures undertaken in this study is presented along with a presentation of the practical and ethical issues involved. Finally, the sampling techniques employed and the data analysis procedures are considered. The chapter commences with an examination of the philosophical assumptions that underpin the major research paradigms.

2.2 RESEARCH AND THE PARADIGM DEBATE

In order to arrive at a suitable methodological strategy for this study, the researcher had to engage in a process of constant reflection. The adoption of an interpretive approach evolved after the careful consideration of numerous ontological, epistemological, practical and ethical issues. As the research progressed, the methodology adopted had to be constantly reviewed and refined. As a result the methodology adopted for this study is more along the lines of Lincoln and Guba's (1985) emergent designs since the methods eventually adopted were not premeditated but evolved as the study progressed. One of the major considerations was to arrive at a suitable epistemological and ontological stance, one that would allow the enquiry to proceed effectively. Each researcher brings a set of epistemological assumptions into the research process, sometimes unconsciously, and these influence how the researcher will collect and interpret the data (Travers, 2001).

Researchers (Sarantakos, 1988; Sekeran, 2002; Wickens, 1999) are continuously debating the merits of the two main methodological approaches to research. These approaches are underpinned by two contrasting paradigms. A paradigm, according to Maykut and Morehouse (1994: 4), "has come to mean a set of overarching and interconnected assumptions about the nature of reality". These assumptions form the framework within which empirical enquiry takes place and provide two different perspectives about how data should be collected and analysed. Methodological paradigms are based around a number of ontological (assumptions about the nature of reality) and epistemological (assumptions concerning the origins of knowledge) postures that provide two different perspectives from which knowledge is constructed and defined (Lewis, 2002; Wickens, 1999; Wickens, 2002;). The focus of the following discussion is a critical assessment of the assumptions that underpin these two competing paradigms.

2.2.1 The Positivist Paradigm

Traditionally the positivist paradigm has tended to dominate research in the social sciences (Burns, 2000). Positivism is concerned with the scientific exploration and the objective collection of facts in order to derive the 'positive' truth and to make predictions and generalisations about a phenomenon (Sekeran, 2002). Positivism is further underpinned by a number of ideological tenets. It is based around the argument that all sciences should be founded on the principles of the physical and natural sciences and that the same methods could be used for the study of social phenomena. Durkheim (1964: xlv) argues that the social scientist should study social phenomena: "…in the same state of mind as the physicist, chemist or physiologist when he probes into a still unexplored region of the scientific domain".

Positivism, therefore, is founded on the assumption that the laws governing nature and social reality are the same. It views humans as beings that are governed by 'social laws' with no 'free will' (Sarantakos, 1988). Humans are objectified and assumed to have no control over their world or behaviour. It is perceived that the world is orderly, lawful and predictable and that by dividing and studying parts the whole could be understood (Maykut and Morehouse, 1994: 12). Human behaviour is, therefore, seen as a stimulus-response mechanism so that once certain conditions exist generalisations and predictions can be made about human life in the same way as they can about nature.

According to positivists, reality is 'out there' independent of any consciousness and all members of society define the world in the same terms (Sarantakos, 1988: 36). As Crotty (1998: 27) asserts: "objects in the world have meaning prior to, and independently of, any consciousness of them". This point stresses the notion of objectivity

12

where emphasis is placed on the collection of factual and quantifiable information derived from phenomena that can be observed and measured. Blaikie (1993:15) contends: "... unobservable entities may not be offered as causes because reality is what can be observed and observed regularities are all that can be verified". Objectivity is thus derived from a clear separation between the 'subjective' knower and the 'objective' world so that the knower can stand 'outside' of what is to be known and true objectivity can be attained (Maykut and Morehouse, 1994: 12).

Positivism is also grounded in the notion of verification and proof, which is concerned with the deductive proving, or falsifying of the hypothesis. There is an emphasis on precision, which deals with the degree of accuracy of the results on the basis of the sample chosen to what actually exists (Sekeran, 2002). Data is collected on observable entities that can be measured through direct observation and with the aid of instruments. Data collection thus utilises structured and precise procedures that can be duplicated by other researchers, so that once exposed to the same data, they should be able to draw the same conclusions. These philosophical notions underpin the quantitative approach to research. Quantitative research is prominent in the study of leisure and tourism (Dunn, 1994; Walle, 1997). It involves the collection of factual data that is presented in a numerical, measurable form. It is mainly deductive in that the researcher tries to arrive at a reasoned conclusion based on logical generalisations (Sekeran, 2002). The phenomenon is broken into measurable units; data is collected and subjected to empirical scrutiny. The researcher then seeks to explain or establish causal relationships between the independent and dependent variables in order to arrive at 'value free' conclusions (Lewis, 2002). The main strength of quantitative research lies in precision and control. Control is achieved through the sampling design and precision through the use of quantitative and reliable measurements (Burns, 2000). The advantages of quantitative research are discussed in the section that follows.

2.2.1.1 Advantages and Limitations of Quantitative Methods

Quantitative research offers many advantages to the social sciences. It can facilitate the identification of factors associated with a problem or situation through correlations. The stating of the hypothesis at the beginning and the development of a conceptual framework means that there is a clear focus and clarity of purpose, providing a framework for the collection, analysis and interpretation of

13

the data (Sekeran, 2002; Robson, 1993). This gives the researcher the scope to design the research along structured lines by stating from the outset how the data will be collected and analysed. In the leisure and tourism industry the emphasis on statistical analysis and numerical presentations means that industry managers can use the information to make decisions in an informed context (Brunt, 1997). For instance, quantitative research is particularly useful in the areas of forecasting and predicting demand in the hotel sector and in the study of tourists' behaviour (Dunn, 1994).

However, opposition to the domination of quantitative measures is voiced by researchers who argue that understanding social action from the actual 'players' and 'actors' cannot be achieved with rigid and highly structured research designs (Blaikie, 1993; Riley, Wood, Clarke, Wilkie and Szivas, 2000; Tribe, 2001; Walle, 1997). Such a view stems from the recognition that there are fundamental differences between the natural and social world and consequently quantitative methods would be inappropriate for studies concerned with a social phenomenon. Tribe (2001), for instance, argues that human actions cannot be researched in the same way as the natural sciences since the laws of nature are constant but social life is plural and irregular in nature. Riley, Wood, Clark, Wilkie and Szivas (2000: 15) concur and comment:

> The social world is also prone to greater variations than the natural world: while humans do exhibit regular, systematic patterns of behaviour (like certain molecules), these patterns cannot be assumed to be fixed forever.

Human values, beliefs and cultural systems change over time and as a result it is difficult to replicate them. Blaikie (1993: 18) argues:

> Social life, however is much more complex than natural phenomena and cannot be usefully isolated artificially. In social situations, similar conditions occur only within very limited time periods; history never really repeats itself. Therefore, social conditions can never be precisely repeated..."

Social reality does not represent laws of nature, but laws that are socially constructed and therefore humans have the power to alter and control them. Humans also attach meanings to their social world based on ideas, values, beliefs and cultural norms, which cannot be measured

14

with instruments (Ibid). It would therefore be difficult to study social action based on the principles of positivism, as replication and control of human conditions would present difficulties.

Another problem with positivism is that it neither allows the researcher to capture the rich complexities of human experiences nor does it assist the researcher in accounting for the way humans understand and construct their world. Ryan and Cave (2005:145) argue that quantitative research methods "... impose methodological limitations that cannot capture the complexity and inter linkages of so-called real experiences". The complexity and plurality of the social world is therefore hidden behind the 'mask' of positivism. Quantitative techniques would thus impede the researcher who is trying to establish the subjective meanings that humans use to construct and understand their world. For example, survey questionnaires do not allow the respondents to deviate from the rigid agenda of the questionnaire so important categories may be missed due to the constraints imposed (Lewis, 2002).

Some researchers (Blaikie, 1993; Priest, 1996; Sarantakos, 1988; Tribe, 2001) question if quantitative research can be purely objective. Sarantakos (1988) argues that even where there is a clear separation of the researcher from the object this does not guarantee objectivity. In the formation of hypotheses and the development of research instruments the researcher uses meanings that have been ascribed from the researcher's own preconceptions (Tribe, 2001). Researchers tend to locate themselves within a particular ontological, epistemological and theoretical position which influences the choice of what is studied, how it is studied and what literature is reviewed. Burns (2000:10) contends that quantitative research "....cannot be totally objective, since subjectively it is involved in the very choice of a problem worthy of investigation and in the interpretation of the results".

What is regarded as acceptable evidence, how data is collected and how the results are interpreted will be influenced by the researcher's values, whether intentionally or unintentionally (Blaikie, 1993). Furthermore, the process of choosing what to research can be affected by a multitude of factors external to the researcher. These could include historical or political forces, theoretical or ontological shifts, gender issues and institutional and hierarchical 'webs of power' (Humberstone, 1997a). Priests (1996:4) reinforces this point and states that politics affects the research process, whichever methods are applied:

15

The instruments and techniques that scientists have available to them affect the kinds of experiments they can do and therefore have powerful effects on what kind of new knowledge is created.

Politics usually determines what areas of research will be funded and which areas will be ignored. This will have powerful effects on the kind of knowledge that is discovered and what is left undiscovered. Furthermore not allowing the subjects of research to articulate their views also subscribes to partiality. Ryan (1995b: 214) drew attention to this point when he stated that: "...it is accepted that tourism is concerned with an experience of places and the interactions that occur at those destinations;......then research that denies the opportunity for holiday-makers to speak of their own experiences in their own words - that seeks only reactions to a research determined agenda – is itself limited". It can then be argued that even where the most honourable intentions exist, the values and prejudices of researchers will taint the research process. These arguments demonstrate that in quantitative research bias is possible at all levels.

A further drawback of quantitative methods is that it does not allow the researcher the flexibility to account for the many contingencies that may be encountered during the research process. For example, if a researcher is confronted with the vagaries of fieldwork the quantitative approach may prove too restrictive for him/her to adapt to the evolving conditions. In a perfect world, the researcher can establish a clear focus and a structured methodology a *priori,* however, once the fieldwork commences the researcher may have to adjust and review the research methods to fit the evolving situation (Burgess, 1984; Burgess, 1987a; Burgess, 1987b; Seaton, 1997; Wickens, 1999).

Based on these arguments, and after considering the objectives and nature of this research, it became clear that quantitative measures were not appropriate for this study. Instead, if the objectives were to be achieved, what was required was a flexible approach where the researcher was central to the investigation in the collection and interpretation of the data (See Holstein and Gubrium, 1997; Parker, 1994). At this juncture a closer inspection of the interpretive paradigm is undertaken.

2.3 THE INTERPRETIVE APPROACH

The interpretive approach includes a number of strands known as phenomenology, ethnography, symbolic interactionism and hermeneutics (Mason, 1996). These fall under the umbrella of research methods known as qualitative research methods. While diversity exists between these different approaches, what is common is that emphasis is placed on the subjective interpretation and microanalysis of those being studied.

There are various definitions of qualitative research; however, an appropriate definition for the purpose of this study is: "...the interpretive study of a specified issue or problem in which the researcher is central to the sense that is made" (Parker, 1994:2). Qualitative research is less concerned with the analysis of macro-processes and more concerned with how individuals interpret their world; hence it is interpretive in nature (Decrop, 2006; Lewis, 2000). The focus is on people's lives, stories, behaviour (Strauss and Corbin, 1990), their thoughts, feelings, emotions and other internal experiences. This approach is concerned with understanding the meanings that events have for the persons being studied (Patton, 1990; Thompson and Walker, 1998). Rather than standing back and observing the phenomena, the researcher acts as the 'instrument' of data collection and plays an 'active' role in the entire research process including the collection and interpretation of the data (Allan, 1991; Bryman, 1988; Maykuk and Morehouse, 1994).

The qualitative research paradigm is, therefore, concerned with an examination of the phenomenon from the perspective of those experiencing it. The proximity of the researcher to those being studied means that the researcher can extrapolate an 'enriched' (Veal, 1997) collection of data that illuminates and explains the dynamics of social interaction and experiences. The data provides depth and a more profound understanding of the informants' feelings, attitudes and experiences (Briedenhann, 2004). The data is therefore presented in words with rich descriptions, quotations and conceptual models rather than mathematical equations.

Another important feature of the qualitative approach is the notion of 'flexibility'. Qualitative researchers recognise that non-human instruments are not sophisticated or flexible enough to adapt to complex social settings (Seaton, 1997; Wickens, 1999). Qualitative research starts with a 'focus of inquiry' rather than a hypothesis or a proposition. This 'focus of inquiry' leads the researcher through the research process (Lincoln and Guba, 1985). Rather than the structured, linear approach adopted by quantitative practitioners (Sekeran, 2002), qualitative researchers can adopt methods that evolve over the course of the study. Leads can be identified early in the research, which influence the methods and the approach that the researcher may subsequently adopt and vary as the research progresses (Strauss and Corbin, 1990). Qualitative research designs, due to their nature, are not always specified in advance, but instead they are emergent. Although there will be an initial focus and plans for interviews or observations, the inductive and naturalistic focus of qualitative research does not always render it appropriate to specify rigid operational plans at the outset (Patton, 1990). Instead the research structure may evolve and/or is modified as the fieldwork progresses and decisions are sometimes made in the field (Patton, 1990; Punch, 1998; Wickens, 1999). Qualitative research strategies do, however, have weaknesses, which are now discussed.

2.3.1 Limitations of the Qualitative Approach

Qualitative research has often been criticised on the grounds that it generates 'soft' data, which should only be used as an appendage to the more 'hard' quantitative data (Denscombe, 1998). Whilst qualitative research is frequently used to inform larger and more scientific studies it is not considered to be valid in its own right (Denscombe, 1998). The nature of the research restricts the researcher to small samples and findings cannot be generalised since there are not facts but ideas, experiences and opinions that are applicable only to the set of individuals experiencing the phenomenon. The conclusions drawn are contextual in nature and time specific.

The nature of qualitative research makes it subject to bias in that the researcher may influence the final conclusions and results (Silverman, 2000). The 'active' position of the researcher and his or her closeness to the subjects under study is believed to influence the respondents, particularly in interviews where it is thought that respondents might be intimidated by the researcher's presence or feel threatened by the researcher's closeness (Brewer, 2000). It is also perceived that in some instances respondents may be influenced by what they perceive to be the aims of the investigation (Bryman, 1988). In participant observation, particularly in overt situations, it is argued that the researchers' presence may influence an alteration in the behaviour of those being observed (Brewer, 2000). Qualitative research can be time consuming and sometimes demands much personal sacrifice on the part of the researcher. In addition, there is the

18

risk of collecting meaningless and irrelevant information (Denscombe, 1998; Sarantakos, 1988).

Despite these limitations, qualitative methods are deemed appropriate for this study in that they allowed the researcher the scope to understand and discover the 'whys' of golf event tourism in Barbados. Why did the Barbados Tourism Authority host the Golf World Cup in 2006 and why did international tourists and local residents choose to or not to attend? Crompton (1979) notes that in tourism it is easy to describe the 'who', 'when' 'where' and 'how' of tourism but as far as the 'why' question is concerned, this is more difficult. Crompton advocates that a qualitative approach is best suited to deal with this problem. Hakim (1987: 28) supports this view and states that:

> The question 'why' often cannot be asked, or answered, directly and may involve a variety of circumstantial and contextual factors, creating links between or choices between, apparently unrelated matters. Whether one is seeking explanations at the social-structural level or at the level of individual choices and life styles, qualitative research can be extremely valuable for identifying patterns of associations between factors on the ground, as compared with abstract correlations obtained from the analysis of large-scale surveys and aggregate data.

In this study, qualitative methods assisted the researcher in uncovering the 'richness' and complexities of the 'why' question. The rationale for a qualitative approach in this study was also encouraged by a range of studies in leisure and tourism, particular those pertaining to motivation and consumer behaviour. Bowen (2002), Crompton (1979), Dann (1977), Ryan (1995c), Sealy and Wickens (2008), Wickens (2002, 1999) and Wilson (1996) have all used qualitative methods to study leisure and tourism. Interviews were an integral part of the data collection process for these researchers while Bargeman and Van der Poel (2006) and Ryan (1995c) used a combination of participant observation and conversations to collect data from tourists. Researchers, such as Green and Chalip (1998), used an ethnographic approach to gain insights into the expectations of participants at a women's football tournament. The success of these studies, and the recognition that they have achieved in academia, inspired the methods undertaken in this research. The following section introduces the data collection methods employed in this investigation.

2.4 DATA COLLECTION STRATEGIES EMPLOYED

Since this study was influenced by the interpretive paradigm, consideration was given to the range of qualitative methods available to the researcher. These methods include historical analysis, life histories, observation, participant observation, focus groups and interviews. Life histories are concerned with gaining an insider's view of cultural change through the history of an individual's development (Marshall and Rossman, 1995). In tourism research historical analysis can be useful in showing how and why tourism practices and policies have evolved over time. In staying true to the dictum "fitness for purpose" (Wood, 1999) it was established that the focus of this research was not concerned with past events or past behaviour, which ruled out these approaches.

Another method considered was the focus group. Focus groups are an effective way to stimulate discussion and to collect rich data; however, they can be problematic in that some individuals may dominate the discussion whereas others may resist expressing their true feelings because of the presence of others (Decrop, 2006). Although there were initial plans to organise focus groups with the help and sponsorship of the Barbados Tourism Authority, these plans did not materialise. Since this event did not attract many packaged tour tourists, those tourists relevant to this research could not be easily identified. The tourists visiting Barbados for this event were scattered across the island in various hotels and resorts and consequently could not be adequately identified. It was at this time that attention became focussed on participant observation and the semi-structured interview as a means of data collection.

2.4.1 Participant Observation

Participant observation is an ethnographic technique for data collection (Punch, 1998). It differs from simple observation in that the researcher changes from a detached observer of the situation to the dual role of active participant and observer of the situation. Jorgensen (1989: 13) contends that participant observation is appropriate when a study meets certain conditions. These include:

1) When the research is concerned with human meanings and interactions viewed from an insider's perspective.

2) When the phenomenon is observable within an everyday life situation or setting.
3) When the researcher is able to gain access into such a setting.
4) When the phenomenon is sufficiently limited in size and location to be studied as a case; and
5) When the study questions are appropriate for the case study and the research question can be addressed by qualitative data gathered by direct observations and other means pertinent to the field setting.

This study fulfils these conditions. Firstly, the research is viewed from an insider perspective, which is the perspective of the stakeholder. This insider perspective could be best accomplished with the researcher taking the role of a participant observer at the Golf World Cup on the island of Barbados. Secondly, since the researcher travelled to Barbados and attended the event, observations were made in the natural setting of the event itself. Additionally, the researcher was conscious of the importance of not manipulating the setting and of achieving a balance between being a passive or at times active observer (Bowen, 2002). The event, which was hosted in a confined setting at the Sandy Lane Golf and Country Club in Barbados over a period of seven (7) days, was sufficiently small to allow for effective observations to be made in a case study context. The access gained as a participant observer was adequate for the observations required. These observations were further supplemented by other data collected in the field setting through semi-structured interviews and articles from newspapers, brochures, statistical documents and documents of state.

Burgess (1984: 79) highlighted one of the key advantages of participant observation:

> The value of being a participant observer.... is that researchers can utilise their observations together with their theoretical insights to make seemingly irrational or paradoxical behaviour comprehensible to those within or beyond the situation that is studied. Observations can also be used to support or refute ideas about human behaviour and to generate questions that can be used in future research.

In turn, observation and participant observation can help the researcher to understand the experiences of people in event tourism. In addition, observations can help the researcher to identify with informants' experiences and to observe events as they unfold.

Through the use of participant observation the researcher was able to move freely amongst the other participants covertly and overtly at the Golf World Cup. By being a participant observer and, thus, part of the group of spectators, conversations developed and flowed naturally, enabling the information required to emerge. The researcher was able to establish a common ground with other patrons by initiating conversations with questions such as " are you enjoying the golf?"; "is this your first day?"; "where are you visiting from?". At times it was the informant that initiated the conversation. By utilising participant observation it was easy to observe the functional workings of the event and the activities and behaviour of the visitors. These observations created the context in which the interviews took place and helped to determine who was interviewed, how, when and where. The participant observation worked well because the researcher was able to blend into the environment in an unobtrusive way; so although her reason for being in Barbados and attending the Golf World Cup was significantly different from many of the other participants, this did not intrude upon the participants' enjoyment. This is where the researcher was able to draw on years of hospitality training – being able to strike up conversations with international tourists and residents in a friendly and natural way. As stated by Jorgensen (1989: 28):

> The participant observer interacts with people under the ordinary conditions of their daily lives much like any other participant. The participant observer's interests in research, though different, is not unlike any number of special interests people have in interacting with one another.

Drawing on Ryan's (1995c) advice, the preparation of an interview guide in advance provided an advantage, in that it was possible to identify and explore the main themes while simultaneously building on new concepts that were emerging in the field. Significantly, although there was no initial observation agenda when the research entered the field on the first day of the golf event, the exploration of themes through the pre-prepared interview guide, determined the observation agenda. As a participant observer, the researcher was able to relate to the participants' experience and impressions of the event. For instance, when some informants commented about the 'lack of atmosphere' the researcher was able to attach meaning to the statement by also experiencing the same phenomenon through constant observation. At this stage the researcher was prompted to observe the design and layout of the areas where spectators tended to converge in order to understand this 'lack of atmosphere'. Observations included the landscape, the position of tents, bars, food stalls and seating areas. Similarly, when visitors at the Golf World Cup complained about the food, this also prompted an observation of the culinary offers on display in the respective food tents.

One advantage that was particularly useful is that it was possible not only to see, watch, record and mingle, but eavesdropping became a technique used to gather information about what people were actually feeling and experiencing at various points. This provided an opportunity for an 'authentic' (Silverman, 1993) account of people's experiences without the influence of researcher presence. Thus, experiencing the phenomenon first hand, the preparation of an agenda, establishing a friendly rapport and determining a strategy for note taking provided the skills that achieved the desired result in the field (Ryan, 1995c).

2.4.1.1 Limitations of Participant Observation

Like all other research methods, participant observation has limitations. One of the main challenges in observations is that the researcher is able to maintain a virtually unobtrusive role (Cresswell, 1994). It is often argued that participant observers tend to change the situation under study due to their mere presence (Frankenberg, 1987). It is also argued that the personal characteristics of the researcher may draw them to certain types of individuals who may provide an undue amount of information that may be biased towards a particular point of view. In such a situation the researcher may not be inclined to explore opposite points of view (Dean, Eichhorn and Dean, 1969) to get a more holistic impression of the situation under study. Participant observation can be demanding mentally, physically, personally, socially and legally (Denscombe, 1998; Gans, 1987; Marshall and Rossman, 1995). When observations must be undertaken in harsh conditions there could be a level of discomfort or danger (Marshall and Rossman, 1995). In this study the researcher had to combat the pouring rain, the scorching sun and 30-degree centigrade temperatures.

The researcher's role in the field was constantly changing. One minute as a fellow spectator, then a friend and then a researcher. Consequently this was mentally and physically exhausting.

One other concern put forward by researchers (Denscombe, 1998; Gold, 1969; McCall and Simmons, 1969) is the danger of 'going native'. Participant observers could become so immersed in the situation or group under study that they lose sight of their real purpose – that of conducting research. The success of participant observation depends on being able to walk the 'tightrope' between the involvement and the passion associated with full participation and the detachment required in order to get the job done. If researchers 'go native' they tend to lose focus and their original sense of purpose and this in turn can jeopardise the research. In this study the researcher was not at threat of 'going native'. The researcher is not a fan of golf or any participating player; neither does she understand the game. As a result, the researcher was not caught up in the euphoria and excitement that accompanies sport events. Visits to the golf course and other sites on the island were strictly for the purpose of collecting the data required. For this reason the researcher was able to remain detached by maintaining a professional and focussed outlook, thereby executing the research as efficiently as possible.

Another criticism of participant observation is that the researcher is limited to observing small groups that may not be typical of the society under study as a whole (Frankenberg, 1987). Furthermore, the participant observer is constrained by the physical limits of the role and the location. As a result the researcher can only record a small selection of activities and events. The basis of this selection is often non-random and is influenced by the conditions under which the observations take place (Brewer, 2000). Lone observers are bound to be selective because of the impossibility of recording or observing everything. Consequently, it is acknowledged that participant observation presents only a partial view of a way of life compiled from selective records. It is perceived as partial because it is the personalised view of a single or several individuals. Conversely, Brewer (2000) notes that ethnographers recognised that the participant observers' view is still a view, which is better than no view at all. Researchers, however, advocate that participant observation should not be a stand-alone method but should be complemented by other data collection strategies. Consequently, participant observation in this case was used to complement other data collection techniques (See Fontana and Frey, 2005; Robson, 1993) and it facilitated the execution of the interview schedule. In this case participant observation was not used as a single method but more as a 'research enterprise', a style of combining several methods to achieve a particular end (McCall and Simmons, 1969:3). Thus, participant observation worked favourably when combined with semi-structured interviews. This combination assisted the researcher in gaining a sense of context in understanding what people do and why they do it. The interviews were particularly helpful in getting inside people's minds to understand their perceptions and expectations. It is for this reason that this study adopted the use of semi-structured interviews to complement participant observation strategies. The next section acknowledges the advantages and limitations of semi-structured interviews.

2.4.2 Conducting Interviews

The interview is a type of conversation (Patton, 1990; Robson, 1993) which is defined as any interaction in which two or more people are brought into direct contact in order for at least one party to learn something from the other (Brenner, Brown and Canter, 1985: 3). Arksey and Knight (1999) identify three types of interviews – the unstructured, the structured and the semi-structured. Unstructured interviews are of a freestyle nature in that there are no pre-determined questions and the researcher is free to guide the interview in any direction required. Structured interviews involve a set of pre-determined questions. These types of questionnaires are mainly used in public opinion and government surveys. They, however, tend to be geared towards the collection of quantifiable data and are usually standardised with closed-ended questions which the researcher must rigidly follow. The rigidity of this approach means that the researcher is bounded by a set of questions without the freedom to digress or probe with additional questions and to add topics that are deemed appropriate to obtain the information being sought.

Semi-structured interviews involve a set of pre-determined questions or topics in the form of an interview guide, which guides the discussion but does not confine the researcher. The researcher has more freedom to deviate by asking probing questions far beyond the pre-determined ones (Berg, 1989; May, 1993; Robson, 1993). The freedom to probe can facilitate exploration, clarification, illumination and elaboration of the respondents' experiences, feelings, opinions and attitudes that would not be possible with structured interviews (Burman, 1994; Denscombe, 1998). The main strength of the semi-structured interview lies in the fact that it is targeted; that is, it focuses on the topic directly (Briedenhann, 2004). Semi-structured interviews were particularly useful for this study because they allowed the researcher to explore the topic in depth and detail (see Denscombe, 1998; Robson, 1993). They allowed respondents to express their personal thoughts, feelings, perceptions and opinions freely and were appropriate for revealing information about behaviour that could not be obtained merely by participant observation. At the same time the researcher had the opportunity for face-to-face clarification of responses.

Semi-structured interviews can provide a source of 'rich' data from which the researcher can discover new categories, concepts and meanings. However, the technique is also criticised on the basis that the data may be distorted as the presence of the interviewer - their personality, attitudes (Oppenheim, 1992) gender and race (May, 1993) may influence the responses. In the light of these criticisms the next section examines the limitations intrinsic to semi-structured interviews.

2.4.2.1 Disadvantages of Semi-Structured Interviews

There are limitations and challenges associated with the use of semi-structured interviews. Interviews involve personal interaction, so cooperation is necessary from the interviewees who may be unwilling or uncomfortable in participating, or simply may not be aware of recurring patterns or events in their lives (Marshall and Rossman, 1995). Additionally, respondents may not have the information that the researcher requires; or, if they do, they may not be able to articulate this effectively (Oppenheim, 1992; Cresswell, 1994). Arksey and Knight (1999) also caution that what respondents say they do, or intend to do, might not necessarily be congruent with their actual actions and that interviews can only be a tool to uncover beliefs and meanings and not necessarily actions. Conducting interviews involves a substantial commitment of time, energy and money on the part of the researcher. In this case, the researcher was required to spend every day of the two-week period in Barbados seeking out opportunities to collect data. Of the time available to the researcher, four full days were spent at the Golf World Cup conducting interviews and observations. Because of the richness and complexities of the data, data analysis can be a laborious process (Marshall and Rossman, 1995) and transcribing can be tedious, lengthy and expensive (Veal, 1997).

One of the major limitations associated with semi-structured interviews is that the findings cannot be generalised. However, this study is not about establishing generalisations and making predictions but rather about discovering the conceptual meanings that will inform other studies, tourism marketers and policy makers. Another concern is that the interpretation of the data may be subject to researcher bias in that the values and beliefs of the researcher may influence interpretation (Punch, 1998). It is argued that semi-structured interviews leave the research open to human error in that poor recall, misinterpretation or inarticulate responses may distort the data (Yin, 1994). However, in this study, this problem was minimised through the establishment of 'ecological validity' (Burns, 2000) where the researcher was able to forward the transcripts to a select group of informants for confirmation of accuracy (See Gibson Wilming and Holdnak, 2003). The issue of validity and reliability will be dealt with in more detail in section 2.10.

It is argued (Aaker, Kumar and Day, 1995; Malhotra, 1999; Punch, 1998) that the success of interviews is dependent on researcher skill and adequate training. Without the appropriate training the interviewer may not ask questions that inspire long narratives from the respondents or they may lack familiarity with the local culture or language. Interviewers are therefore required to constantly think on their feet in order to adjust to the social dynamics of the interviews and to ask the appropriate questions that will generate the data required (Jennings, 2005). In this research, efforts were made to minimise many of these shortcomings. For instance, the researchers' twenty-year industry experience in Barbados worked to her advantage. The researcher has extensive management training and experience derived from the event industry in Barbados, the United States and the United Kingdom where she has conducted marketing research on numerous occasions. Being educated in Barbados, where English is the first language, and subsequently in the United Kingdom, means that the problems of interviewer skills, cultural and language barriers were minimised.

2.5 PREPARING THE INTERVIEW SCHEDULE

Although the research methods evolved as the study progressed, the researcher found it necessary to prepare a set of questions in advance. The questions were arranged in the form of interview guides that would lead the discussion rather than be rigidly applied. Although there was a pre-determined set of questions for each group of respondents, as unexpected themes and issues emerged it was necessary to digress from some of the questions in order to explore these themes fully. Furthermore, the questions asked were dependent on their relevance to the informant and the context under which the interview took place. However, the preparation and memorising of a pre-determined set of questions helped to ease the pressure on the researcher in initiating conversation and alleviated the embarrassment of silent gaps during conversations.

2.5.1 Testing the Interview Guide.

Hammersley and Atkinson (1995) stress that although qualitative research strategies cannot always be predetermined, this does not mean that the researcher should adopt haphazard behaviour. Instead they recommend the need for fieldwork preparation and constant reflection (see Burman, 1994). This advice was heeded and an interview guide was prepared for each group of individuals to be interviewed.

The interview guide should ideally have been tested on a small group of informants who bear similar characteristics to those persons in the actual study (Gill and Johnson, 1991). However, this was not possible. Studies in event tourism tend to face logistical issues not necessarily present in other studies. For example, most special events have fixed dates and times, they may be of very short duration and of a one-off nature. This makes it virtually impossible to carry out pilot studies or to anticipate all of the dimensions and logistics in advance (Getz, 1997; Nicholson and Pearce, 2001; Seaton, 1997). Furthermore, the geographical distance between Barbados and the United Kingdom meant that it was not possible to conduct pilot tests on the interview guides on the subjects. Instead, the interview guides were tested on lecturers and fellow PhD colleagues at Buckinghamshire New University, all of whom have varied expertise in tourism and research. This location was chosen because of the geographical convenience for the researcher. Time and financial constraints also prevented this pilot test from being conducted at another similar event and on subjects similar to the ones in the actual research.

Berg (1989) suggests that interview schedules be pre-tested on two levels. Firstly, the schedule should be critically examined by experts familiar with the area of research. Secondly, the instrument should be pre-tested to assess its effectiveness and appropriateness for the investigation (also see Stacey, 1969). The first level of testing required lecturers to comment on the questions in the interview guide. The second level of testing involved scenario based interviews with five PhD colleagues and residents of High Wycombe, Buckinghamshire. These five colleagues had all travelled within the last year and as a result were able to relate the questions to their own travel experiences.

The purpose of the pilot study was to test the average length of the interview and the wording of each question in order to ensure clarity and to identify possible ambiguities. It was also necessary to ensure that the questions were addressing the issues that needed to be explored. Finally, it was necessary to establish whether the sequencing of questions allowed a logical flow of discussion while motivating the respondents to participate. The pilot test also allowed the researcher to rehearse the administering of the interviews and to memorise the questions.

2.6 ETHICAL ISSUES

The British Sociological Association and the American Sociological Association are some of the organisations that provide ethical guidelines for researchers to follow. Higher education institutions also have their own research ethics and committees, whose codes of conduct are aimed at protecting the participants and the institution. Institutions endeavour to protect themselves from any legal implications or bad image that may emanate from unethical research practices. As a student of Buckinghamshire New University, it was extremely important that this research be conducted at the highest level of propriety. Perhaps the most important ethical issue involved in this research was to gain permission to conduct this type of study in Barbados and access to the golf course at the Sandy Lane Hotel. Early attempts at gaining access and permission to conduct research involved approaching the management of the Sandy Lane Hotel who initially refused access. Instead, access had to be negotiated through the Barbados Tourism Authority, the major sponsor of the Golf World Cup, who granted conditional access to the event in return for a report on the findings of this research.

Other ethical issues revolved around the respondents' rights to informed consent, right to privacy and confidentiality. Kellehere (1993) asserts that it must be made clear to all participants that they have the right to refuse to participate in any research. Consent to participate was sought from all participants and confidentiality of privilege information was guaranteed. For instance, the names of all participants were concealed, except in situations where the expressed permission of the participant was received. During the fieldwork all refusals, albeit few, to participate in the semi-structured interviews were duly respected. Some local tourism stakeholders were very adamant that their identity be concealed to prevent reprisals which is why the publication of this work was long in the making.

2.7 CARRYING OUT THE FIELDWORK

The fieldwork for this study took place on the Caribbean island of Barbados. The fieldwork began on December 2, 2006 on arrival at the Grantley Adams Airport in Barbados and ended on December 18, 2006 when the researcher returned to the United Kingdom.

The Golf World Cup was hosted at the Sandy Lane Golf and Country Club, which forms part of the facilities offered at the Sandy Lane Hotel on the west coast of Barbados. Sandy Lane Hotel is regarded as one of the island's most luxurious resorts. The official dates of the Golf World Cup were December 4th to December 10th, 2006. However, the practice rounds for the competition took place from December 5th to 6th, while the competitive rounds took place from December 7th to 10th, 2006. While the researcher spent the first five days on the island interviewing tourism officials and local residents, the period of December 7th to 10th - the official dates of the competition - were spent on the golf course observing the event and interviewing the local and international spectators. A total of 85 interviews were conducted with foreign visitors to the event and local tourism officials/stakeholders and residents.

2.7.1 From Observation to Semi-Structured Interviews

Ethnographic research is not necessarily a linear technique but instead it is a dynamic process (See Patton, 1990). This view was certainly illustrated in this research as the researcher's role was constantly shifting from a participant observer to that of an interviewer during the entire fieldwork exercise.

The first data collection exercise commenced on December 2nd 2006 as soon as the researcher arrived on the island of Barbados. Much of the data collected on December 2nd and 3rd involved the researcher taking on the role of a participant tourist. These initial observations involved car trips to various parts of the island observing how the island was preparing for the Golf World Cup. It was during this time that the billboards on the ABC highway advertising the Golf World Cup were first observed. During these early observation

30

exercises the extensive road-works programme taking place in Barbados and the consequent inconveniences were observed and experienced. These types of observations took place initially the first two days of the researcher's stay in Barbados until they were halted by the first set of semi-structured interviews with tourism officials which commenced on 4th December.

Early data collection exercises at the Sandy Lane golf course were in the role of a participant golf visitor. Immediately on arrival at Sandy Lane initial observations involved standing back and examining the physical and social environment in which this event took place. This involved observing the landscape, the flow of people as they entered and exited the compound, observing the ways in which people organised themselves and how they interacted with the social setting. This preliminary observation was necessary in order to best determine how and where the semi-structured interviews would take place. It also provided the researcher with an appreciation of the complete social setting in which people functioned by recording the context in which they operated on the golf course. Many critical observations pertinent to this project were observed at this time.

A major challenge on the golf course involved how and where to solicit participants for interviews. In the early stages of soliciting for interviews the role of participant observer was adopted as golf visitors appeared more comfortable interacting with other golf tourists or spectators rather than officials. This role seemed the most effective way to approach individuals for interviews which involved initial 'small talk' about the event, the weather or Barbados in general after which the researcher would reveal who she was to any willing participant. Once the interviews on the golf course commenced these interviews tended to take place simultaneously or alternatively with the observations of the surrounding, therefore, after a few interviews the researcher's role would shift again to a participant observer as she went about observing the food, the landscape or some other phenomenon critical to the research. These shifting of roles characterised the entire field work exercise until the researcher departed the island to return to the United Kingdom on December 18th 2006. This field work exercise certainly demonstrated how one must be flexible in the field in order to adapt to evolving situations (Wickens, 1999).

Many critical observations were made during the field work exercise at Sandy Lane. A major observation on the golf course was that were no spectator stands or seating areas so as a result many spectators tended to follow their favourite player as they played 'hole' to 'hole'. Consequently, many spectators were not in any one place for more than ten minutes at a time; once the ball was played they moved on to the next hole. In addition, while the ball was 'in play' spectators and officials had to be absolutely silent and still; one was even discouraged from sneezing. There were officials around the parameters of the 'hole' to ensure that these restrictions were observed. It soon became evident that in order to conduct an interview the researcher might have to be constantly mobile with the informant while tolerating constant interruptions. On the first day, many conversations with visitors took place while on the move. For example, while walking from 'hole' to 'hole' or while travelling together on golf carts from one end of the golf course to the other. Consequently, on a few occasions, the researcher was not able to explore all the themes in the interview guide, but this is a common problem in some ethnographic research (Wickens, 1999). However, in many instances, the researcher was able to 'pin down' visitors for conversations while they were socialising at one of the bars. On the second day of the event it was observed that spectators tended to gather for extended periods at the 18th hole. This was apparently because all competitors had to play the 18th hole so it provided a good vantage point where observers could sit on the grass and watch the players as they each reached this stage of the competition. It was at this location that the researcher was able to procure a number of more in-depth semi-structured interviews since informants tended to be stationary for extended periods rather than in a rush to follow any particular player around the golf course. These interviews lasted between 30 minutes to one hour.

Once the semi-structured interviews on the golf course commenced, the researcher was constantly interviewing golf visitors in one instance and then in the other observing various phenomena on the golf course in order to understand the context in which participants were describing their experiences during the interview sessions. Bowen (2002) notes how observations of this sort allow the researcher to validate people's actions since very often people may say that they do one thing but actually do something else. The observations at the Sandy Lane golf course provided the researcher with much descriptive and analytical data that was later useful when analysing the data from the semi-structured interview data. For instance initial observations involved observing the flow and direction of human traffic at the Sandy Lane hotel which later helped in making decisions about where and when to interview participants. This is consistent with the argument put forward by Seaton (1997) who noted that when researching event tourism it is not always possible to anticipate beforehand the logistical challenges that may confront the researcher's data collection efforts due to the one-off nature of most events. Seaton (1997) in this instance had to modify the data collection agenda by combining participant observation with questionnaires in order to collect meaningful data. The experience of this researcher and the Seaton (1997) experience further emphasises the view of other researchers that we must be flexible in the field (Hammersley and Atkinson, 1995; Maykut and Morehouse, 1994; Patton, 1990; Punch, 1998).

While a substantial amount of research was conducted on the golf course, other observations were made as the researcher travelled around the island during her two-week stay in Barbados. These observational activities involved the researcher leaving her residence as early as 10.00 AM and returning around 7.00 PM at night. During these trips the researcher adopted the role of simply 'observer'. These round the island observations were necessary as a follow up to what participants highlighted in their interviews. Visits to Sandy Lane Hotel and a tour of the West Coast validated much of what participants highlighted in the interviews about West Coast tourism. During these travels local residents and other tourists visiting Barbados were also interviewed. These interviews were conducted at sites including, Holetown, Bridgetown, Accra Beach, the Hilton Hotel, the Bougainvillea Beach Resort, Miami Beach and at selected residents' homes in Christ Church. With the exception of the interviews conducted at the Sandy Lane Golf and Country Club, the choice of the interview sites was not pre-meditated but based on opportunities that were presented at the time in terms of available and willing informants. Interviews with tourism officials and industry managers were much easier to procure as these were pre-arranged by appointment before leaving the United Kingdom.

2.7.2 Recording the Data

Data from the field work were recorded in a field diary. Initially there were plans to video record all observations and to tape record all interviews. However this was not possible since electronic equipment was banned from the golf course. This ban included cell phones, cameras and video recorders. Due to these restrictions handbags were searched at the entrance and each visitor was subjected to electronic scanning by event personnel. The fear of these expensive items being confiscated influenced the decision not to tape or video record the interviews and observations on the golf course.

When approaching individuals for interviews, outside of the Sandy Lane golf course, a decision was also made not to approach any potential informant with evidence of officialdom such as note pads, clipboards or tape recorders. This decision followed an incident where the researcher was met with suspicion by tourists at Miami Beach and with hostility at the Hilton Hotel. In both cases the tourists thought that the researcher was trying to sell them time-share accommodation. In the end, the researcher had to adopt a policy of interviewing the informants and then recording the notes at the next possible opportunity. Public sector officials, although willing to be interviewed, did not submit to a tape-recorded session and wanted assurances that their names would not be mentioned in the publication. This is because at the time event tourism was a contentious, political issue on the island and although much of the debate involved the Cricket World Cup rather than the Golf World Cup, most people preferred not to be quoted. In these instances condensed notes were taken during the interview.

Tape recording has the advantage of enabling the researcher to become familiar with the data through the constant replaying of tapes. Tape recording is superior to note taking in that it prevents the researcher from using his or her own words in the recording of data or in the citing of quotations. Tape recording facilitates the accuracy of data collection and allows the interviewer to be more attentive to the respondent (McCall-Simmons, 1969). However, the presence of a tape recorder could also be intimidating and people may generally not want to be recorded when discussing sensitive issues (Patton, 1987). The presence of a tape recorder can also make people uncomfortable resulting in stilted or unnatural behaviour (McCall-Simmons, 1969). In this research, the issue of intimidation and harassment raised by the Barbados Tourism Authority, as well as the need to be unobtrusive, led to the decision not to use a tape recorder, particularly at the Sandy Lane Golf Course. However, good note-taking skills were employed, a skill that the researcher had developed from management experience. Wickens (1999) did note that the most practical recording by the researcher is note taking. A good observation or interview recorded with less than perfect accuracy is generally preferable to a mediocre interview with high quality recording. Notes taken during the interview involved the recording of key words and phrases with detailed notes at the earliest possible opportunity (See Oliver, 1997). However, it is recommended that even when a tape-recorder has been used, comprehensive notes should still be taken in the event that the tape recorder breaks down, the tapes become distorted or data is lost (Wickens, 1999). The next section examines the strategies employed in the selection of informants.

2.8 SELECTION OF INFORMANTS

In qualitative research, the researcher follows rules that are different from those followed in quantitative research, but does not do so haphazardly. As (Honigmann, 1987: 81-84) explains:

> Judgement and opportunistic… sampling represents degrees of deliberateness exercised in choosing informants, subjects, situations or behavioural events…. Opportune social contacts may be exploited for the special knowledge they possess…

In qualitative research the objective is to explore a range of experiences, patterns and issues. The nature of qualitative research requires that the researcher employs sampling techniques more along the lines of 'deliberate' sampling (Punch, 1998). It means sampling in a 'deliberate' way with some focus or purpose in mind. There are no precise strategies for sampling in qualitative research due to the wide range of research purposes, approaches and settings. The basic ideas guiding sampling strategies vary considerably and reflect the purposes and the objectives guiding the study. Miles and Huberman (1994) for instance presented a typology of sixteen (16) sampling strategies to match different settings, purposes and situations.

This researcher adopted a purposive and theoretical sampling strategy (see Wickens, 1999). The strength with purposive sampling is that it enables the researcher to select 'information rich' cases to be studied. Information rich cases are those from which a great deal can be learnt about issues that are of central importance to the purpose of the research (Patton, 1990). In this case, the fact that the researcher was able to travel to Barbados and visit the Golf World Cup meant that the foreign visitors to Barbados and local tourism officials were purposely sought to provided cases with 'rich' and 'authentic' (Silverman, 1993:10) information about the phenomenon being studied. Being in the right place at the right time meant the researcher was able to procure information from those persons actually experiencing the phenomenon. Purposive sampling provided the opportunity to follow new leads and to take advantage of emerging opportunities in the field.

In qualitative research the need for more flexible research designs is recognised (Hammersley and Atkinson, 1995; Maykut and Morehouse, 1994; Patton, 1990; Punch, 1998). The approach adopted in this study is thus in line with the concept of 'emergent designs' where adjustments and refinements to the sample occurred once the data collection and analysis was in progress. At the Golf World Cup sampling decisions were made while the researcher was a participant tourist at the event. In addition, sampling local stakeholders sometimes involved 'snowballing' techniques. Snowballing techniques involved using key informants to gain access to other key informants (Sekeran, 2002). In some instances, the researcher had to use insider contacts to gain access to public officials and this resulted in further 'snowballing' techniques of public officials.

Proponents of traditional theories of sampling might have 'raised an eyebrow' at the lack of 'representativeness' of the sample. However, as Honigmann (1987: 83) notes: "The validity of the sample depends not so much upon the number of cases as upon the proper specification of the informant". In this research it was particularly important to select individuals that represented Barbados' key tourism markets. In this regard, it was important to talk to individuals from the United States of America, the United Kingdom and the Caribbean. In the case of the Caribbean, the informants included individuals visiting the event from Jamaica and Trinidad and Tobago - Barbados's key regional markets. Interviews with major decision-makers included those at the top of the decision-making hierarchy in Barbados' tourism industry, including the then Minister of Tourism.

Strauss and Corbin (1990) and Wickens (1999) defended the issue of sample size suggesting that researchers using qualitative techniques should be guided more by conceptual concerns and not necessarily by 'representativeness'. As the research progressed and themes emerged further sampling decisions had to be made. For instance, the theme of 'civic pride', which emerged through interviews with local residents, prompted the researcher to utilise 'theoretical sampling' (Strauss and Corbin, 1990) in order to confirm the emerging issues by interviewing more local residents. This type of sampling continued until the theory that the researcher was trying to establish was 'saturated'.

The issue of sampling in this study was also dependent upon human cooperation. The willingness of tourists, tour representatives, officials and residents to participate was critical to the research going ahead. In one instance tourists at the Hilton Hotel refused to be interviewed and, in another, a public official and a manager of a Bridgetown hotel refused to cooperate. Issues pertaining to access also had an impact on sample selection. Had access been less restrictive and institutional support obtained from the Professional Golfers Association, this would have provided the scope to approach a wider range of individuals. It would have been valuable to collect data from the competing golfers, their families, media personnel and officials of the Professional Golfers Association. As a result, the sampling employed in this study cannot lay claims to generalised findings. However, as stated at the outset, the main objective of this study was to identify the participants' perceptions and expectations associated with golf events in Barbados and not to generalise but to conceptualise. The type of sampling strategies employed by qualitative researchers tends to raise concerns about validity and reliability in qualitative research. This issue is discussed in the following section.

2.8.1.1 Trustworthiness in Qualitative Tourism Research

The use of qualitative approaches and multiple data collection methods in research is often criticised because of the perceived lack of objectivity and generalibility (Burgess, 1984). This brings to the fore issues of validity and reliability. These issues were acknowledged and every effort made to counteract any factors that might have contaminated this study.

Thompson and Walker (1998: 69) argue that there are four factors for assessing the rigor of qualitative studies. These include credibility, transferability, dependability and conformability. Credibility deals with the true value of a study when the descriptions or interpretations presented are recognised by people who had that experience, whereas transferability is achieved when findings 'fit' samples and settings beyond that of the particular study. Dependability refers to the stability of the findings and the ability to track variances in the data over time. Conformability deals with the issue of bias and suggests that when others, not involved in the research, can confirm the results, it is then possible to verify that the findings are not based on the perceptions of the researcher.

However, Silverman (1993) argues that qualitative researchers need not concern themselves with the issue of validity and reliability in the same sense as quantitative research but should instead be concerned with the issue of 'authenticity'. Authenticity refers to collecting information from those individuals that are actually experiencing the phenomenon. In this study, every effort was made to collect data that provided an 'authentic' representation of the stakeholders' expectations and perceptions. It was an advantage that the researcher had access to the entire golf course where the event was taking place so that those individuals experiencing the event could be interviewed and observed. Reliability was achieved by keeping a written record of all steps taken in the research, justifying what was done at each stage, so that other researchers could follow the same decision trail (Silverman, 1993). Fieldnotes were taken at the time of a specific observation or interview or as soon as possible thereafter. A fieldwork journal was used to record problems and ideas that arose in addition to the records pertaining to analysis and interpretation of the data (Silverman 1993).

Training of interviewers and the pre-testing of interview schedules help to make studies error free. In this study, the piloting of the interview schedule helped to identify problems and ambiguities before they occurred in the field. Another technique recommended is the use of an independent analyst whose task is to analyse a set of data from the study in order to ascertain if they reach the same conclusions as the researcher. This is known as 'inter-rater reliability' (Silverman 1993). In this study, the supervisor of this study at Buckinghamshire New University was asked to review all of the data obtained for an independent analysis and subsequently concurred with the themes that emerged.

Validity is concerned with the extent to which the data collected is a true picture of what is being studied (McNeill, 1985). The nature of qualitative research makes it susceptible to misinterpretation and misunderstandings that could present a distorted picture of reality. There is the question of whether respondents are telling the truth. This is complicated by the fact that people sometimes believe they are telling the truth but their actual behaviour is not always congruent with their stated behaviour. Memory is also a factor, especially in cases where individuals are asked to recall certain events. In this study, the researcher had the advantage of conducting interviews and making observations at the actual event on the island of

Barbados so that respondents were not necessarily totally dependent on memories of their event experience.

Cresswell (1994) suggests that the researcher should discuss the issue of validity and what measures are taken to validate the data from the outset. He further suggests that researchers can take the categories and themes back to the informants and ask whether the conclusions are accurate. Alternatively, transcripts can be forwarded to the informants for confirmation that they present a true and accurate picture of what was revealed to the researcher (also see Gibson, Willming and Holdnak, 2003). In this study the researcher was not able to send interview notes to all informants for validation since many were from overseas or unknown. However, the notes were emailed to local informants for whom email addresses were known. However, where possible, the researcher was able to establish 'ecological validity' (see Parker, 1994) with foreign informants and industry stakeholders by constantly restating what the respondents had said, in order to verify that there was a mutual understanding of the issues being addressed and to obviate misinterpretations. In reality, validity and reliability depend on the professional and personal skills of the researcher: their methodological skills, their knowledge, sensitivity and integrity. It is about being open and possessing a willingness to listen to others and representing their views as accurately as possible (Strauss and Corbin, 1998). Thus, the credibility of the researcher is central to deriving reliable and valid findings. Humberstone, (1997b: 200) notes: that "...the visibility of the researcher's personal experience and a self-interrogation of their own values and motivations embedded in the particular research process are pivotal". It is at this juncture that it becomes appropriate to engage in the process of personal reflexivity.

2.9 REFLEXIVITY AND RESEARCHER DECLARATION

Blaikie (1993) and Humberstone (1997a) assert that researchers need to declare up front their values and attitudes as comprehensively as possible so that other researchers would be aware of any factors that may impinge upon the objectivity of the findings and interpretation of the study. Personal reflexivity is the process by which the researcher reflects on how his or her personal interests and values affect the research. It is a process of in-depth reflection and a critique of the research process by the researcher (Humberstone, 1997a). To make this process visible, all procedures throughout the research process are carefully documented and the limitations and perspectives are made transparent so that others may judge the quality of the research (May, 1993). This is not to undermine the value of this work but rather it serves to highlight the fact that in research it is difficult to be totally objective and to separate the researcher's beliefs and assumptions from the issue under investigation (Lewis, 2002). In fact, in the paradigm it is the researcher's background and experiences that make an important contribution to the construction of knowledge. The task of making the problems encountered during the research process explicit and the way in which these issues are tackled will enable a greater degree of credibility since the exposing of the researcher's values exposes the study to the critical analysis of the audience (Humberstone, 1997b). Reflexivity is therefore critical since it will equip readers with more comprehensive insights into the role the researcher played in shaping, interpreting and theorising the data (Humberstone, 1997a). As Humberstone (1997b: 204) asserts, providing a reflective account "...makes visible the ways in which the researcher, who is central to the research, influences and is influenced by it. It highlights the ways the researcher weaves her way through the webs of power whilst attempting to remain true to her principles.... Clearly then such an autobiography will not try to hide 'problems' but will wish to explore and expose them". In the light of this, it is necessary to give a reflective account of the researcher's background and its relation this to study.

The researcher is a stakeholder in Barbados' tourism having been born and educated on the island. She has worked for over 20 years in various managerial capacities in the tourism industry in Barbados, the United Kingdom and the United States of America in the areas of public relations, sales, promotions, marketing, conference, event management and environmental management. This experience involved positions at Marriott Hotels and Resorts, Island Magic Barbados (an event management company), the Almond Beach Resorts and Bougainvillea Beach Resort in Barbados and Jarvis Hotels in the United Kingdom. The researcher's interests in mega events stems from the decision by the Caribbean Heads of Government to support a bid for CARICOM (Caribbean Common Market) member states to host the Cricket World Cup, 2007. From that time the topic of event tourism became a popular topic of political and public debate on the island. This debate stimulated the researcher's interest in learning more about the mega sport phenomenon. The researcher thus had the advantage of understanding Barbadian society and the nature of the tourism product and was familiar with the research surroundings. She also owns and manages a tourism business called 'Hospitality Solutions' which is a company that provides specialised advice to small tourism businesses in the area of marketing, training and event planning and research. Today she is the Programme Coordinator for the BA (hons) event management at the University of Chichester. Having personal friends and contacts in the industry in Barbados meant that the researcher was able to use these contacts to gain access to the golf course at Sandy Lane and high-powered personnel in hotels. However, this closeness to the research environment, although it worked to the researcher's advantage, raises questions about the researcher's own biases and values contaminating this study. The next section discusses the issue of objectivity and subjectivity in this research and considers to what extent objectivity could be achieved.

2.9.1 Objectivity versus Subjectivity

Although many researchers, operating within different paradigms, endeavour to achieve objectivity during their research, social research is not conducted in a vacuum and therefore the extent to which it could be totally objective is questionable (Patton, 1990). Human life is a complex phenomenon and the values of the researcher and the researched are socially and culturally constructed (May, 1993). According to Denzin and Lincoln (2005) objective reality cannot be captured because we only know a thing through its representations. Research is thus mediated by the complex dynamics of social forces so that although researchers seek to achieve total objectivity the researcher's subjective meanings, as well as those of the informants, will penetrate the research. After all, subjective meanings and interpretation are a fundamental part of human existence. As Priest (1996: 3-4) notes:

> How is it possible... to study important social phenomena objectively when subjective individual thought and interpretation was so characteristically human?

The nature of tourism as an experiential product means that it can only be subjective. Ryan (1995b and 1995c) notes that because tourists have their own unique experiences research can only be subjective like a list of individual case studies which may serve to help others derive their own meaning.

In qualitative research, however, a primary purpose is to understand the subjective meanings that people hold of their

41

experiences. In this sense objectivity is not what is necessarily important but the subjective opinions and experiences of the subjects. Employing a fusion of participant observation, semi-structured interviews and the examination of documents, will have neutralised any bias that might be inherent in this study.

The methodology for this research was thus chosen not with the view of imposing rigidity but with the objective of developing a flexible design that would allow the researcher and the participants' total freedom to explore and relay the subjective meanings and experiences of those being studied. It is therefore the goal of this researcher to report truthfully the different perspectives as put forward by the participants.

However, it is nevertheless prudent that a reflective account be taken of the participants' views. As stated earlier, there is concern within the research community as to the extent that the views expressed by participants accurately represent the participants' true feelings or impressions of the phenomenon. While some researchers contend that the researcher's presence can influence what the participants choose to express or how they choose to express it (Brewer, 2000; Burgess, 1984; Punch, 1998), there is concern in this particular study regarding the extent that political and public debate in Barbados affected the views of those who participated in the research, in particular the local perspective. As stated in chapter one, at the time of the fieldwork the Cricket World Cup finals were due to take place the following April. This event was a controversial issue which dominated much public and political debate. In fact, the controversy concerning the impacts and alleged benefits of hosting mega events was used as a political weapon by most opposition parties in Barbados. In such circumstances, it is plausible to assume that some of the views expressed by the local participants might have been politically motivated or politically biased.

Concern regarding bias in the information given by participants was also raised on the golf course when soliciting interviews. On the Sunday (December 10, 2006) of the event when the rain fell, participants were willing to give interviews about their experience and were thus lining up to talk to the researcher. This opportunity occurred mainly due to the heavy rain that fell and the subsequent temporary suspension of play due to a water-logged golf course. With no activities available to fill the time many spectators were happy to grant interviews. Although this occurrence opened up the possibility of biased views, it must also be acknowledged that human cooperation and willingness to participate in research is a major challenge for qualitative researchers (Strauss and Corbin, 1990; Wickens, 1999, 2002). The researcher of this golf tourism event was fortunate to be presented with participants who were willing to express their opinions and experiences of the golf event to her. However, at this stage, the researcher decided that conceptual issues and the need for authentic and rich narratives should take precedence over concerns of possible bias (also see Silverman, 1993; Wickens, 1999).

It is evident that all research is methodologically flawed and socially constructed and therefore can only be viewed in context (Blaikie, 1993), as in this case the context of those individuals who participated. What is important in exploratory research however is its potential for identifying the range of issues that are associated with a specific phenomenon that acts as a stimulus for further research. An idea expressed by one individual may be critically important to the success of the final or future studies (Peterson, 1994). However, the combining of the interviews with participant observations and the examination of documents would have helped to minimise the potential for bias in participants' narratives of their experiences and feelings. The next section explains how the qualitative data was organised and analysed.

2.10 DATA ANALYSIS

This section pertains to the final component of this chapter – the data analysis procedures. As Miles and Huberman (1994) point out, data analysis is an iterative process, which occurs both during and after collection of the data (also see Cresswell, 1993; Dey, 1993; Hammersley and Atkinson, 1995).

Although the data analysis for this study was iterative in nature it nevertheless occurred at three distinct levels, which began during the commencement of the fieldwork and continued until the end of the project in August 2008. The first stage of analysis in the field involved the continuous process of identifying and connecting categories and themes after each interview and observation. This early analysis involved organising and summarising the notes from the observations and interviews conducted on a daily basis. Engaging with the data at this early stage allowed the researcher to become sensitive to a large array of important ideas, concepts and themes as they emerged from the fieldwork exercise. This process was particularly useful as it guided the further data collection strategies that were subsequently employed. For instance, as the theme of 'atmosphere' emerged in the data, the researcher was led to continuously explore this theme, amongst others, during the next fieldwork exercise.

As previously mentioned the use of a tape recorder was not permitted within the confines of the golf course and some local officials and residents did not agree to be tape recorded. Under these circumstances condensed notes were taken during the interviews and then elaborated, edited and organised into topics subsequent to the preceding interview. Consequently, the filling in of some missing data was reliant on the researcher's memory. However, the fact that this early coding and analysis took place immediately after each interview meant that any missing data was immediately recalled. This early analysis and on the spot interpretation of data is recommended by qualitative researchers, and is common practice in ethnographic studies (Burgess, 1984; Hammersley and Atkinson, 1983; Maykut and Morehouse, 1994; Strauss and Corbin, 1990; Wickens, 1999). Early analysis was aided by the use of analytic memos. Analytic memos are brief notes that represent the insights that the researcher achieves as they progress through the data analysis process (O'Brien, 2006; Strauss, 1987). Memos were particularly useful for documenting ideas, views, questions and intuitions as they occurred through the analysis of the data (see Robson, 1993; Strauss and Corbin, 1990).

The second stage of analysis involved the constant comparative method for qualitative analysis. This is a method of combining inductive category coding with a simultaneous comparison of all of the units of meaning contained in the data. As each new meaning of data is selected for analysis it is compared to all other units of meaning and subsequently grouped with similar units of meaning (Maykut and Morehouse, 1994). This stage of analysis occurred after the data collection was completed but remained an on-going process until the end of the project. This second level analysis occurred once the researcher had returned to the United Kingdom. The mass of qualitative data collected during the fieldwork was mainly textual in nature and therefore had to be condensed, organised and coded in order to achieve structure, coherence and manageability. At this stage the typing of all interview and observation notes were undertaken. At the same time, all secondary data from promotional material, state documents and newspapers was thoroughly examined and organised through a filing system according to the themes represented and those that matched the interview and observational data.

Hammersley and Atkinson (1995) recommend that researchers immerse themselves in the data and then try to seek out patterns, identify possible surprising phenomena and be sensitive to inconsistencies or divergent views between individuals and groups. To facilitate this, the field-notes were thoroughly examined, read and re-read. It was at this stage that the researcher realised that analysing qualitative data involves a process of interpretation. As stated by Wickens (1999:43), "participant's words often have multiple meanings and therefore have to be understood through the process of interpretation". Finding the meaning behind all the textual data was facilitated by an exploration of the data through an early coding process which assisted in identifying the many themes that emerged and which helped to form the basis for a workable descriptive framework (Robson, 1993). Coding is a system used to categorise the data. It assists in identifying patterns and themes by giving them provisional names. This preliminary coding also assisted in reducing the data, by eliminating data that was not relevant to the study (see Dey, 1993) while helping to identify the salient, relevant issues. It is the process of breaking down, examining, comparing, conceptualising and categorising the data. Numerous codes were generated while reading through responses without concern for the variety of categories. Some of this early coding was influenced by 'open coding'. Open coding is a term normally associated with grounded theory methodology. It is the process of developing categories, concepts and themes emerging from the data without making any prior assumptions about what you might discover. The data is broken down into discrete parts, closely examined, compared for similarities and differences, and questions are asked about the phenomena reflected in the data (Strauss and Corbin, 1990). To this end the data in this study was examined word-by-word and line-by-line and coded accordingly.

Miles and Huberman (1994) suggest that the researcher can being the coding exercise using a 'start list' of codes that emerge from the conceptual framework and list of research questions that the researcher brings to the study. Strauss and Corbin (1990) argue however that the purpose of 'open-coding' should be to open the study to all possible new concepts and dimensions that are embedded in the data. So, although some codes were informed by the extensive literature review and conceptual framework the researcher was conscious of the importance of allowing the codes and subsequent themes to flow naturally from the data without the influence of the researcher's prior knowledge. While codes such as 'IE' for image enhancement and 'SP' for self-perception were informed by the literature review other codes such as 'SE' for social exclusion and

'CE' for Celebrity Effect were influenced by the phenomena that were emerging from the data.

After the preliminary coding process a further coding system was employed where codes were related to each other through the identification of core code categories and sub-categories (Hammersley and Atkinson, 1995; Robson, 1993). For instance, the core category of 'poor local spectator attendance' was related to sub–categories of 'awareness', 'perception' and 'celebrity effect'. From an international perspective, the core category of 'poor international attendance' was related to the sub-category of 'atmosphere'. This coding processed was influenced by axial coding. Axial coding is the process of relating categories to their subcategories (Strauss, 1987; Strauss & Corbin, 1990). Subcategories also are categories, but they are categories that answer the questions of ''when, where, why, who, how, and with what consequences (Strauss and Corbin, 1990).

The identification of core categories and sub-categories led to the identification of other categories or dimensions that related to the core categories or sub-categories (see Maykuk and Morehouse, 1994). The sub-category of 'awareness' was related to the dimension of 'advertising and promotion' while the sub category of atmosphere was related to the dimensions of event design, arena layout/design and social atmosphere. Strauss and Corbin (1990) recommend linking the sub-categories to dimensions in the data that further illuminate or explain the core categories or sub-categories under study. This is done through a process of continuously trying to relate the core categories in the data to other categories that may help to clarify their meanings. In this procedure the researcher examined each piece of data coded in terms of a particular category and noted its similarities with and differences to other data that had been similarly categorised. In this way more categories or sub-categories emerged resulting in some reassignment of data (see Hammersley and Atkinson, 1995). Where a chunk of data did not relate to any other units of meaning or categories, this was used to form a new category (Maykut and Morehouse, 1994).

Once all of the core categories, sub-categories and their dimensions were identified, the process of making comparisons between the different groups was undertaken. A considerable amount of time was spent engaging with the data through the process of re-reading the interview notes, the observation field notes and the documents. Reviewing each script enabled comparisons to be made between the data collected from each group of informants. Each script was reviewed and convergent, parallel and diverse experiences between the groups of informants were noted and organised into topics or themes based on the core and sub categories identified earlier. When comparing responses between the different groups, particularly the international visitors and local stakeholders, care was taken to ensure that the responses to specific questions were analysed in the context in which the data was produced (see Wickens, 1999). Significant statements were identified according to the core categories and sub-categories and placed into a filing system according to the group represented in the data. This involved a system of cutting and pasting material from the field notes whereby chunks of texts were cut out and pasted with other chucks of text that fit under a specific theme or heading. Care was, however, taken not to lose sight of the contextual relevance of the transplanted data in the final analysis (see Bryman and Burgess, 1994).

Once all the themes were identified, and the data sorted and organised, the third level of analysis commenced. As Wickens (1999) pointed out, the analysis of qualitative data is a daunting linguistic exercise. In other words, the researcher has to make sense of the data collected through constant interpretation. This was facilitated through a prolonged process of relating the themes back to the literature in order to derive a coherent understanding of each informant's experience. This involved a constant dialogue between the researcher, the analytic notes and the views and issues as addressed in the literature.

2.11 CONCLUSION

This chapter provided insights into both the research experience and the philosophical and practical considerations associated with this project. The research techniques of participant observations, semi-structured interviews and the examination of documents adopted, elicited a 'rich' and comprehensive body of data that would not have been possible with a single method of data collection. The utilisation of these methods facilitated the accommodation of diverse and paralleled perspectives solicited from a range of actors associated with the Golf World Cup.

The utilisation of diverse methods is essential to the credibility of the research findings. It is, nevertheless, acknowledged that the results of this study are based on the representations of the reality experienced by the respondents and the interpretation of the researcher (see Wickens, 1999). As a result, the findings reported in chapters five and six do not represent generalisations to a wider population but are limited to the individual respondents who provided the information relevant to their own expectations and perceptions of the Golf World Cup. The findings are limited therefore to the respondents selected, the biography of the researcher, the methods used and to a specific place at a specific time (Wickens, 1999).

However, all research is methodologically flawed and socially constructed (Blaikie, 1993) and therefore can only be viewed in context. The value of qualitative research lies in its potential for identifying the range of issues that are associated with a specific phenomenon that acts as a stimulus for further research. As Peterson (1994:488) points out "...an idea expressed by one individual may be critically important to the success of the final study". It is in this vein that qualitative research is fundamentally important.

3 -CHAPTER THREE
THEORETICAL PERSPECTIVES ON MEGA EVENTS

3.1 INTRODUCTION

This chapter highlights the many similar but also divergent theoretical approaches that exist in the event management field. It also highlights the fact that although events have been studied from an economic, social, cultural, psychological and tourism perspective, there are many overlaps and dependencies in event management in terms of the scholastic domains used to analyse them.

The most prominent perspective, the economic perspective, dominates the literature but very often scholars link the economic perspective to the tourism and commercial implications. The tourism implications are also often analysed in accordance with the social and cultural impacts that mega events have on destinations. Despite the range of disciplines used to study these events, serious gaps in our knowledge continue to be evident. Firstly, studies in the sports tourism and the event arena hardly give the key players in the phenomenon, the stakeholders, a voice. The stakeholders represent one of the most neglected areas of research in the events industry. The multitude of stakeholders who comprise the event organisation may range from politicians to volunteers to hoteliers, but their voices are hardly heard. This continues to be the case due to the preference of structured methodologies which do not allow the subjects a voice. Secondly, also notably absent from the multiplicity of studies in sport event tourism, are studies dedicated to golf. Golf continues to receive scant attention from scholars and event researchers; and thirdly, studies dedicated to the study of mega events on small islands are limited if not non-existent.

This literature review critically examines the theoretical perspectives put forward by scholars concerning the staging of mega events. These are examined from an economic and tourism perspective and the physical legacy perspective. Socio-cultural and political perspectives also receive attention. The media impacts and destination image theory are also discussed at length; and finally, motivation to attend events is critically examined.

3.2 THE EVENTS INDUSTRY

Events are occurrences out of the ordinary, limited in duration and infrequently staged (Getz, 1997). The term special event has been coined to describe specific rituals, presentations, or celebrations that are planned to mark special occasions or to achieve specific cultural, social or corporate goals and objectives (Allen, O'Toole, McDonnell, Harris, 2005). Special events have been parts of cultures and civilisations for many years dating back to the Babylonians of 9th and 7th centuries BC (Hede and Jado, 2005). By the 20th century special events have been used to celebrate a range of achievements, including the landing of explorers, coronations of kings and queens and the launching of new governments or legislation. Today events have become essential components of private, local, regional and national economic portfolios. Events and festivals have become strong demand generators, making a considerable contribution to the tourism, travel, leisure and hospitality industries. Events and festivals play a multiplicity of roles in enhancing the social fabric of a community and as generators of economic activity. Whatever the aims and objectives of events or festivals, they are becoming increasingly popular vehicles for achieving diverse outcomes in the communities that stage them.

There is no one universally accepted definition for an event. This presents numerous challenges for scholars and researchers, making it difficult to impose specific demarcations between different types of events. This problem is partly due to the range of events staged, the variances in size, scope and purpose. Special events include an exhaustive list of activities that fall into a variety of classifications making definitional attempts difficult. Thus, events are often classified according to their purpose or the particular business sector to which they belong. These include religious and sacred events; cultural events, including festivals and carnivals; historical milestone events including the Australian Bicentenary and the 500th anniversary of the Sailing of Columbus. Commercial events such as world fairs; political events, such as visits by foreign dignitaries, political leaders and royalty are all included under the many different classifications. Sporting events are prominent events ranging from small national championships to mega events like the Olympic Games (Hall, 1992a).

However, the literature acknowledges that smaller, more private events have become instrumental in contributing to the multibillion-dollar events industry. Corporate events including meetings, seminars and incentive travel events are some of the most prominent events in the corporate world. The conference market in the

United Kingdom is said to be worth over £7 billion a year (Allen, O'Toole, McDonnell, Harris, 2005). Weddings, funerals and private parties have become part of the daily operations in resorts and convention facilities worldwide. In the wedding industry, it is not uncommon to host an event over a period of three days including the actual ceremony. Wedding guests travel miles to attend these events and hotels capitalise on the business opportunities by offering special discounts to guests travelling for the weddings, thus taking advantage of room revenue opportunities as well as the food and beverage aspect of the business (Goldblatt, 2002).

In reviewing the event management literature several definitions have been put forward by scholars as to what constitutes a special event. However, because of the diversity of events and the purposes that they serve, definitions are often far from exact and the distinctions are blurred. To deal with this problem Shone and Parry (2001: 4) offer a general definition of a special event:

> Special events are that phenomenon arising from those non-routine occasions which have leisure, cultural, personal and organisational objectives set apart from the normal activity of daily life, whose purpose is to enlightened, celebrate, entertain or challenge the experience of a group of people.

Goldblatt (1990) chose to highlight the celebratory aspect of special events. For him a special event recognises a unique moment in time with ceremony and ritual to satisfy specific needs. Although this definition clearly works for weddings, parties, festivals and carnivals, it is restrictive for some commercial events like exhibitions and corporate board meetings where people may attend primarily to conduct serious business. To resolve the problem Getz (1997: 4) developed a definition of a special event from a supply and demand perspective. From the supply side: "a special event is a one time or infrequently occurring event outside normal programmes or activities of the sponsoring or organising body"; while from the consumer's perspective: "a special event is an opportunity for a leisure, social or cultural experience outside the normal range of choices or beyond everyday experiences". Events should therefore occur infrequently and possesses a degree of 'specialness' and uniqueness which is part of their appeal.

The events that have achieved widespread attention in the literature are the 'hallmark events'. Large-scale events with a tourism

51

focus are usually referred to as 'hallmark events'. Ritchie (1984: 2) describes hallmark events as:

> major one-time or recurring events of limited duration developed primarily to enhance the awareness, appeal and profitability of a tourism destination in the short or long-term. Such events rely for their success on uniqueness, status or timely significance to create interest and attract attention.

For destinations ranging from small towns and islands to large metropolitan areas, the hallmark event has become a key aspect of tourism development. A major function of a hallmark event is to provide the community with an opportunity to secure a position of prominence in the tourism market for a short or well-defined period of time. A hallmark event distinguishes itself from other events due to its propensity to focus attention, both national and international, on a destination through the media that they attract. However, its ability to do so will depend on the uniqueness of the event, its status and the extent to which it is successfully marketed (ibid). Ritchie's (1984) definition is restrictive since many hallmark events are also used as catalysts for redevelopment plans or re-imaging strategies.

On reviewing the event management literature many studies make reference to a variety of terminology - hallmark events, major events and mega events and these terms are used interchangeably by scholars. Allen, O'Toole, McDonnell, and Harris (2002: 13) define hallmark events as:

> ....those events that become so identified with the spirit or ethos of a town, city or region that they become synonymous with the name of the place and gain widespread recognition and awareness.

According to this definition, Carnival in Rio, the Kentucky Derby in the United States of America, the Chelsea Flower Show in London and Oktoberfest in Munich are examples of hallmark events since their names are synonymous with a specific place. They further describe major events as "events, that by their scale and media interest is capable of attracting significant visitor numbers, media coverage and economic benefits (ibid: 14). They describe the Australia Open Tennis tournament and the Australian Formula One Grand Prix as significant annual major events. They distinguish between mega events and other events on the basis that mega events are so large that they affect whole economies and reverberate in the global media. Such definitions tend to be confusing since they indicate no clear quantitative demarcations between the different terminologies used.

Clearly, the major problem in distinguishing between hallmark events, special events and mega events is that of scale. An attempt to alleviate this problem was offered by Marris (1987) who posited a quantitative and qualitative definition of mega events by arguing that mega events must be viewed in terms of their cost, volume of visitors and psychology. Their volume of visitors should exceed one million, their capital cost should be around US$500 million (£250 million), and their reputation should be of a 'must see' nature (ibid). However, this definition is problematic because it assumes that all mega events are hosted in locations with the capacity to attract at least one million visitors and require financial inputs valued at US$500 million (£250 million). Many events are hosted within facilities that are already in existence, particularly events that are staged annually. Furthermore, size is a relative term and although many events may not attract these numbers they may still be 'mega' relative to the time, space and environment in which they are held.

Rooney (1988) concluded that mega sport events should be loaded with tradition, and have profound historical significance. They should have developed a mystique or have taken on mystical proportions; they benefit from media overload at the international level and are usually accompanied by parades and festivals. Roche (2001) states that mega events are best understood as large scale, cultural, including commercial and sporting events, which have a dramatic character, mass popular appeal and international significance. Roche (2001) distinguishes between a mega event, special event and hallmark event in terms of the target audience, attendance, market targeted and the type of media interest generated.

According to Roche (2001), a mega event would be a large sporting event that attracts a global audience and global television coverage. These would include the Olympic Games and the Football World Cup. Events like the Grand Prix or the Pan American Games would qualify as special events since these events attract more regional or national audiences and international and national media coverage. Hallmark events tend to target a national or regional audience and national or local media coverage and are therefore smaller in terms of geographic interests and less significant in terms of media coverage. But can mega events only be defined in terms of target audiences and media attention and if so what are the quantitative measures? To compensate for the different terminology used and the diverse purposes for which events, including mega events are staged, Hall (1997: 1) offers an extended definition of a mega event:

> Mega tourists events, otherwise referred to as hallmark events or special events, are major large-scale fairs, festivals, expositions, or cultural and sporting events that are held on a regular or one-off basis, which often require substantial input of public funding and/or support that serve as mechanisms for the physical redevelopment and/or re-imagining strategies.

Two central features of mega events are evident. Firstly, they have significant consequences for the host city, region or nation; and secondly, they must attract significant media coverage. Researchers also tend to neglect the fact that many of these events must be bid for. However, some mega events may not necessarily attract large numbers of visitors but still generate enormous media coverage. Mega events as 'media events' are becoming increasingly popular mainly due to the power of television coverage to attract large, global audiences and target markets (Hargreaves, 1986). The ability to transmit promotional messages to billions of people via television is an essential feature of a mega event (Hede and Jado, 2005. By 1990 the Olympic Games, the World Championships of Athletics and the Soccer World Cup were televised in over 200 countries (Maguire, 1999), while the cumulative audience for the 2004 Olympic Games was 40 billion people (Horne and Manzenreiter, 2006). So an event can be 'mega' if it generates exceptional levels of media interest or fosters a strong positive image for the host location (Getz, 1997).

Clearly, attempts to define and classify mega events have not been able to capture the multi-dimensional and synergistic character of mega sport events. Consequently, there is   no universally accepted definition. What constitute a mega event then is more a question of its relative significance to the host location and the overall goals and objectives of the host (Getz, 1997). For the purpose of this study, the definition posited by Hall (1997) will be accepted as it clearly embraces the goals and objectives that Barbados' tourism authorities wished to achieve from the staging of mega events on the island of Barbados. As the semi-structured interviews will show, the Golf World Cup would qualify as a mega event. Firstly, it was a one-off event designed to enhance the awareness of Barbados as a tourist destination and was part of a re-imaging strategy designed to launch the island as an up-market tourist and golfing destination. Secondly, it required the input of public funds in the amount of US$3 million (£1.5 million) which was paid to the Professional Golfers Association to bring the event to Barbados; and thirdly, it attracted considerable international media attention. The Golf World Cup was broadcasted in 140 countries before a television audience of over one billion by major television networks including ESPN and ABC in the United States and Sky in the United Kingdom (Spooner, 2006b). This event was initially projected to attract over 8000 visitors to the island and over 200 journalists specifically for the event, utilising approximately 66% of Barbados' overall accommodation stock. This figure is unmatched by any single event ever hosted in Barbados, besides cricket test matches and the subsequent Cricket World Cup final. The following section examines the nature of mega events.

3.3 THE NATURE OF MEGA EVENTS

One type of mega event that has received much attention by researchers is the mega sport event. Sport events of this nature include the Olympic Games, FIFA World Cup and Cricket World Cup, among others. These events are worthy of study because they are associated with the emergence of new forms of entrepreneurial governance at the local, regional and international level as cities and regions seek to devise strategies to attract new capital flows and to engage in urban re-development processes (Olds, 1998).

The mega event has distinct features that make it stand out from other events. In many instances they are biddable (Hudson, 2003). This is illustrated by the aggressive and competitive bidding employed by countries, cities and regions to host prestige events (Getz, 1998; Gibson, 1998; Legacy Barbados, 2006). Some countries have also formed companies and agencies whose main function is to identify and bid on these events (Getz, 1998; Gibson, 1998). Mega events are of a 'high profile' nature with an element of prestige (Hall, 1992a), which attracts corporate sponsorship and hospitality for the promotion of other related or non-sport related products, including tourism. Their international appeal coupled with the selling of broadcasting rights is important and significant. The support of the media prior to and during the event guarantees exposure and worldwide awareness. This exposure is likely to attract more tourists than other regularly scheduled events and they can be used as catalysts for attracting spin-off tourism through training camps, conferences and

55

exhibitions. Furthermore, the exposure can be a springboard to attract investment and other business opportunities.

More significantly, their organisation from the bidding stage to the actual production requires technical competencies and skills such as technologically advanced facilities and skilled personnel. The pressure placed on host countries to deliver services required to host a superior event is different to that of other events (national or regional). The standards are related more to the technical standards set by international federations who are usually located abroad. These include standards dedicated to competition including high technologically advanced sporting facilities. Non-competition elements include accommodation, transport and skilled personnel in competition management and event management. Consequently, the host location must draw on the support from direct and indirect stakeholders. Overall approval must come from government and other business related sectors. Since much of the public purse is invested in the bidding and the subsequent staging of events, support from the wider public is imperative (Getz, 1997; Masterman, 2004).

Mega events receive an abundance of attention by researchers and the press due to their controversial nature. A key trend is that many mega sport events have been accused of not meeting the expectations of stakeholder groups – government, tourism officials, tourists and residents. For instance, the recently hosted Golf World Cup and Cricket World Cup, both of which were hosted on Caribbean islands, failed to attract the anticipated number of international visitors. From the tourists' perspective, the Cricket World Cup was lacking in Caribbean flavour due to excessive security measures (The Legacy of Cricket World Cup, 2007). The Montreal Olympics of 1976 have been accused of incurring an enormous debt and the 2006 FIFA World Cup was accused of disenfranchising German beer and sausage in favour of the official licensees Anheuser Busch and McDonald, both foreign products (Hall, 2006). These occurrences have produced a climate characterised by distrust, scepticism, discord, confusion, and a lack of credibility (Goldblatt, 2000).

Finally, mega sport events are associated with large scale public expenditure for the construction of new facilities and urban redevelopment and revitalisation strategies that have long term negative consequences for the public stakeholders, while providing short term financial and other gains for corporate interests (ibid). Consequently, many researchers have asked the question, who benefits from the staging of mega events? It is often perceived that the host community bears the financial and social burden while the wealthy reap the benefits. These issues will be discussed in more detail in the following sections.

While the mega event has been the focus of much research, particularly from the economic perspective, the work in this area tends to neglect the viewpoints of the major stakeholders. We still do not understand what their expectations and perceptions are of mega events. This is partly due to the quantitative nature of work in this area which does not allow the stakeholders' perspectives to be heard. As will be demonstrated in the following sections and subsequent chapters, the many underlying contextual forces driving the way stakeholders respond to mega events are missing from the literature. Unfortunately research in this area tends to be biased in the assessment of the economic impacts. However, research into mega events must be undertaken within the socio-cultural and political environment in which they are hosted. This research is different not only because it explores the contextual forces from specific stakeholders' perspectives but it also examines a single event in a specific place and time in a holistic context; hence, it is context specific taking into consideration the social, cultural and political environment in which it is held. It is also the first study of its kind in golf tourism with special relevance to island tourism.

3.4 THEORETICAL PERSPECTIVES

Up until 1980 it was felt that the hosting of a major sporting event was a recipe for administrative and financial burdens to the host city and organisation (Gratton and Dobson, 1999). More recently mega events are viewed by academics, politicians and tourism officials as significant assets because they can induce travel to the destination in the short and long term due to the media attention they attract (Laws, 1993). Other benefits proclaimed by proponents include economic stimulation in tourism-related and other non-related sectors, urban regeneration (Jones and Stokes, 2003) and 'civic boosterism' (Waitt, 2003). However, little reliable and consistent data exists to support these perceptions. With the lack of consistent concepts and definitions, as well as data, it is impossible to measure the industry accurately. As a result divergent and conflicting perspectives appear in the literature regarding the viability of mega events. This situation is further exacerbated by the tendency of researchers to concentrate their efforts towards the economic perspective and on events that are staged in large metropolitan areas.

Although decision-makers tend to concentrate on the positive economic impacts in an effort to justify the cost incurred in preparing to host a mega event, the impacts of mega events seem rather paradoxical in nature when analysed in the context of their business characteristics. Mules and Faulkner (1996) point out that the hosting of a major sporting event is not always an unequivocal economic benefit. They explain that these events often result in the city authorities losing money even though the city itself may benefit through additional spending. In addition, some scholars contend that the losses tend to accrue to those who can least afford them – the host community. While the positive impacts are often important and relevant, the literature highlights significant negative impacts such as increased public debt, inflation, congestion, cultural degradation amongst others that are the consequences of hosting mega events (Jones, 2001; Whitson and Horne, 2006). Furthermore, many perceived positive impacts are intangible. Impacts derived from media exposure, such as the opportunity for place marketing and image enhancements, are not only intangible but also difficult to measure (Gratton, Shibli and Coleman, 2006). The emphasis on economic impacts means that there continues to be little empirical evidence that validates the social, political, and cultural implications of these projects. Mega events should not be studied in isolation of their social, cultural or political milieu since the impacts that mega events have on the host locations are largely multidimensional, ranging from economic to physical-infrastructural, social-cultural or psychological, political and commercial impacts (Ritchie, 1984). The following section discusses the various theoretical perspectives on mega events in more detail focussing first on the economic perspective.

3.4.1 Economic and Tourism Perspectives

Claims of significant economic benefits dominate the literature and it is the major justification used by tourism authorities to stage mega events. Euro 1996, hosted in the United Kingdom, attracted 280,000 overseas visitors to the eight host cities and surrounding regions (Gratton and Dobson, 1999); while Korea, for the 2002 Football World Cup, attracted over 230,000 foreign soccer fans (Kim and Petrick, 2005). Madden's (2002) evaluation of the Sydney Olympic Games revealed that the games impacted the Australian gross domestic product by AUS$6.5 billion (£3.25 billion), representing an increase in economic activity of 0.12 percent over a 12 year period from 1994 to 2004; while creating between 5300 to 7500 jobs in an average year over the same period (Madden, 2002: 18). The hosting of training teams prior to the games also generated 40,000 bed nights and injected AUS$16 billion (£7.5 million) into the economy (Hinch and Higham, 2004). It is estimated that overall the games generated £3 billion into the Australian economy and would be responsible for attracting an additional one million visitors to Australia between the years 1994 to 2004 (Neirotti, 2003).

The revenue generated from mega sport events have significant multiplier potential that impacts positively on other tourism related or non-related industries such as food sales, transport, merchandising and retail. Gratton and Dobson (1999) reported that the city of Sheffield in the United Kingdom generated £120 million in revenue and attracted 61,000 visitors for Euro 1996. However, although only 24% of these visitors spent at least one night in the city, the income that they generated was significant. They estimated that these day visitors spent on average £50 per day, which resulted in overall additional spending of £5.8 million. Other multipliers and spill-over effects for Euro 1996 on the British economy were derived from the £40 million made from VAT on ticket sales, £5 million from betting tax, £3 million from taxation on the incomes of event organisers and £16 million from companies paying corporation tax on commercial profits (Gratton and Dobson, 1999).

However, opponents and independent researchers tend to be sceptical about claims of positive economic impacts. It is felt that mega sport events do not always meet the economic expectations and at times the perceived benefits are often exaggerated (Getz, 1991a; Horner and Manzenreiter, 2006; Jones, 2001; Whitson and Horne, 2006). Montreal for example incurred a loss of £692 million in staging the 1976 Olympics while Munich in 1972 made a loss of £178 million for that year's Olympic Games (Gratton, Dobson and Shibli, 2000: 17). The losses from the Montreal Olympics had to be covered by the City of Montreal and it is anticipated that taxpayers will be paying off the debt well into the 21st century (Preuss, 2003). The 1991 World Student Games, in Sheffield, was entered into without a proper impact study. The result was a loss of £180 million and an extra £100 on the yearly council tax bills of city residents (Horne and Manzenreiter, 2006). In Wales, Jones' (2001) study showed that the economic impact from the staging of the 1999 Rugby World Cup was negative. It was found that of the projected £78 million in revenue expected, £48 million was retained by World Cup Limited while the remainder was split between the five host regions. This meant that

Wales' share of the profits was not commensurate with the expenses incurred as the official host since the expenses for accommodation, meals and media management had to be met by Wales.

Critics of mega sport events further question the claims of positive economic benefits on the basis of the methodologies used by evaluators, planners and analysts (Hall, 1992a). Opponents argue that credibility is tarnished both by the questionable independence and the inaccuracy of the methodologies used in the estimation of economic impacts (Burgan and Mules, 1992; Gelan, 2003; Mazitelli, 1989; Mules and Faulkner, 1996). They point to the propensity of policy makers to produce figures that produce positive net economic outcomes which are relatively easy to obtain given the incorrect calculations of the direct expenditure triggered by the event and the dubious use of economic multipliers. Many figures in the literature are not explained in terms of how they were calculated and many are derived from secondary sources without a proper analysis. Gelen (2003) agrees that unless there is a carefully structured methodology regarding the types of tourists and their expenditure relative to the event, the economic impact could be overestimated.

In order to arrive at the approximate economic impact of a mega event, it is suggested that economists try to demarcate the economic activity that would have occurred without the event taking place from that which occurred as a direct consequence of the event. In this regard, Crompton, Lee and Shuster (2001) state that economic impact studies for events need to exclude expenditure incurred by local residents and what they refer to as 'time switchers' and 'casuals'. 'Time switchers' are international visitors who would have visited the destination regardless of the event but chose to switch their visit to the time of the event. 'Casuals' are those international visitors who visited the destination during the event but were motivated to do so because of other attractions. To include expenditure from these groups would present an overestimation of expenditure directly attributed to the staging of the event.

Attention is also drawn to the importance of accounting for economic 'leakages' when estimating economic impacts. Economic leakages in this sense would refer to leakages that occurred in excess of general economic 'leakages'. In this regard, Gelen (2003) questions the viability of developing nations hosting mega events. In developing nations revenue can be siphoned away by multi-national corporations and other leakages, particularly imports and debt repayment that will negatively impact the economic viability of mega events.

60

Developing nations like Barbados import goods to service the tourism industry and this exercise results in foreign exchange leakages. As will be discussed further in the following chapter, Barbados requires foreign exchange in order to maintain acceptable standards of living. Hosting mega events requires investments in infrastructure, which has to be paid for in foreign currency. Thus, leakages can occur from importing goods, services, foreign workers expatriation of income and expatriation of profits by transnational firms, all of which will reduce the money that stays in the economy (Matos, 2006). In the case of Barbados, a total of US$3 million (£1.5 million) was paid to the Professional Golfers Association to bring the Golf World Cup to Barbados, representing a drain on the country's foreign reserves. In order to justify such cost, the event was required to generate an equivalent amount in foreign exchange revenue. This means that the event needed to attract foreign visitors in order to compensate for the foreign exchange expense. However, as Matheson and Baade (2003) notes, developed nations tend to be able to attract larger numbers of foreign fans to mega events than developing nations. Foreign visitors to developing nations tend to experience trepidation due to worries about crime and the quality of infrastructure and accommodation. Furthermore, island travel is relatively expensive particularly if long haul travel is involved (Reid and Reid, 1994) and it is already established that cost is a major deterrent of travel to a mega event (Delpy, 1997). It was evident from the semi-structured interviews and the observations that this event did not attract many international visitors. As will be discussed in chapter five the evidence showed that many international visitors at the Golf World Cup were casuals and time shifters. This evidence lends credibility to many of the arguments posited in the literature which claim that mega events do not necessarily attract new visitors (see, Jones, 2001; Lee and Taylor, 2005; Pyo, Cook and Howell, 1991).

The tourism authorities in Barbados hosted the Golf World Cup on the pretext that it would attract tourists to Barbados during a traditionally slow period. Owing to the poor international spectator turnout at this event, there is still much doubt as to whether mega sport events do have a positive impact on international tourism. A study of the 1984 Olympic Games in Los Angeles concluded that the city lost tourist visits as a consequence of hosting the games (Pyo, Cook and Howell, 1991). In Los Angeles 600,000 tourists were expected but only 400,000 arrived whereas the Tokyo Olympics were expected to attract 130,000 visitors but only 70,000 arrived (Lee and Taylor,

2005). In the case of Los Angeles, Pyo, Cook and Howell (1991) believe that out of town residents and other tourists stayed away from the Olympic areas due to the anticipated congestion predicted in the pre games media coverage. They also believe that price gouging[3] and the unavailability of quality tickets to support tour operator sales might have had negative impacts on tourist arrivals. In some instances, destinations may find that inflated prices, or the perception of inflated prices for tourism and related services, can also deter potential tourists from visiting the host location (Hall, 1992b).

In the case of Wales and the 1999 Rugby World Cup, Jones (2001) found that as the event was hosted in different regions, tour operators were able to transport people into Cardiff to watch the games and then transport them out on the same day. The nature of the event and the fact that it was hosted in different regions meant that the event attracted 'day trippers' who arrived just to watch the games and left immediately after. Consequently, hotels were left with spare capacity and many auxiliary services such as restaurants, bars and shops were under-utilized. Likewise, the 2007 Cricket World Cup, which was staged in nine Caribbean islands, including Barbados, in March and April of 2007, failed to attract the anticipated number of international visitors: This quote from a Barbados newspaper tells the story:

> The fans appear not to be coming out in anticipated numbers for Cricket World Cup matches. This situation was evident yesterday when at the first Super 8s match between West Indies and Australia in Antigua, the newly-built stadium was nowhere close to its 19 000 capacity. Here, the scattering of spectators in the North Stand told the story (Fan-tasy, 2007: 1).

Just months before, the Golf World Cup also failed to attract the projected numbers of international tourists. Unofficial statistics obtained from the Barbados Tourism Authority anticipated that the event generated only 200 of the 8000 international visitors initially expected to travel to Barbados. This issue will however be discussed further in chapters five and six.

Other studies demonstrate the complexity of predicting international tourism flows for mega events. In a study to evaluate the economic impacts of the 2002 Football World Cup, Lee and Taylor (2005) concluded that the scheduling of matches and the progress of

---

[3]   Price gouging is a pejorative term for a seller pricing goods or services much higher than is considered reasonable or fair.

certain teams through the competition might have had a negative impact on tourist arrivals. They concluded that the nationality of teams playing in South Korea could be linked to the tourist arrivals during the fourth round of games in which the United States and several European teams played. As Japanese teams played almost exclusively in Japan, this decreased the incentive for Japanese tourists to visit South Korea. Japanese tourists account for more that 40% of the Korean inbound market and this meant a decrease of 44.6% in Japanese arrivals, representing a significant drop in the Japanese market. Furthermore, Korea's advancement to the third place match at the expense of a foreign-based team acted as a disincentive for foreign tourists to visit, so that travellers comprised mainly domestic supporters and this had a negative impact on international tourist arrivals.

Getz (2003) cautions that some events may attract 'sport junkies'. A 'sports junkie' is an individual who travels just to watch a sporting event and as result does not take part in any tourist related activities and is unlikely to return. Pyo, Cook and Howell (1991), after investigating the impacts of the Olympic Games held between 1964 and 1984, concluded that visitors who travelled to be spectators at the event tended to be less affluent and spent less than other travellers. Sport junkies tend to be interested in the sport alone or in following their favourite competitors, hence, for them it is the sport that is important rather than the destination experience. The 'sport junkie' concept was illustrated during the Cricket World Cup of 2007 when the early elimination of the Pakistan and Indian teams resulted in the cancellation of thousands of fans from these countries; including the cancellation of an entire Air India charter (World Cup Comes Up Short, 2007). These cancellations were attributed to the propensity of Asian spectators to support their cricket stars rather than the sport itself. The motivation to travel was therefore the opportunity to see the cricket stars and not necessarily to see the destination. This phenomenon clearly illustrates a particular behaviour pattern of potential sport tourists, a tendency which event planners and tourism officials should note. This evidence, as well as those mentioned previously, show that the staging of a mega event for tourism gain is a high risk venture as it is difficult to predict which teams or competitors will advance to subsequent rounds and how the fans will respond.

3.4.2 The Legacy Perspective

Legacy refers to the short and long term benefits that a community can expect from the staging of a mega sport event. Tourism and other government officials support the staging of mega sport events on the basis that they require investments in the building of sport and related facilities and services. These in turn can be used to stimulate other financial and social benefits (Glyptis, 1991). Substantial evidence exists of infrastructural developments stimulated by mega events. Sydney, in preparation for the 2000 Olympic Games, built new sport facilities and upgraded existing ones. New roads were built, the Sydney airport was expanded and hotel room capacity was increased by 25% (Chalip, 2002). Barcelona, in preparation for the 1992 games, constructed a new airport and a derelict waterfront area was redeveloped for an Olympic village (Laws, 1993). Seoul, in preparation for the 2002 Football World Cup, undertook 16 projects aimed at city beautification including the enhancement of restroom quality, repair of shop signs and improvements in lighting and waste management (Kim and Petrick, 2005). England's bid for the 2012 Olympic Games included a proposal to regenerate a 500-acre site in Stratford - one of London's most depressed areas. There will be the main 80,000-seat Olympic stadium, a world-class aquatic centre, a hockey centre, the Velodome and the Olympic Village. An enhanced transport system for London that will deliver up to 240,000 people an hour to the Olympic Park by tube, train and bus and via park and ride schemes http://www.london2012), forms part of a multi-billion dollar regeneration plan.

Commentators claim that the significance of this type of regeneration and improvements in infrastructure is that it looks good on camera and presents an attractive first impression for event visitors. It also increases the location's tourism marketing potential since an adequate infrastructure is an essential part of a tourism destination's development programme and is vital to the growth of the industry in the host location (Cooper, Fletcher, Gilbert, Shepherd and Wanhill, 1998). It is also argued that enhanced civic pride from these improvements can positively impact business confidence and community satisfaction, which in turn can stimulate economic activity and increase household income (Gelen, 2003). The existence of additional sports facilities also enhances the location's chances to host other major events and can act as training venues for sport teams.

New sporting facilities are also built under the notion of promoting nostalgia tourism. It is argued that these facilities leave a legacy of places where heroes once played and legends were made. Sports stadia can serve as tourist attractions, which along with modern technological applications can create exciting visitor attractions (John, 2002). These would include the 'sports hall of fame' concept where sports stadia museums offer visitors a unique and new experience. Examples of such facilities include the Nou Camp in Barcelona, the Australia Gallery of Sport and the Wimbledon Lawn Tennis Museum in London. These are equipped with souvenir shops, galleries, screen projects and other facilities to entertain visitors. In some cases, sports stadia can be put to multiple uses by not only catering to sport events but to events such as concerts and conferences (John, 2002). An example of this is the Sky Dome in Toronto, Canada where a 350-bedroom convention hotel was incorporated into the Sky Dome facility to complement its multi-faceted use as a conference and exhibition facility (Glyptis, 1991). Despite this evidence, the literature on nostalgia tourism has not identified the type of tourists that use these facilities and the characteristics they possess. We still do not know if sports tourists are likely to return as nostalgia sports tourists. Consequently, there is doubt whether visitors to the Golf World Cup are likely to return to play on the Sandy Lane Golf course and whether the gates will be opened for local residents to play golf at Sandy Lane notwithstanding the resort's exclusive policy. Even where facilities are put to use after the event, no research could be found assessing the financial viability of these projects. Mega sport events have also gained attention among academics due to their perceived social impacts. The next section is a critical examination of the social and cultural perspectives of mega events.

3.4.3 Social and Cultural Perspectives

The idea that the long-term viability of tourism is dependent on local support and good relations with the local community has been cited by many authors (Cooper, Fletcher, Gilbert, Wanhill, and Shepherd, 1998; Fredline and Faulkner, 2000a; Hall, 1992a). Theoretical models, such as the irridex model (Doxey, 1975) and the resort life cycle (Butler, 1980), have been recognised by tourism researchers. Both models suggest that intensified tourism development can induce a resident backlash that could work unfavourably against the industry. The various work in the area of residents' perceptions of the impacts of events tourism have highlighted key social costs and benefits. Special events for instance may have an advantage over other types of tourism in that they provide residents with the opportunity to participate directly through volunteering, attending as a spectator, and working at the event or by engaging in commercial activities (see Ritchie & Lyons, 1990). However, it is important to determine how these benefits can be nurtured and how the host community may respond to them.

Studies on the impacts of mega events have focused mainly on residents' perceptions of such impacts on the host community (Fredline and Faulkner, 2000a; Fredline, 2000; Kim and Petrick, 2005; Mihalik, 2000; Twynam and Johnston, 2004; Waitt, 2003). Many of these studies pay attention to the notion of 'psychic income' (Emery, 2002; Waitt, 2003). 'Psychic income' refers to the feelings of confidence, euphoria and pride that community members may experience as the result of hosting a high profile event (Hall, 1992a). One study of note in this area is that of Waitt (2003) who examined the social impacts of the 2000 Sydney Olympic Games. Waitt found that mega sport events have the ability to generate patriotism and a sense of community belonging. While investigating the changes in enthusiasm that occurred between the period 1998 and the period immediately after the 2000 Sydney Olympic Games, Waitt (2003: 204) found more positive responses on items such as "desire to be a volunteer at the Sydney Olympics", "feelings of a sense of community spirit as a result of Sydney 2000", "feelings of pride in Sydney and Australia" and "feelings of excitement". However, this study failed to address the causes of this euphoria, the length of time that it lasts and how it actually benefits the community as a whole.

Soutar and McLeod (1993) examined community views before and after the America's Cup in Fremantle, Australia. Surveys in 1985, 1986 and 1987 were conducted to explore residents' perceptions on the levels of impacts, and to investigate changes in expectations over time. Soutar and McLeod found residents' expectations of the positive and negative impacts of the event were more extreme before the hosting than their perceptions after the event. Perceptions in the two pre-event surveys were similar but these differed from the post-event survey. Following the event, the majority regarded the hosting positively and felt no major disruption from it. This study showed that the perceptions of impacts change over time and are dynamic rather that constant.

Another prominent study is Fredline and Faulkner's (1998) evaluation of the Indy Car Race in Australia. They found that residents of the Gold Coast appreciated the tourism benefits of the event while at the same time they also recognized the negative consequences.

Fredline and Faulkner explored residents' reactions and they identified six factors that explained the variation in responses. These included a factor called 'showcase effects'. 'Showcase effects' refers to the spectacle factor, the images and dramatization of the event. They also identified a factor describing amenity and facility benefits. These include promoting the place as a tourist destination and providing an international identity. Deccio and Baloglu (2002) used the social exchange theory to analyze community support for a mega event. They suggested that community support for mega events depends on the perceived cost versus the benefits derived from the event. In this case an examination of non-host residents in a nearby region was undertaken in regards to the hosting of the 2002 Olympics in Salt Lake City. The researchers found that 31% of residents of a county in close proximity to the hosting site supported the hosting of the event while 46% neither supported nor opposed it. In this study, support for the Olympics was positively influenced by perceived spillover benefits, but many residents did not perceive that many spillover impacts would occur. A study on the impacts of the 1996 Atlanta Olympics found that residents rated the intangible impacts more highly than the economic impacts. This study by Mihalik (2000) also found that local residents, although satisfied with the attention that Atlanta was receiving in the international media, were discouraged by perceptions of increased crime, price gouging and traffic congestion. Mihalik concluded that these perceptions reduced resident support for the event and their willingness to attend.

There is a further body of literature that adopts a critical approach to analysing the social dimensions of mega events. For instance, some studies have reported on the propensity of mega events to violate the civic rights of host residents. Gelen (2003) drew attention to event related evictions to make way for new money, new people and new facilities. The Olympic Games is probably the most notorious in this regard. It is reported that the Games are responsible for the eviction of over 20 million people worldwide (Fair Play for Housing Rights, 2007). In Seoul for the 1988 Olympic Games, 720 000 room renters were forcibly removed and in Barcelona thousands of low income tenants and small businesses were forced out of Barcelona before the 1992 Olympic Games. In Atlanta, more than 9000 homeless people were arrested prior to the 1996 Olympic Games (Shapcott, 1998). In Australia, in order to provide adequate security, the New South Wales State Government introduced special legislation that gave the security forces powers that they would not ordinarily

67

have had. Under this legislation, police were given the power to search citizens in the central district and to tap telephones (Chalip, 2002).

Researchers however agree that the social impacts of mega events grow out of political processes that lead to their staging. The next section examines the political processes that guide the decision to host mega events and their political implications.

3.4.4 The Socio-Political Perspective

Mega events are largely political affairs. However, the tendency to focus on the economic impacts of mega events has resulted in little or no research into the political and planning process which underlies such events (Roche, 1994). This is particularly exacerbated by the unwillingness of researchers and individual political actors to acknowledge the significance of mega events to the micro and macro political process (Hall, 1997, 1989). Furthermore, the sensitive and ideological nature of politics would make research into this area difficult, as political figures may be reluctant to be observed.

The importance and prestige attached to mega events by governments is evident. This is emphasized by the strategic deployment of political leaders, prime ministers and royalty at the forefront of the bidding process to stage important events (Horne and Manzenreiter, 2006). Politicians, particularly in developing nations, often seek to use mega-events to meet specific political or foreign policy goals (Cornelissen and Swart, 2006). It is a way of signalling messages to the international community and engaging in international activities far beyond their capacity. It is a way of compensating for the developing nation's lack of resources and power within the international sphere. This often results in a fast-track approach, which ignores community resistance to either the hosting or the associated construction of facilities (Hall, 1989). Of particular importance and lacking in the research area, is how decision-makers rationalise their decisions to host mega events. This calls into question issues concerning where the power is centred and whether it is hierarchical (centred at the top) or level (equally distributed) among stakeholders.

Andranovich, Burbank and Heying (2001: 120) concluded that the decision to stage or not to stage mega events is often influenced by the political agendas of the authorities. Their study of the bidding processes behind the Olympic games in three cities notes:

The Olympic bid in all three cities shared two common features. One was that the Olympic bid was a product of regime politics. The driving force behind the Olympic bids in each city was influential members of the city's business elites with the endorsement of elected officials to provide public legitimacy.

Roche (1994) highlighted the view that prestige projects, such as an important hallmark event, are usually the product of influential elites or a particular powerful individual. This view was also supported by Emery (2002) who, in a study of the bidding processes employed by authorities in various countries worldwide, concluded that the desirability to host major events was guided more by personal and political convictions than by an objective appraisal of the project. Other researchers make the point that decisions to host are often made by undemocratic and anarchic processes that are characterised by secrecy and a lack of transparency (Horne and Manzenreiter, 2006). In this respect they represent a shift in public funds to satisfy private interests and in support of global touristic and monetary flows. According to these researchers they represent an ideological assault on citizenship, preferring global consumers to the local public. Sack and Johnson's (1996) study on the processes involved in bringing the Volvo International Tennis Tournament to New Haven, Connecticut in 1989, concluded that the main policy decisions had been made long before the general public become involved. Many events thus go ahead without any evaluation of cost benefit projections, community consultation or the relevant consumer research. As a result, events can fail to meet the expectations of the stakeholders, decision-makers and the tourists.

Westerbeek, Turner and Ingerson (2002), in a study to observe bidding procedures, concluded that the staging of a mega event is very often a political leveraging strategy used by politicians to support their own political ambitions and often results in a struggle for power between individuals, interest groups and organisations. Mega events are designed to create playgrounds for the bourgeois while the long-term benefits are accrued to the wealthy. (see Horne and Manzenreiter, 2006). Jennings' (1996) study, on the Olympic bidding process, presents an intriguing and alarming insight into the political processes that developed within the Olympic Movement. Jennings (1996) wrote about the bribery involved in the bidding for the Salt Lake City Winter Olympic Games where bribes of first class travel, gifts and credit cards to Olympic Committee officials resulted in a scandal. This is a case that confirms Hall's (1993: 583) analysis that "hallmark events may be used for personal political ambitions". Jennings' (1996) chronology of unethical practices within the International Olympic Committee (IOC) hold serious implications for the widely espoused benefits of hosting sporting events. These findings lead to questions concerning whether Jenning's observations are transferable to other sporting events of significant scale. Jenning's findings certainly raise the question: 'why and for whom are these events held'?

Much work on the political and social implications of mega events stresses the view that the success of mega events is dependent on local support and participation (Fredline and Faulkner, 2000a; Getz, 1991a, 1997; Hall, 1992a; Hiller 1989, 2000; Twynam and Johnston, 2004; Westerbeek, Turner and Ingerson, 2002). Without local support several sanctions may be imposed by the host community such as unwillingness to work at the event, lack of enthusiasm in promoting the event by word-of-mouth and possible hostility to visitors (Turco, Swart, Bob and Moodley, 2003). The need for local involvement in the decision-making process has been echoed by commentators in the tourism planning and development disciplines (Hall, 1992a; Hiller, 2000; Swarbrooke, 1999; Westerbeek, Turner and Ingerson, 2002). Hall (1992a) notes how traditionally tourism planning tends to be based on a top-down approach to planning that has left destination communities with little input or control over their destinies. Hiller (2000) also recognises that sometimes local communities have to accept arrangements geared to promoting sport that were foreign to the local culture.

Hall (1992a) rightly points out that if governments are to use these events as part of a tourism development strategy they simply cannot afford to ignore the resident community. This is because, "tourism, like no other industry, relies on the goodwill and cooperation of local people because they are part of the product" (Murphy, 1985: 153). Brohman, (1996) notes that tourism should be treated as a local resource and therefore the needs and interests of local communities ought to be the principal criterion on which its development is evaluated. He further notes that community based tourism development would seek to strengthen institutions designed to enhance local participation and to promote the economic, social and cultural well-being of the population. However, it is recognised that creating synergies in the planning and marketing of tourism products is difficult due to the multiplicity of interest groups that must be represented (Buhalis, 2000).

More importantly, one of the major political justifications for staging mega events is that of imaging. Civic leaders and politicians perceive them as significant tools for the branding and marketing of a tourist destination based on the attention that they attract in the global media. This media attention is often seen as an opportunity for the host destination to project positive images that will result in increased investment and tourism. The section that follows critically examines these assertions.

3.4.5 Place Marketing, Media and Image Perspective

Government and tourism authorities evaluate the viability of mega events on the basis of their perceived intangible benefits. During these events the host community is able to highlight certain images, themes and values through the staging of a 'spectacle'. Spectacles are those phenomena of media culture that embody contemporary society's basic values and serve to acculturate individuals into its way of life. They promote values, lifestyles and perpetuate ideologies. They include not only sport events but also political happenings which are transformed into attention-grabbing occurrences called news (Kellner, 2003). In contemporary media culture, professional sports are a major field of the spectacle since spectator sports involve the consumption of images of the sports spectacle (*Ibid*, 2003).

The atmosphere that the event creates means that state interests and politically dominant values and ideologies are represented and transmitted to a global audience. The mega event transmits images and messages about a place through the period of time that it may be the focus of international attention. Thus, it is regarded as an opportunity for the marketing of place. Place marketing is one of the prominent justifications used by politicians to stage mega events. Place marketing is a phenomenon derived as a response to the international competitiveness of urban centres (Kotler, Haider and Rein, 1993). With increasing competition in tourism, regions and countries must strive to re-establish their position as principal places for business, leisure and economic activity. Place marketing therefore represents the techniques utilised by governments and tourism organisations to raise the awareness of their particular destination to specified target markets to entire tourism and investment.

Place marketing is particularly important to island tourism. The marketing of island destinations is often challenged due to limited

71

awareness in international markets. International tourism marketing budgets are usually too small for large promotional campaigns and islands like Barbados tend to fall back on tour operator and travel agent promotions to gain referrals and build awareness (Pattulo, 1996; Reid and Reid, 1994). Sport attracts large audiences and in advertising terms it does so relatively cheaply when compared to the comparable cost of traditional advertising to target the same audiences. It is in this regard that islands like Barbados find the hosting of mega events viable entities for building destination awareness.

Support for the use of mega events as a destination promotion tool is documented in several studies (Butler, 1990; Hall, 1992a; Tooke and Baker, 1996). It is argued that advertising messages need to break through a veritable mass of other advertising messages from competing products. In order for one destination's advertisement to be heard it must therefore have a unique quality. It is argued that the high intensity nature of the mega event is unique enough for advertisers to grab the attention of audiences. Hall and Selwood (1989: 105) assert that:

> A tourist promotion must carry a significantly different message than the standard imagery used to attract the visitor.... The hallmark event with its high intensity coverage and its concentrated time exposure can achieve that objective.

The strategies used by media personnel to cover these events provide a unique forum through which these messages can be transmitted. Sporting events undergo a transformation when they are presented in the media. What appears on the television screen is not necessarily what the spectator or performer at the event experiences (Hargreaves, 1986). Mega event television coverage is characterised by special effects and expert analysis that provide an exciting build-up to the event, which may foster an interest to attend (Maguire, 1999). Emphasis is placed on 'dramatisation' in which the media creates stories around the event and the individuals involved. The event is scripted so as to provide excitement that will enhance the programme's appeal to the audience (Stead, 2003) and the city or location provides the backdrop or the stage for these effects. The intensity of the media coverage attained through such strategies is perceived to provide an atmosphere where the promotional message can be unique enough to break through the barriers of 'noise' and 'clutter' that is a constant challenge for advertisers and promoters. The 'noise' and 'clutter' in advertising refers to the distraction caused by other advertising messages or entertainment products that may prevent the intended message from reaching the target audience. In advertising for instance, anything that obscures the message from gaining the attention of the prospective consumer is regarded as 'noise'. This could occur where the reader of a newspaper is inundated with a multitude of advertisements for travel holiday packages but only those that are unique or unusual stand out and those that are not are therefore lost in the 'noise' (Smith, Berry and Pulford, 1997). All channels used by marketers contain a considerable amount of noise and it is a constant challenge for the marketer to ensure that their messages are loud and attention-grabbing.

The images projected of event venues are also derived through news stories, features and documentaries in the media as well as the event broadcast and opening and closing ceremonies. Opening and closing ceremonies are opportunities for the host nation to showcase its culture to the world (Pruess, 2003). Barcelona, for the 1992 Olympics, used the opportunity to present itself as a modern city, which welcomed economic activity and initiative. It was the desire of the Spanish authorities that Barcelona be perceived as a thriving and cosmopolitan city rich with history (de Moragas Spa, Rivenburg and Garcia, 1995). The opportunity was also utilised to show the city's scenic assets. Certain venues for diving were designed to offer television cameras scenic backdrops for events and 'beauty' cameras were set up around the city to provide colourful visuals of the city's characteristics for international broadcast (ibid).

Further support for these arguments is found in the work of Tomkovich, Yelkur and Christians (2001) who in their study of Superbowl advertising in America, found that advertisements shown during the Superbowl had greater recall impacts than those presented in alternative forums. They contend that the Superbowl is an emotionally charged, high intensity event and that advertisers who can capture the right emotions with their advertisements have a greater chance of higher advertisement recall. They claim that:

> In advertising during special events….it is critical for advertisers to get viewers emotionally involved in their advertisements. Since viewers of special events are typically very highly emotionally involved in the programme, the challenge for advertisers is to capture this intensity and

immediately channel it towards their commercials (Tomkovich, Yelkur and Christians, 2001:93).

Emotion can be defined as a state of arousal involving conscious experiences and visceral or physiological changes (Mullen and Johnson, 1990:75). Since tourism is an experiential product it therefore follows that its consumption would be associated not only with cognitive or rational information processing but also in accordance with certain feelings of fantasy and fun, as encompassed by the 'experiential' nature of the tourists' experience (Williams, 2006). According to Holbrook and Hirschman (1982: 132), vacation is a phenomenon that includes "various playful activities, sensory pleasures, daydreams, aesthetic enjoyment and emotional responses". Advertisers tend to prey on the emotional responses of individuals in their advertisements through the use of repetition; classical conditioning, humour and fear appeals and the Tomkovich, Yelkur and Christians (2001) study shows that advertising effectiveness depends on the emotional context in which the message is delivered. Sport spectating is an emotional pastime. Watching sport provides opportunities for fans to vent their emotions (Masterman, 2004). However, the role of emotion in sports spectating or travel decision-making is not a widely studied phenomenon and further studies are required to identify its role in understanding consumer behaviour in relation to golf event tourism.

The destination therefore falls into the background in this high intensity, emotionally driven, media coverage and audiences would have been given a glimpse of the destination's tourism assets in the process. This can have the impact of forming favourable images of the destination in the eyes of the audience and studies have shown that a favourable image is linked to destination choice (Alhemond and Armstrong, 1996; Bigné, Sanchez and Sanchez, 2001). As explained by Hiller (1989:121):

> The emphasis on image is not meant to suggest that a false construction of reality is established but that the media transforms the sporting event into an urban 'happening' by exposing their audiences to numerous other facets of the city's non-sporting life, from cultural life to culinary activities and unique landmark and traits. The attachment of the city's name to the event enhances not only global recognition but suggests

74

that the success or failure of the global event reflects on the city.

The audience becomes exposed to aspects of the city's culture and life in a way that may not have been possible with commercial advertising. It is these images which destination managers hope will be converted into motivation to travel (Laws, 1993). However, claims of image enhancement after an event continue to exist without much empirical validation. Despite this image continues to be one of the major reasons for the staging of mega events. The next section critically examines the image perspective of mega events as expounded by leading scholars.

3.4.6 Mega Events as Image-Makers

The emphasis on positive imagery is one of the often-cited opportunities derived from the hosting of mega sport events (Getz, 1991a; Hall, 1992a; Laws, 1993). Creating a positive image and the perception that a place is worth visiting can be achieved through publicity, particularly by attracting media coverage of high profile events (Getz, 1997). Although many events do not have the capacity to attract many visitors, they may, however, attract a large media audience through the media; hence, the media is the cornerstone through which an image shaping opportunity can be exploited in favour of the host community. It is therefore felt that the global coverage of a one-time, major event has the ability to enhance the awareness, appeal and image of a destination (Riley and Van Doren, 1992; Ritchie and Smith, 1991).

The concept of image is a prominent theme in destination marketing (Laws, Scott and Parfitt, 2002). It is important to tourism marketers because it is regarded as one of the major factors in the travel decision-making process (Alhemoud and Armstrong, 1996) since the image that an individual holds of a destination will influence whether or not they choose to visit. In tourism marketing, an appropriate image can establish a meaningful and advantageous position for the destination in the minds of the potential visitor, which could eventually lead them to visit. Understanding the images that potential tourists have of a destination and how they evolve can help destination managers to identify those special attributes that distinguishes the destination from its competitors in a favourable way. Such understanding can also assist in the formulation of effective promotional strategies that would have the effect of attracting those visitors that the destination wishes to attract (Laws, Scott and Parfitt, 2002).

There is no one accepted definition of what constitutes a destination image. Some of the words used to sum up what destination image represents are beliefs, ideas, impressions, feelings, knowledge, prejudices and emotional thoughts (Pikkemaat and Peters, 2004). Crompton (1979) contends that destination images are ...'the sum of beliefs, ideas and impressions that a person has of the destination", whereas the definition posited by Lawson and Baud-Bovy (1977) is that the destination image is the expression of knowledge, impressions, prejudices and emotional thoughts an individual or group has of a particular object or place. Morgan and Pritchard (1999) relates destination image to an organised representation of an object, person or place in an individual's cognitive system. It embraces both a definition of that object, person or place and recognition of their attributes.

Some authors (Baloglu and Brinberg, 1997; Baloglu and McCleary, 1999; Faykaye and Compton, 1991) tend to view destination image as a reasoned and emotional interpretation based on the perceptive cognitive evaluations and the affective appraisals of the prospective tourist. The cognitive and perceptive evaluation refers to the individual's own knowledge and beliefs about the object while the affective components refer to the feelings or emotions that the individual has towards the objects. From a tourism perspective, cognitive evaluations are assessed based on those resources or attractions at the destination that hold some sort of appeal. These may include scenery, activities or experiences. Such attractions provide the 'pull' forces or the motivations necessary to persuade an individual to visit (Alhemoud and Armstrong, 1996). The affective component refers to the emotions associated with the place, such as the aura or atmosphere or other feelings intrinsic to the individual (Wickens, 2002).

All individuals have images of destinations that would have accumulated over time whether or not the desire to travel exists. Gunn (1988) conceptualised destination image at two levels, the organic and the induced. Books, novels, movies, newspaper reports or word-of-mouth recollections usually influence the organic image. These images are regarded as 'organic' since the images have not been influenced by the direct and conscious efforts of marketers to influence that image. It is often argued that the news stories surrounding a mega event is an ideal way to transmit organic images to potential tourists.

Once a favourable organic image is formed and a potential traveller decides to travel he or she may seek information on the particular destination and may refer to advertisements in newspapers, magazines or television, and travel agent and tour operator promotions, brochures and guidebooks (Gunn, 1988). The images that are encountered at this stage are said to be 'induced' because they are the result of a conscious effort by destination managers to persuade the individual to visit the destination. Fakeye and Crompton (1991) discussed the role of a third image level, which they called the 'complex image'. The complex image is developed at the time of visitation and consists of the pre-experience and post consumption images. The image of the destination perceived at this stage will influence satisfaction and intention to repeat the experience (Beerli and Martin, 2004).

However, image is a complicated, multi-dimensional construct that is difficult to capture. Echtner and Ritchie (1993) in an attempt to enhance our understanding of destination image conceptualised destination image as having six components along three continua, which they presented as three, bi-polar extremes including functional-psychological, common-unique and attributes-holistic characteristics. The functional and psychological characteristics may be perceived as individual attributes or as more holistic impressions. On the attributes side, the perceptions of the individual characteristics of the destination range from the functional to the psychological, while on the holistic side the functional impression consists of the mental or holistic impressions of the physical characteristics of the destination. The psychological impression can be described as the atmosphere or mood of the place. In terms of the common-unique continuum, destinations can be rated by common psychological characteristics such as level of friendliness or quality of service. Images of tourist destinations can also contain unique features such as iconic monuments or landscapes and events (functional characteristics) or auras (psychological characteristics).

Although the model presents us with a more thorough understanding of destination image, it is still difficult to break down the psychological or the affective components into measurable units. When research is geared at conceptualising the affective components of destination image such as exciting, gloomy, relaxing, and unpleasant, or the atmosphere, auras or feelings associated with a place, these cannot easily be operationalized. This shortcoming is due to the type of methodologies used in most image studies. There is a strong preference for more structured methodologies such as the likert or semantic differential scales where respondents are asked to rate a set of *a priori* list of attributes, which is inadequate for image studies. Instead the affective components require access to 'rich' data that can only be captured through qualitative techniques.

Destination image is an important area for managers pursuing the hosting of mega events. As stated earlier, images projected of the event through the news are aimed at soliciting future visits from those who may watch the event on television (Chalip, Green and Hill, 2003). However, holistic images may not hold any value for the tourism practitioner who may be interested in targeting specific markets. In order for a destination's image to have an impact on the travel decision-making process there would have to be a positive change on those dimensions that are important to the individuals within that market segment. The problem then with the image thesis is that studies in sports marketing fail to address which dimensions of destination image are tapped by mega event media and which type of images would influence travel. Answers to these questions are critical in the planning of mega events if the correct visuals are to be displayed during the telecast. Tapachai and Waryszak (2000) stress that often image studies do not address the actual image characteristics that influence purchase decisions. Thus, research needs to identify and focus on factors believed to attract attention and interest among potential visitors. In other words, promotional messages need to concentrate on those features that would 'trigger' the decision in favour of the destination. Similarly, Chen and Hsu (2000) made the point that promoting favourably perceived characteristics may not be effective in convincing tourists that a destination is a good place to visit. Their study was concerned with measuring the attractiveness of overseas destinations among Korean tourists. Although they found that the attractiveness of destinations was associated with adventurous atmosphere, scenery, environmental friendliness and the availability of tourist information, the attributes that exerted the most influence in inducing travel were trip planning time frame, budgeted travel cost and the length of trip. Researchers are still to discover which images are tapped by mega event media and which of these images are likely to induce travel to the destination (Sealy and Wickens, 2008).

To date very few attempts have been made by researchers to understand the effects that sport media have on destination images and subsequent destination choice. Instead the role of movies as a hallmark event and destination marketing tool has achieved the most attention in the literature. Consequently, empirical evidence exists that

78

support the view that movies can influence visitation to the locations in which they were filmed (Busby and Klug, 2001; Kim and Richardson, 2003; Kinkead, 2002; Riley, Baker and Van Doren 1998; and Tooke and Baker, 1996). Visitation to historic Fort Hays is said to have increased by 25% during 1990-1991 coinciding with the release of the movie *Dances with the Wolves* (Riley and Van Doren, 1992). Tooke and Baker, (1996) conducted four case studies on the effects of certain films on location visitation. In the case of the film *To the Manor Born* they found that although access to the primary location, the Cricket St. Thomas Estate in Somerset was restricted, visitation at the adjacent site increased by 37% over a two year period. Rocking Castle in Northamptonshire experienced a 93% increase in visitation due to the film *By The Sword Divided.* However, the images portrayed of a destination during a mega event may not be analogous to images presented in a movie. Movie media is completely different to mega event media in the sense that movies are based around a storyline theme, exciting sequences and human relationships, which may induce visitation to the filming location. In the movies the place and scenery is built into the storyline but with mega events, the place is not usually what the event is about (Chalip, Green and Hill, 2003). Movies also have the advantage of being recurrent events and the re-release or re-screening on nationwide television networks and their conversion onto videotapes or DVD's means that repeated exposure is possible whereas mega-sport events tend to be 'one-off' relative to the host location with the focus shifting to another location in anticipation of the next event. Consequently, it may be wrong for destination managers and events planners to expect that mega event media would impact destination visitation in the same way as movies.

One of the few studies dedicated to the impacts of mega event media on destination image is Ritchie and Smith's (1991) longitudinal study aimed at evaluating the level of awareness of Calgary as a tourist destination in the United States of American and European markets after the 1988 Winter Olympic Games. Although they found a substantial increase in Calgary's attractiveness during and immediately following the event, the increase was only sustained for a short period and there was an attrition of awareness over time. Mossberg and Hallberg (1999) measured the impact of the media coverage of the World Championships of Athletics in Gothenburg, Sweden on the image of Sweden as a tourist destination and of Swedish products among Dutch, German and English travellers. They surveyed travellers en route to the city before and after the games and found that the event did not initiate a change in image and that pre and post event images remained constant. The exact cause of this is uncertain but they concluded that the media coverage of the event was insufficient to generate a change. In markets where the destination is already well known, communications about an event may simply add another exposure to the frequency of communications about the destination. In such a case the effect may simply be redundant due to other marketing messages in the environment (Butler, 1990).

In another study, Kim and Morrison (2005) found that destination image could be enhanced due to the hosting of a mega sport event. They found that visitors to Korea for the 2002 Football World Cup had more positive images of Korea after than before the World Cup. On the contrary, an exploratory study by Sealy and Wickens (2008) sought to explore the images created by the media coverage of Euro 2004, which was hosted by Portugal. The study revealed that participants' image of Portugal remained constant. The participants in this study indicated that they paid attention to the coverage of the football rather than incidental coverage of the destination's attractions. Many participants thus claimed that they could not remember what images they saw of Portugal. In addition, the majority of respondents indicated that they were not inspired to visit Portugal because of Euro 2004.

Another study by Chalip, Green and Hill (2003) explored the effects that the media coverage of the Honda Indy 300 had on the image of the Australian Gold Coast among American and New Zealand visitors. They tested the effect of the media on nine image dimensions including developed environment, natural environment, value for money, sightseeing opportunities, safety, novelty, climate, convenience and family environment. Their findings found that the pattern of effects were different in each country. There was evidence that the media affected all nine dimensions of destination image tested on United States visitors but only three dimensions on the New Zealand sample. A significant finding in this study, however, is that the event media had no direct impact on the New Zealand participants' intention to visit the Gold Coast. They also found that in the United States market, the event media had a negative effect on the image of the Gold Coasts' natural environment. This was disconcerting since Americans' image of the Gold Coast' natural environment plays a significant role in their intention to visit.

Many commentators warned of the potentially negative effects of mega sport media on destination image. Negative publicity can be a threat due to badly organised games or other negative episodes taking place during the event which can have serious impacts on the international attractiveness of the host country. Australia, for example, received negative publicity in 1998 concerning revelations that inducements were offered to various international Olympic Committee members to secure the games for Australia (Burroughs, 1999). Wales's image was tainted when in the lead up to the 1999 Rugby World Cup bad publicity ensued as a result of a ticket black-market (Jones, 2001) while the public transportation chaos and the bombing of the Olympic Park during the 1996 Olympic Games in Atlanta flawed the tourism promotion aspect of those games (Higham, 1999). Likewise, the negative publicity that ensued due to the death of the Pakistan cricket coach during the 2007 Cricket World Cup might have tarnished the tourism image of Jamaica. This indicates that destination managers should recognise that there is a risk of negative publicity when depending on free press or free promotion and as a result the images portrayed of the destination may not always be favourable. Furthermore, as this study will show, positive publicity can be interpreted negatively which in turn can adversely impact spectator attendance. Chapter seven highlights how the positive portrayal of the Golf World Cup in the local media as an 'upmarket', 'high end' and 'star-studded' event, was negatively interpreted. This in turn was blamed for the poor spectator turnout at the Golf World Cup.

Getz (2003) cautions tourism planners that frequently the destination is not featured in the media coverage. As stated earlier, this was a major problem with the staging of the World Championships of Athletics held in Gothenburg, Sweden where it is felt that the media coverage of this event was insufficient to generate any changes in image (Chalip, Green and Hill, 2003). Getz (2003) claims that this might have reduced the tourism effectiveness of the event. Jones (2001) likewise found that the coverage of the 1999 Rugby World Cup did not allow for any incidental coverage of the region's tourism assets. That study confirmed that unless specific arrangements are made with media networks the destination is not always featured. Instead, what is shown of the destination is up to the media producers and verbal mentions of the destination are left to the discretion of the event commentators (Turner, 2005). This Barbados study also supports Jones' (2001) view as it called into question the quality and the frequency of the pre-event media coverage of the Golf World Cup. Many international participants noted that they did not see any news or advertisements related to the Golf World Cup in the international press at any time prior to their arrival in Barbados.

Another caveat worthy of mention is that event organisers may not have control of the images portrayed of the destination by media networks. Whereas advertising messages can be manipulated in order to convey the message that the advertisers would like the receivers to receive and the quality and quantity of the message can be controlled, a destination manager may have no control over the messages and the images conveyed of the destination by event commentators during an event (Hoek, Gendal, Jeffcoat and Orsman, 1997). In Barbados local stakeholders noted how other Caribbean islands not involved in the staging of the Golf World Cup were receiving publicity at the expense of Barbados' taxpayers. de Moragas Spa, Rivenburg and Garcia (1995) also highlighted that sometimes commentators could misinterpret the messages intended in opening and closing ceremonies. They found this to be the case with the Brazilian commentators during the opening ceremony of the 1992 Barcelona Olympics. Destination managers also need to be aware that it may be wrong to assume that each event telecast is the same in every country. Turner (2005) draws attention to the practice where television broadcasters receive what is called a 'clean-feed' with no commentary and little or no graphics and it is then up to the host network to insert this additional information. The consequence is that the destination may not be promoted at all.

Some commentators argue that mega events may not necessarily enhance destination image and even when destination image is enhanced this is not a guarantee of the destination being included in the 'consideration set' of a potential traveller or a traveller's eventual destination choice (Chalip, Green and Hill, 2003; Sealy and Wickens, 2008). A 'consideration set' is the list of destinations that the potential traveller considers before arriving at a final choice. Even when the publicity from a mega sport event is positive there can be negative connotations that may discourage event visitation or discourage tourists from visiting in the immediate or even distant periods after the event. For example, a study by Deccio and Baloglu (2002) notes how negative connotations and perceptions of crime, loss of authenticity, smuggling, prosecution, alcoholism, additional policing cost and congestion discouraged support for a mega event. In another study, Pyo, Cook and Howell (1991) suggested that out of town residents and other tourists stayed away from the Olympic Games in Los Angeles due to the anticipated congestion perceived from the pre-games media coverage.

Morley (1995) notes that the audience is active, critical and powerful receivers of media messages and thus they construct their own meanings. The audience does not simply accept or reject media messages but instead interprets them according to their own social world – their culture and individual interests (Milner, 1995). For these reasons media effects can be best understood only with reference to the strategies that viewers and readers apply to the media. This includes the social context though which meanings are constructed and elaborated. Thus, how people interpret the media is contingent on prior perceptions of the destination and the event, previous experiences with travel or the destination, selective perception, values and interests and pre-dispositions. Much more work is needed to identify and explore the ways that audiences interpret what they see, hear and read about the host destination and event through mega event media outlets. There is a need to understand audience interpretations in terms of the motives, interests and values that they bring. However, despite the lack of evidence to support the view that the sports media is capable of fostering positive images and inducing travel, supporters of these ventures continue to contend that destination managers should exploit the opportunity as a 'tool' to be used for destination promotion (Faulker and Tideswell, 1999).

For any sporting event to be successful it not only needs to attract competitors, officials or the media but it also needs spectators or attendees (Gibson, 1998). Marketers need to be aware of and to appreciate the driving forces which influence these spectators to take the time, effort and expense to be a spectator either locally or internationally. Spectators will often arrange their yearly holiday to coincide with a sporting event and so there will be many influencing factors such as the time of year, destination and cost to name a few. The mega event as a tourist attraction is another widely cited justification for hosting a mega event but the reasons for visitation by spectators is also another area that has been neglected by the research community. The following section surveys the literature concerned with event visitation.

3.5 MEGA EVENTS AS TOURIST ATTRACTIONS

Sport event tourism is a growing global industry with important economic implications for the sport, the event and its impact on travel and tourism. It is the tourism benefits that are of concern to the event planner since it is argued that mega events act as an attraction that 'lure' potential travellers to the destination. Although a great deal of attention has been given to the economic perspective and to a lesser extent the social perspective of mega events, not much attention had been directed to the supply-demand system and as a result many specific issues have been ignored. While the supply side is characterised by sport event venues and the destinations in which they are hosted, the demand side encompasses many groups beginning with the sports leagues, competitors, officials, the media and the spectators (Getz, 1998). It is important to devote some time to understanding how the demand side responds to mega events. Media, sport officials and competitors are very important; however, the findings in this research highlighted the importance of the spectators in the success of any mega event. On the demand side, although some events are more competitor driven than others, the Golf World Cup in Barbados 2006 was a spectator event, with the spectator being critical to its overall success. The poor turnout of international and local spectators confirms that attention must be given to understanding the spectators of mega events. Their expectations and perceptions play an important role in understanding why they choose to or not to attend a mega event.

Getz (1998) and Ryan (1997) suggest that event visitors are attracted to the leisure, social and cultural experiences that special events can provide. They claim that special events provide the visitor with the opportunity to participate in an experience which is different from everyday life experiences. Some commentators argue that mega events have a global appeal which attracts visitors (Cassidy, 2006). Others argue that their global appeal stems from their prestigious nature or 'once in a lifetime' factor (Hall, 1992a; Laws, 1991) whereas Zauhar and Kurtzman (1997) propose that travel to an event is influenced by the concept of the religious pilgrimage. Whatever the reason an individual may have for travelling to attend a mega event, many questions still remain. For instance, we do not know what type of activities designed around the event would satisfy the social and leisure needs of the visitor. Questions still arise about what makes an event a "once in a lifetime opportunity' or exactly what contributes to its global appeal. Unfortunately, many reasons put forward by researchers are either lacking empirical validation or are under-researched.

Nogawa, Yamaguchi and Hagi (1996) found scant research focussing on the event spectator whose main purpose of travel was to attend events. Efforts dedicated to understanding why people attend events are mainly designed around theoretical frameworks using motivation theory. This study will show that motivation is insufficient as a concept for understanding why individuals attend mega sport events. Furthermore, studies in event motivation are fragmented as researchers tend to investigate sport attendance, event attendance and event tourism motivation as though they were separate domains. Studies on sport spectators, for instance, tend to ignore the travel component; whereas studies on travel motivation do not necessarily explore the role of attractions like mega events in the decision making process. Thus, it is not known if mega event motivation differs from traditional sport consumption or travel motivation.

A review of the tourism literature reveals an abundance of studies on tourist motivation (Crompton 1979; Crompton, 1979; Dann 1977; Gnoth 1997; Iso-Ahola, 1982; Mansfeld, 1992). Theorists and tourism researchers assert that motivation is the fundamental reason behind most tourists' behaviour and is critical in understanding the travel decision-making process and subsequent event visitation. From a practitioner's perspective, understanding motivation is critical for the marketing of tourism experiences and the designing and planning of tourism attractions like mega events. However, the study of motivation is a complex area due to the intangible nature of the tourism product and the issues of multiple motives across different individuals, time and space (Nicholson and Pearce, 2001). The issue of measurement and interpretation have also plagued motivational studies in the leisure and tourism sector. As a result various theories and models of motivation have appeared in the tourism literature.

A generally accepted definition of motivation is provided by Murray (1938: 7) who defines motivation as: ".....an internal factor that arouses, directs and integrates a person's behaviour....". Murray further explains that a motive is: "....not observed directly but inferred from his behaviour or simply assumed to exist in order to explain his behaviour". Crompton and McKay (1997: 427) offer a definition of tourism motivation that embraces the concept of 'homostatis'. They claim that: "....tourism motivation is conceptualised as a dynamic process of internal psychological factors (needs and wants) that generate a state of tension or disequilibrium within individuals".

Iso-Ahola (1982) argues that travel motivation is related to disequilibria in the individual's socio-psychological environment in which they seek intrinsic rewards in destination settings. According to Iso-Ahola, travel motivation to destinations does not only differ among individuals but individuals also seek to satisfy their needs for escape and their search for new experiences in ways that may be personal or inter-personal. Personal motivations include rest/relaxation, prestige, competence and learning about other cultures. Interpersonal motives include social interaction with residents and experiencing their culture and lifestyles. Crompton (1979) identified nine travel motivators. These include: to escape from a perceived mundane environment; exploration and evaluation of self; relaxation; prestige; regression; social interaction; enhancement of kinship relations; novelty and education. Researchers such as Lundberg (1971) developed a list of 18 motivations, which they categorised into four sub-sections: education and cultural motives; relaxation and pleasure motives; ethnic motives; and other motives which they describe as weather, health, sports and sociological motives. It is not known though which of these motives are tapped by mega sport events or which motives an event visitor may seek to satisfy from being a spectator. Although these studies explain in part why an individual may want to travel, they do not provide insights into why individuals choose a particular type of vacation or may choose to travel to one destination over the other.

Dann (1977) developed a theory that is prominent in the testing of hypotheses related to travel choices. The theory, known as the 'push' and 'pull' concept suggests that a person is motivated to travel because they are pushed to do so. The 'push' factors relate to those things that stimulate the desire to travel. These may include psychological factors such as the desire to get away, the desire to experience something new or the desire to experience a new culture. Dann (1977:186) states:

> …while a specific resort may hold a number of attractions for the potential tourist, his actual decision to visit such a destination is *consequent* on his prior need for travel. An examination of 'push' factors is thus logical and often temporarily, antecedent to that of 'pull' factors.

Push factors are usually studied in reference to travellers reasons for travelling but studies in this area have varied considerably depending on the type of vacation, the destination and the context in which the vacation is taken. For instance, Kim, Lee and Klenosky (2003) identified the need to experience a new culture, friendly people and to partake in recreational activities as motivators for visiting Korean national parks. A survey of visitors to the island of Barbados identified the need for rest and relaxation as a key factor in their desire to visit Barbados (Barbados Stay-Over Visitor Survey, 2005). However, it is the 'pull' factor that is prominent in understanding the choice of destination. The 'pull' factor refers to those attributes or characteristics that a destination possesses that the prospective tourist finds attractive. Thus, it is the pull factor that acts as a magnet for him/her to visit that destination. These may include the climate, the beaches, culture or the atmosphere or aura. Practitioners in the event arena are particularly concerned about the mega event as a 'pull' factor in order to achieve the increased international demand that an event is expected to draw to the destination. 'Push' and 'pull' factors are, therefore, thought to work together to determine travel intention and ultimate destination choice.

It is thus crucial to understand motives specific to event visitation. Invariably where travel is involved it is reasonable to suggest that the event planner will have to tap into an individual's desire to travel and then convince them, through promotional outlets, that a specific event can satisfy those needs. In turn, the event itself would have to be designed around these needs so that it provides the nexus through which the travellers' needs and desires are adequately fulfilled. McDonnell, Allen, and O'Toole, (1999) suggested a framework that can be used by event planners for understanding event motivation. They claim that individuals are motivated to attend events due to social, organisational, physiological and personal motives. As social creatures, people have the desire to be with others. This is known as the affiliation motivation. Affiliation refers to the act of developing and maintaining relationships with others (Handy 1993). Often spectators' association with sport is motivated by a desire to confirm their sense of identity through affiliation. It is a time to construct and/or confirm one's leisure identity by interacting with others who share the ethos of the activity. Green and Chalip (1998) found, for example, that participants at an American college football event were attracted to the opportunity to celebrate the group's subculture by dining out and taking in the night life together. Other researchers have noted that events can bring together people who otherwise would have little in common (Melnick, 1983) and can also instil a feeling of national pride or a sense of community (Getz, 1997; Masterman, 2004). Further social motives are explained in terms of the opportunity to socialise or to be part of the community spirit which takes place during an event or to be a volunteer. This factor of event motivation was evident in this study. This study, like McDonnell, Allen, and O'Toole, (1999) study, showed that socialising with friends, family or other visitors was important to the spectators at the Golf World Cup. By understanding the nexus of serious leisure, social identity and subculture, we are better able to describe and explain participation in mega events; however, the area remains largely untouched by researchers.

Organisational motives tend to include the desire of spectators for status conferment due to recognition that they have been a participant at a prestigious event. Thus some individuals may seek social acceptance by attending a prestigious event. The Olympic Games is used as an example of an avenue for the conferment of status or prestige that may be connected with attending the games. The Golf World Cup in Barbados was promoted as a prestigious event. Promotional material and press reports constantly referred to this event as being 'high end', 'star studded' or 'upmarket'; however, the extent to which this prestigious image might have encouraged or discouraged spectator attendance is a contentious issue which will be further discussed in chapters five and six. Physiological motives include the need for relaxation or exercise, depending on the type of event. Golf spectating is particularly known for the exercise and fitness challenge of following golfers around the golf course. Personal motives relate to the need for new experiences that may be the consequence of a mundane existence. Although the McDonnell, Allen, and O'Toole, (1999) study provides a useful framework for understanding why people are likely to attend events, other studies show that event motivation can be multi-dimensional and may vary from event to event. Hence, the need for more context specific research in event tourism geared at particular sports and particular destinations.

Other studies illustrate the issue of multiple motives although a few commonalities exist. Neirotti, Bosetti and Teed (2001) found that the major factors influencing the decision to attend the Olympic Games of 1996 in Atlanta were: "once in a lifetime opportunity; availability of housing and availability of tickets". Other research clearly suggests that the attractiveness of a sporting event will be a function of the fans' level of interest. For instance, Kim and Chalip's (2004) study investigated the factors influencing visitation to the FIFA World Cup 2002 in Korea and found that visitors to the event cited interest in football as a major motivator. A study by Wann, Melnick, Russell, and Pease (2001) identified eight dimensions of fan interests including: group affiliation, sharing with family, aesthetic appreciation, self-esteem, gambling on sport, excitement, arousal ("eustress"), escape and entertainment. A further study by Funk, Mahony, Nakazawa, and Hirakawa (2001) notes that fan motives may not necessarily be good predictors of attendance. They instead identified ten dimensions to predict attendance at a sporting event. These include: being a fan of the sport, vicarious achievement, excitement, team identification, supporting women's opportunities in sport, aesthetics, socialisation, national pride, drama and interest in particular players. However, many of these studies were conducted at different events, some of which were not necessarily 'mega'. Another weakness is that they were all conducted with the use of structured instruments which do not necessarily allow all relevant concepts to be explained. Of particular concern is the lack of data on golf event tourism and the motives that attract golf spectators. Golf event motivation may be influenced by factors alien to those identified in the above-mentioned studies.

Motivation is inextricably linked to theories of consumer behaviour and decision- making. Planners and researchers must, however, recognise that motivation is insufficient a concept to understand why people travel to mega events. This Barbados study confirms Moutinho's (1987) view that the desire to travel is influenced by the individual's personality and lifestyle, group influence, reference groups and culture, which are all concepts rooted in consumer behaviour theory.

Consumption patterns are particularly influenced by cultural orientation. Culture is not instinctive but is learned. Humans learn cultural norms through imitation or by observing the process of rewards and sanctions to those who conform with the acceptable norms relevant to that society. Culture refers to 'a set of values, ideas, artefacts and other meaningful symbols that help individuals communicate, interpret and evaluate as members of society' (Engle, Blackwell and Miniard, 1995: 611). Culture is a shared set of beliefs that provide individuals with a sense of identity and an understanding of what is acceptable or desirable behaviour. Some of the most important attitudes and behaviours that are influenced by culture are: sense of self and space; communication and language; dress and appearance, food and feeding habits, time and time consciousness, relationships, values and norms, beliefs and attitudes, mental processing and learning, work habits and practices. Culture is passed from generation to generation primarily by the family, or by religious and educational institutions. Most cultures possess a characteristic known as *ethnocentrism*, which is the belief that their own culture is right or superior while that of other groups is a poor imitation or an 'evil travesty' (Blythe, 1997: 91). Culture influences the way people behave as tourists. Sport for instance, has often been cited as an important cultural value in western countries to the extent that it influences the content of the holiday experience (Decrop, 2006, Standeven and DeKnop, 1999). For many Europeans and Americans, golf, tennis, skiing and scuba diving are primary motives for leisure travel (Decrop, 2006; Weed and Bull, 2004).

3.6 CONCLUSION

This chapter provided a thematic discussion on the theoretical perspectives contained in the literature on mega sport events. The perspectives expressed in the literature reveal contradictory arguments about the benefits and costs of staging these events. One such argument is that on the positive side, they can contribute additional expenditure, new and improved facilities, enhanced infrastructure and act as a tool for 'civic boosterism'. On the negative side, they can cause social dislocation and inconvenience due to construction and other violations of human rights. It is also doubtful if these events do increase tourist visitation to the host location in any significant way. The dubious nature of economic impact studies has left academics sceptical about the claims of increased economic and tourism activity. In terms of publicity, events can be used as a tool to improve the image and awareness of a tourist destination; however, much of this publicity may be haphazard or may not occur in any effective way. Sceptics argue that locations are always at a risk of being exposed to negative publicity and it is still not clear to what extent positive images can actually encourage visitation to the location in the short or long term. Positive media effects do not simply happen automatically and the role of the media in persuasion appears to be a complex and complicated issue that requires further research. However, the impact of mega event media on destination awareness and the travel decision-making process is still not understood.

Clearly from the foregoing review it can be seen that many theoretical perspectives on mega events have not been empirically verified. Studies on mega events in general lack a solid stakeholder perspective. This is in part due to the restrictive nature of the positivist methodologies that characterise these studies. Such methods do not allow stakeholders a voice. What is also evident in this chapter is that many of the perspectives expressed tend to be based on studies and observations made of events in large metropolitan countries. This literature review simultaneously highlights the gaps that exist in the study of sport events on small islands, particularly golf tourism events. Consequently, how the golf event tourist and local residents respond to

90

golf events on a small island needs further illumination. It is the island context that forms the basis of the next chapter.

4 -CHAPTER FOUR
TOURISM, THE GOLF WORLD CUP 2006 AND THE ISLAND CONTEXT

4.1 INTRODUCTION

Small island states like Barbados share features that are different from more developed mainland territories. One distinct feature is the role that tourism plays in the economy and the resources upon which the industry is dependent. In Barbados tourism is the mainstay of the economy but it is affected by a high degree of external influence which presents challenges for the local tourism decision-makers. Tourism, on the one hand, is recognised for the role that it plays in wealth creation where no other viable alternatives exist but, on the other hand, it is sometimes perceived negatively due to its perceived association with the socio-cultural structures of the past.

This chapter examines the historical and cultural context in which the Golf World Cup took place by giving an account of the historical forces that shaped the Barbadian society and economy. It will also provide the reader with a historical analysis of tourism in Barbados by focussing on the internal and external problems and issues facing the industry. In addition, this chapter provides the reader with a background to the development of event and golf tourism in Barbados. Finally, the reader will benefit from an introduction to the Golf World Cup event.

4.2 BARBADOS - THE HISTORICAL CONTEXT.

Barbados is a former colony of the United Kingdom. Its socio-cultural structure and economic development is a manifestation of its colonial past. The legacy of slavery and the plantation society underpins much of the contemporary culture and values that pervade many aspects of the tourism industry (Lewis, 2002). The plantation is a type of settlement in another place that serves metropolitan interests in their colonies of exploitation (Knight, 1990). In the colonial setting the plantation was created by metropolitan capital to serve the interests of metropolitan enterprise. In colonies like Barbados the plantation evolved around the production of cash crops, mainly sugar, for sale exclusively to an overseas market (Beckles, 1990). The plantation was a monopolising institution that hoarded the best land and smothered other forms of production that threatened its labour supply. The labour force on the plantation was coerced labour or in other words it was slave labour or indentured labour. The slave labour comprised Africans who were brought forcibly to the West Indies during the notorious 'middle passage' trade of the 16th, 17th and 18th centuries. The plantation was characterised by a racially rigid and hierarchical society that lent itself to centralised power that was vested in the British planter who maintained ultimate power and control. The social forces inherent in the plantation system served to perpetuate its very existence and its hegemonic control. The attitude of Barbadians to tourists and tourism development is significantly influenced by their colonial history (Lewis, 2002). The genesis of this history is European colonisation, indigenous destruction, slavery, indentureship and the struggles for freedom, migration and independence.

After independence colonial ties to the mother-land remain intact in the form of foreign imports and tourists. Barbados, which once relied on the United Kingdom for food and other supplies and its overall economic well-being, now depends on the United Kingdom for its tourists and to a lesser extent on the United States of America. Barbados also relies on transnational organisations to fuel the tourism industry, particularly the airlines, tour operators and to a lesser extent the hotels. Because most tourists come from the United Kingdom and North America, many of these tourists are white. Tourism is therefore an industry where frequently black workers serve a white clientèle. Lewis (2002) notes that as a result the distinction between service and servitude is difficult to maintain due to the history of race relations in former colonial states.

Tourism is not a recent phenomenon in Barbados, but it has become a prominent feature of the economy since the 1950s. Significantly, many of the features of the former colonial structures pervade the tourism industry today despite the attainment of political independence and economic self-determination. In fact, the industry has been labelled the new 'plantocracy' by historians and writers of Caribbean history (Beckles, 1990; Lewis, 2002; Pattulo, 1996). Many Caribbean intellectuals question the co-option of the Caribbean region by foreign interests viewing it as demeaning and as a form of recolonization. Strachan (2002) concurs that the same type of exploitation that occurred during colonial times has resurfaced in various forms all over the world. Strachan notes that tourism is run by transnational organisations that depend on the local bourgeois to serve as caretakers. Consequently, the tourism industry has become part of government policy in that tourism ministries and boards become extensions of foreign enterprises who routinely serve to protect and facilitate the growth of a foreign owned industry. Like the plantation economy, the tourism industry is the major monopoliser of land, particularly along the shoreline. Tourism is also the first-born of the plantation system and the social dynamics that it perpetuates. Many authors of Barbadian and Caribbean history have alluded to the view that tourism fosters social exclusion and perpetuates social divisions in society (Pattulo, 1996; Strachan, 2002). Pattulo (1996: 137) illustrates the exclusive and snobbish nature of Barbados' tourism in this quote:

> The west-coast tourists like luxury in bucketfuls...They stay in places such as Sandy Lane, tucked away from normal life behind heavily guarded perimeter gates...Even more exclusive are the private homes. An example is Heron Bay, the US$20 million {£10 million} holiday home of Sir Anthony Bamford, whose family made money out of steel beam supports. Guests such as Joan Collins drop in to stay in a cottage in the grounds for New Year and to party with the likes of Rocco Forte... David Frost and Robert Sangster at the Carambola Restaurant. For those who care winter in the Caribbean retains its snobbish ring.

Today hotels like Sandy Lane and the Royal Westmoreland Golf Club use class and wealth to exclude certain segments of the population through excessive fees and other forms of snobbery. Strachan (2002) notes how tourism has reinforced the snobbery of whites, encouraged black subordination and rigidified class divisions of the past. Sandy Lane, in particular, is notorious on the island for its policy of excluding the general public from playing golf on their famous 'blue monkey' course (Its Tee Time, 2006). Furthermore, the public is not accorded free entry to the facility without first acquiring the permission of management. Once entry is attained you are escorted by security or other personnel.

The control of the industry by foreign enterprises and local elites fosters a situation where the masses of the population have no say in the type of tourism development that it wishes. The failure to recognize the importance of local involvement in the industry is acknowledged in many tourism documents but hardly ever practised in Barbados (Barbados Legacy, 2006; Sustainable Tourism Policy, 2002). The need for foreign exchange and employment opportunities has resulted in tourism development that has been uncoordinated and sporadic (Lewis, 2002). The leaders of the industry seem generally unconcerned about the local dimensions of the industry and the type of tourism development that local residents desire. Consequently, the need to protect the authenticity of local art and dance forms, cultural heritage and local traditions are largely ignored (Lewis, 2002). Today, in the Caribbean, including Barbados, much of what is acceptable in terms of dress, music, technology, the visual arts and personal behaviour is foreign, mainly North American. Pattulo (1996) notes about the tendency of hoteliers to promote and serve foreign food to tourists while local delicacies are ignored. There is an underlying assumption that tourists to Barbados and the wider Caribbean want what they can get at home (*ibid*). McAfee (1991) notes, however, that the damaging effects of tourism on Caribbean communities and values are now being voiced by citizens. This quote from Pattullo (1996: 182) tells the story:

> If we ignore our history and the cultural legacy that it has left us, we run the risk of developing tourism as an industry which puts the dollar first and our people last. We are saying to ourselves, perhaps unconsciously: we are the field labourers on the modern plantation of the tourism industry.

While the negative impacts of tourism are acknowledged, political figures, economists and academics agree that it is a necessary evil mainly due to the economic benefits derived from the industry. While the plantation structure and sugar cane production remained after the attainment of political independence from Britain, high production cost, cane fires, labour shortages and the measures adopted by foreign governments to protect their own beet-root sugar resulted in a new economic strategy (McAfee, 1991). As a result there was, and still is, a continuous struggle to identify activities which can contribute to long term economic development. Barbados, like many island micro states, did attempt to develop export markets in merchandise, but these were unsuccessful or not as successful as anticipated. It is this combination of a limited array of economic activities and restricted resources that places even greater emphasis on the tourism industry as a tool for social and economic advancement. The natural attractions, including the climate of many small islands, often gives them a competitive edge in tourism markets. For this reason, many governments of small islands give tourism top priority and attempt to maximise their island's tourism potential by further developing the industry through promotional campaigns, building of hotels and other tourist facilities, and enhancing their air and sea links with other countries.

The importance of tourism to the economy of Barbados is reflected in the way that the industry is organised. Decisions regarding the tourism industry are a primary function of Government. The Barbados Ministry of Tourism is the ultimate governing body of the tourism industry. According to the Barbados Ministry of Tourism website, the ministry's role is to provide leadership in the sustainable development of Barbados' tourism industry through the formulation of policy, the provision of timely and quality research, the development and maintenance of industry-wide standards and the facilitation of appropriate product development whilst ensuring maximum economic benefits to Barbadians. The ministry, with the Minister of Tourism as the head, functions as a research centre, facilitators of the tourism industry and as a partner for private sector initiatives. The Barbados Tourism Authority functions as an arm of the Ministry of Tourism, but this agency is primarily responsible for marketing. The Barbados Tourism Authority is headed by a President who together with a board of directors, appointed by the tourism minister, are the key decision-makers of all matters that affect the marketing of Barbados' tourism product. Although these agencies are in place, tourism planning in Barbados has been a major weakness of these agencies. Wilson (1996) notes that very often, the scramble for the tourist dollars has seen development determined by short-term fancy rather than a coordinated long-term strategic approach. Another major weakness is that statistical data is hardly ever up to date and lacks appropriate attention to detail (Pattulo, 1996). The fact that no post impact studies have been conducted on the Golf World Cup and the Cricket World Cup is testament to this statement. The lack of up to date and detailed research presents challenges for researchers and evaluators. We now turn our attention to the importance of tourism to Barbados and the challenges facing the industry.

4.3 CHALLENGES FACING BARBADOS

Since independence from Britain in 1966, successive governments have sought to diversify the economy from an agrarian-based economy to a more diversified one characterized by light to semi-heavy manufacturing and services (Hoyos, 1978). A relatively stable economic climate has provided an attractive environment for foreign investment and a growing offshore services industry. Over the years, tourism and financial services have grown from insignificant levels to become major contributors to the gross domestic product (GDP), employment generation and the country's capacity to earn foreign exchange. By the 1970's manufacturing and tourism emerged as major foreign exchange earners. Barbados is now acknowledged as one of the most mature tourist destinations in the Caribbean (Sustainable Tourism Policy, 2002).

Like other island states lacking in mineral resources, Barbados has recognised that self-sufficiency and economic stability can be attained through tourism (Conlin and Baum, 1995; Croes, 2006; Dann, 1992; Fagence, 1997; Pattulo, 1996; Poon, 1988; Wing, 1995). Large-scale tourism in Barbados developed mainly as a substitute for the declining sugar industry. Barbados' beautiful beaches and its social stability have been important factors in attracting an increasing number of tourists since the late 1970s (Strategic Development Plan, 2005). Through tourism, Barbados has achieved significant economic and social growth. Between 1965 and 1976 Barbados became one of the fastest growing economies in the Caribbean, moving up from 11th to 3rd place among Caribbean island states (Hoyos, 1978). Tourism now ranks as the major foreign exchange earner contributing 70% of exports (Sustainable Tourism Policy, 2002). Tourist expenditure in 1990 amounted to US$ 493.5 million (£246 million) and reached US$ 0.7 billion (£3.5 billion) by 1999, reflecting an increase of over 41.8% in the nine-year period (Barbados Ministry of Tourism, 2002). By 2003 tourism expenditure stood at US$ 0.747 billion (£0.373 billion) with a contribution to GDP of 27.4% (Caribbean Tourism Organisation, 2003). According to the Barbados Economic Report (2006), by the end of 2006 tourism earnings were approximately US$1.8 billion (£1 billion), representing a growth of 2.7% compared to the US$1.7 billion (£0.85 billion) a year earlier. Despite the island's small size, by 2006 Barbados was considered one of the better performing countries of the Caribbean with a Gross Domestic Product, per capita, of US$18,700 (£9,350) making it the number one economy in the Caribbean and Latin America region (International Monetary Fund, 2006). In 2013 Barbados is recognised as having one of the highest standards of living in the western hemisphere ranking 3rd behind the United States and Canada and ranking 31st on the human development index.

Tourism expenditure creates direct employment in hotels, restaurants, nightclubs, cafés, retail outlets, transport and sightseeing

97

operations and for arts and crafts entrepreneurs. In 2006 it was estimated that tourism provided direct employment for approximately 14,000 individuals from a total work force of 148,200 (Barbados Ministry of Tourism 2006). In addition, there are other sectors in the Barbadian economy linked to tourism which benefit from indirect employment stimulated by the industry. These include printing and publishing, food processing, real estate, communication services, agriculture, fishing and construction, amongst others (Barbados Private Sector Trade Team, 2004). In addition to providing employment, the government also depends on tourism to generate revenue through taxes and other direct and indirect revenue. For example, there is a 7.5% value added tax (VAT) on hotel rooms; a 15% VAT on food and beverage services; and an airport tax of US$30.00 (£15.00) per person (*Ibid*). These taxes are important as they facilitate the repayment of foreign debts, pay for national imports and maintain and expand social services.

As stated in the introduction, tourism in island micro states is conceptually different from that which exists in mainland territories that are a part of larger geographical areas. In island tourism territories the constraints of size presents a number of challenges. Size is an important consideration when analysing the viability of an event to a small island state. The size of an event thus has to be considered in the context of the size of the host environment. A major city may routinely play host to a multitude of small events with the collective impacts being perceived as general tourist activity. However, in a small community like Barbados such an event may have significant impacts on the limited resources of the community in a substantial way.

Size also limits the volume of tourist visitations required to sustain particular levels of capital investment in tourist enterprises. Island micro states depend almost exclusively on international markets for tourists since size rules out any potential for domestic tourism (Reid and Reid, 1994). The dependence on inward tourist flows means that the tourism industry is largely controlled by external forces. Major players in the inward flow of tourists are the tour operators and airlines. Tour operators are very powerful entities as they have the bargaining power to dictate hotel rates and marketing strategies (Pattulo, 1996). They deal with large volumes and they are shrewd negotiators who put pressure on hotels for large discounts. These foreign-owned establishments make decisions that may lead to developments which are not always in the long term interest of the

98

island. For instance, while they have the power to direct the inward flow of tourist traffic they can also withdraw it. The strength of tour operators lies in their marketing power, their ability to generate large numbers, their familiarity with diverse market segments and their capacity to shift tourist flows from one destination to another (Lewis, 2002). They have the financial clout to produce colourful brochures and to engage in extensive trade advertising. However, the tour operator is not loyal to any particular destination but promotes all destinations under the strength of the tour operator brand (Reid and Reid, 1994). A destination dependent on tour operator promotions tends to have limited awareness in the tourism generating countries since all promotions tend to come through one channel – that of the tour operator. The limited advertising budgets of small island states and the high cost of go-it-alone advertising means that micro states find it difficult to conduct large scale promotions in tourist origin markets such as those conducted by their larger counterparts (Pattulo, 1996).

Another challenge facing island tourism is that tourism, as an industry, depends on the whims and fancies of foreign travellers, whose decision to visit a particular island is influenced to a very large extent by conditions outside the control of the island itself. These may include economic recession or reports in the popular press in the country from which the tourists originate. Economic recessions in the 1980's and in the early 1990's as well as the events of September 11, 2001, had a significant negative impact on tourist arrivals in Barbados. Press reports about crime, hurricanes and other natural disasters in the Caribbean can redirect tourist flows to other regions of the world. The impacts of these events will be discussed in greater detail later in this chapter.

The effort to remain competitive is also compounded by the tendency of island destinations to sell undifferentiated products with a focus on the sea, sand and sun (Wing, 1995). This means that each island destination is challenged with differentiating itself from the sea, sand, sun and exotic image that characterise many island vacations (Witt and Moutinho, 1989). Another limitation is that island trips can be expensive (Getz, 1995) mainly due to their remoteness and the fact that they are only accessible through the air and sea ports. This remoteness contributes to the difficulty of acquiring adequate airlift out of tourist generating regions. Thus, the decisions made by foreign airline carriers can have a significant impact on an island's ability to attract tourists (Ryan, 1995a). The fall of Eastern Airlines and Pan

99

American Airlines in the early 1990's significantly impacted tourist arrivals from North American into Barbados. Airlines control not only the number of seats and airlift but the routes and the air fares. The demise of the Concorde had a corresponding impact on Barbados' luxury markets.

Barbados has an added disadvantage due to its distance from tourist generating countries in relation to some of its Caribbean counterparts. Its location in the southern Caribbean means that flying time from Miami to Barbados is approximately three and a half hours and four and a half hours from New York and Washington DC. Jamaica and the Bahamas have the advantage over Barbados due to their closer proximity to the United States of America. It takes just 25 minutes to fly from Miami and two and a half hours from New York to the Bahamas while it takes one hour and forty minutes to fly to Jamaica from the Miami area and three and a half hours from New York (Pratt, 2003). The extra flying time implies that visitors must make an extra effort, both physically and financially, to visit Barbados. The extra distance also means higher airfares and this is an on-going issue confronting Barbados' tourism. Getz (1995: 153 citing Holder, 1993) notes: "The high cost of many island trips is a limiting factor. To combat this limitation requires niche marketing and an emphasis on high yield tourists, rather than mass tourism". American tour operators servicing Barbados also raised the issue during a 2006 conference in Barbados:

> tour operators from the North American market have highlighted the price of airfare as being a critical point in the competitiveness of the Barbadian tourist product. Representatives from some of the largest travel agencies in North America have stated that considering Barbados has to compete with some of the most exotic jurisdictions in the world, ticket pricing is key (Brown, 2006:1).

The problems of scale created by the effects of size and geographical location limits Barbados' potential to achieve an appropriate share of the world's fastest growing industry. Traffic volumes are the single most important requirement for receiving a scheduled air service. Thus, the problems of keeping airline seats filled and the route profitable leads to the problem of high airfares or worse, the possibility of the airlines withdrawing their services. Other destinations with larger markets and land masses are in a more advantageous position to negotiate with foreign carriers due to the benefits of economies of scale.

While size and geographical location may present challenges, there are also advantages from which tourism planners can draw. While size limits growth, it can otherwise assist in developing a sense of community and personalised ties among the local population. This makes it easier to preserve the local culture and identity, important elements in creating destination distinctiveness (Reid and Reid, 1994). The small size of island destinations allows for more stakeholder involvement and thus islands like Barbados are in an easier position to be selective in the choice of tourism development that they wish to pursue. One advantage of geographic isolation is that the existence of certain eco-systems creates special attributes that are uniquely different and which carry a special appeal. Currently in Barbados, the rain forest, beautiful coral reefs and turtle breeding grounds are major tourist attractions. Paradoxically, tourism growth through the increase of tourist numbers and the development of commercialised attractions may destroy the very special qualities that made the destination popular in the first place. The next section pays attention to the nature of event tourism in Barbados.

4.4 EVENT TOURISM IN BARBADOS

Small scale events are an integral part of the Barbados tourism product. The social calendar consists of numerous cultural and sporting events. The biggest cultural event is the annual *Crop Over Festival*, which is the Barbadian equivalent of a carnival. This event is hosted in the summer months of July and August and lasts for approximately one month. Events associated with this festival sometimes start as early as May. *Crop Over* promotes the musical and artistic talent of the island and culminates on the first Monday in August with a street carnival called *Kadooment*. This event stimulates significant tourist activity and it attracts migrant Barbadians who return to the island on holiday to participate in the festival (Wilson, 1996). Crop Over is now regarded as a perfect example of an event that has grown to become a destination 'icon'.

Crop Over, as the name clearly suggests, is a festival to signal the end of the once thriving sugar cane harvest. This festival had unrivalled importance in the days of the thriving sugar cane industry but faced a drastic decline in the 1940s due to the social and economic hardships facing not only Barbados but the rest of the world (Beckles, 1990). In 1976, the festival was revived and has grown from strength to strength. The social calendar is packed from as early as May with community fringe events, so during the two-month long festival visitors can arrange their itineraries to accommodate the events that they would like to see or in which they would like to participate. The festival attracts visitors from the Caribbean, the United States of America and Europe. According to statistics from the Caribbean Tourism Organisation (2006) the festival contributed over US$40 million (£20 million) in foreign exchange into the economy in 2006, representing US$3 million (£1.5 million) more than the amount from *Crop-Over* 2005. The average daily spend of visitors amounted to US$152.93 (£76.46), a slight increase over the previous year's spend of US$102.22 (£51.11). Spending was especially high among Europeans, who spent US$187.18 (£93.59) daily, while Americans and Canadians spent US$127.00 (£63.50) daily and other visitors, including those from the Caribbean, spent US$154.00 (£77.00). Foreign visitors who participated in Crop-Over came mainly from North America, Europe and the Caribbean, and outstripped 2005 numbers, with 13,429 visitors participating in individual events like *Grand Kadooment, Party Monarch finals* and *Pic-O-De-Crop finals* last year, compared with 11,615 the previous year. Of those 13,000 plus visitors less than half (5,707) flew in specifically for the festival, compared with 5,660 in 2005. However, although *Crop Over* is one of the biggest festivals in the Caribbean and receives considerable media coverage in the Caribbean media, its impact on the international media is much less intensive than that of other events such as the Sandy Lane Gold Cup or cricket test matches. The Sandy Lane Gold Cup and test match cricket will be discussed later in this section.

Another prominent music festival in Barbados is the *Barbados Jazz Festival.* This event is hosted every January and attracts leading Jazz and musical artists from Barbados and the United States. The festival lasts for one month and culminates with a headliner performance at the Sir Garfield Sobers Complex. One of the highlights of this festival is the two-day, open-air concert held at Farley Hill National Park. Farley Hill was once the site of the stateliest mansion house in Barbados. It was owned by an English planter, Sir Graham Briggs and it is here that he entertained King George V in 1879 on his visit to Barbados. It is also where the movie *Island in the Sun*, starring Harry Belafonte, was filmed. World famous performers at the *Barbados Jazz Festival* have included Lionel Ritchie, Roy Hargrove, Roberta Flack, Anita Baker, Patti Labelle, George Benson, Earth Wind and Fire, Chaka Khan and Nancy Wilson, amongst others.

The *Jazz Festival* was cancelled in 2010 but it is hoped that it will be revived in the near future.

Barbados hosts two major street festivals. These include the *Holetown Festival* and the *Oistins Fish Festival*. Every year Holetown, a small town on the west coast, celebrates the landing of the first English settlers in 1627. The week-long event comprises live orchestras, dance performances, a beauty pageant, calypso steel bands, remembrance talks, an exhibition held in the Holetown Museum, bus tours, street parades and many stalls selling local art and craft, food and drinks. This event is rich in culture celebrating both the English and African heritage of Barbados. Easter weekend greets the opening of the *Oistins Fish Festival*, which is held in the historic fishing town of Oistins on the south coast. Oistins saw the battle between the Royalists and the Roundheads in 1639, and resulted in the Articles of Agreement being drawn up to form the Barbadian Government, which is the third oldest in the Commonwealth. The festival in 2007 celebrated its 30th birthday and is a celebration of fishermen where fresh fish is cooked and the fishermen show off their skills. There are numerous food and craft stalls along the street and pulsating music entertains visitors for the entire duration of the event. The *Oistins Fish Fry* is a spin off from the *Oistins Fish Festival*. The *Oistins Fish Fry* consists of local fish vendors who line the street with their coal pots to cook and prepare fried fish for their customers every Friday night. Customers can enjoy their meals under tented accommodation and enjoy the live entertainment that is provided as part of the activities. In addition to these cultural events, Barbados is also the home to a plethora of sporting events. The next section charts the growth of sports event tourism in Barbados.

4.4.1 The Development of Sport Event Tourism

In 1987, the Barbados government made a commitment to develop a sports event portfolio for Barbados, which commenced with the development of and improvements to sport facilities in Barbados. Within the last 20 years, Barbados has played host to a range of sporting events in football, hockey, athletics, cycling and cricket. At the National Stadium, Barbados has hosted a range of events in the athletics arena such as the Texaco Games, with participants from Europe, North America and the Caribbean; the Shell Cup Football Championships and the Carifta Games; with participants from the Caribbean islands. The Barbados Cup for junior footballers was also hosted for teams from North America and the Caribbean. Teams from all over the world have travelled to Barbados to participate in the Banks International Hockey Festival, which was introduced in 1986, and immediately became one of the most popular field hockey events in the world (Elcock, 2005). The Barbados Tourism Authority and the Barbados Hockey Association have made Barbados the world's leading hockey destination and, since 1980, the numbers of teams that have visited for hockey outnumber those for other sports with the exception of cricket. To date over 100 teams have visited from North America and estimates provided by the Barbados Field Hockey Association indicates that approximately BDS$1 million (£333,000) is accrued in accommodation, meals and transport by visiting field hockey clubs each year (Sporting Barbados, 2006).

The building of the Sir Garfield Sobers Complex opened the door for Barbados to pursue a wider range of sporting events. Constructed in 1988, the sports complex consists of an indoor gymnasium designed to cater to twelve disciplines. These include badminton, bodybuilding, boxing, basketball, gymnastics, handball, judo, karate, netball, table tennis and weightlifting. The multi-purpose complex, due to its capacity to sit over 10,000 persons and its excellent media, sound and lighting systems, is home to many cultural events. The complex is equipped with an Olympic size swimming pool, which has been used by teams from the United Kingdom, Sweden and the United States of America exclusively for training.

Because of Barbados' tropical climate the island is capable of hosting water events all year. The most popular of these is the "Soup Bowl" competition, which is an annual surfers' competition held on the island's east coast at Bathsheba. The event, organised by the Barbados Surfers Association, attracts teams from the United States, Brazil, France, Venezuela, Trinidad and Tobago, Puerto Rico, Martinique and Guadeloupe. Other water events hosted on the island include the Mount-Gay Boatyard Regatta, windsurfing competitions and game fishing.

Events that have become international media spectacles include horse racing and test match cricket. Horse-racing is very popular on the island. It is traditionally a seasonal sport with the first season extending from January to April and the second season from August to November. The races in Barbados attract horses from Trinidad and Tobago, Jamaica and Martinique (Elcock, 2005). The Sandy Lane Gold Cup is regarded as the premier racing event in the Caribbean. Inaugurated in 1982, leading bottlers Cockspur Rum originally sponsored the event which received new sponsorship in

1997 from the Sandy Lane Hotel. It has since been renamed the Sandy Lane Gold Cup (Barbados Information Service, 2006). The race is the highest prized horse race in the Caribbean and it receives extensive media coverage through ESPN, the U.S. total sports channel which feeds its coverage within the United States of America and to audiences in South America. TSN, the Canadian equivalent to ESPN, supplies a version of the race to Sky TV in the United Kingdom. The British Broadcasting Corporation (BBC) also supplies information on the race to its television viewers and international magazines throughout the United Kingdom and Europe (Elcock, 2005). One of the highlights of the Sandy Lane Gold Cup is the parade that precedes the actual race. The parade consists of dancers, regimental bands, police horses, stilt men and 'Bajan characters'. This spectacle of colour, pageantry and energy is followed by the national anthem and the ceremonial bugle calling the horses to the starting line (totallybarbados.com). Other horseracing events in the Barbados sporting calendar include the Barbados United Derby, which is the most impressive race for three year olds in the Southern Caribbean, The Manning Mile, the Barbados Fire and General Insurance Trophy, the Wayne Feeds Junior Creole Championship Trophy and the Hearst International Caribbean Classic (Sporting Barbados, 2006).

Cricket, which was brought to the island by the early British settlers in the 1800's, has a long tradition in Barbados (Beckles, 1990). According to a tourist publication: "We live for cricket...it's not just a sport, it's our culture...we have played it with passion and we have played it with flair in our own Caribbean way. Everything stops when cricket is being played...." (Sporting Barbados, 2006; 64). Cricket is, therefore, regarded as an integral part of Barbadian culture. Cricket test matches are hosted annually, between January and April every year. However, the most significant in terms of tourist arrivals are the test matches involving England and the West Indies. These test matches occur approximately every four years and they attract a large contingent of cricket fans from the United Kingdom who visit to support the British team. Barbados has hosted test match cricket at Kensington since 1930 and teams from England, Australia, New Zealand, Pakistan, India, Sri Lanka, South Africa and Bangladesh have visited to play cricket. Cricket test matches are synonymous with large contingents of tourists who visit to support the visiting teams as they play against the West Indies. Cricket has boosted arrivals from Canada, the United States, Bermuda, the islands of the Caribbean and England. In 1998, the Caribbean Tourism Organization conducted a

105

survey on departing visitors after a test match in Barbados involving England and the West Indies. They found that 8,300 persons, representing 15% of all departing visitors, had come to the island primarily for cricket (Holder, 2003). The survey reported that the average length of stay was ten days and that total expenditure injected into the Barbadian economy was US$12 million (£6 million). Of the 8,300 persons interviewed, 6,474 (78%) were from the United Kingdom. In addition to cricket test matches several visiting clubs have been invited to Barbados by the Barbados Cricket Association to play against local clubs.

The biggest event of international significance that Barbados has hosted is the Cricket World Cup in March and April of 2007. Although the event was hosted in nine different Caribbean territories, including Guyana in South America, Barbados had the opportunity to host the 'super eight' leg of the event in addition to the final at Kensington Oval on April 28, 2007. The Cricket World Cup was expected to attract over 20,000 tourists to Barbados for the final and another 100,000 tourists to the entire West Indies region. Significant investments in the infrastructure required to host this event were made including the redevelopment of Kensington Oval, the official test match ground for Barbados, and several road and beautification projects in and around Bridgetown and other parts of the island. The Cricket World Cup was televised to over two billion people worldwide and was projected to contribute an estimated US$20 million (£10 million) into the Barbadian economy (ITG Barbados, 2005). As well as being a major topic in political debate, the Cricket World Cup was a major feature of the Barbados Tourism Authority's marketing thrust to the point that it overshadowed other important events taking place on the island, including the Golf World Cup. The Cricket World Cup was considered important because the government had hoped the event would leave legacies for the development of sport, business and tourism. However, at the time of writing this report, many commentators described the Cricket World Cup as a failure because it did not generate the anticipated tourist arrivals (World Cup comes up short, 2007). The Cricket World Cup was also deemed a failure on the basis that it culturally alienated the local population (Ibid). To date no economic or social impact studies of the Cricket World Cup have been conducted or documented by the Barbados goverment. This is illustrative of the reluctance of government and official bodies to make event oriented research a priority. Consequently, we do not know how visitors perceive these events and what role they played in their satisfaction. Moreover, research into local residents' perceptions and expectations of mega sport events is lacking in Barbados. The next section examines the nature of golf tourism in Barbados and provides an introduction to the Golf World Cup.

4.5 GOLF TOURISM AND THE GOLF WORLD CUP

Barbados has been host to several golf tournaments in the past but these events have evolved locally without much impact in the international media. The Sir Garfield Sobers Golf Festival is the most prominent golf tournament on the island attracting amateur entries from within Barbados and the Caribbean. The event is organized by, and held annually at, the Barbados Golf and Country Club. Golf tourism is not new to Barbados but there has been a surge of investment lately that suggests that the island is serious about optimizing the opportunities that golf tourism can offer. The following section presents the arguments for and against golf tourism.

4.5.1 Benefits of Golf Tourism

Golf is an industry which attracts millions of tourists to destinations around the world (Petrick , 2002). It is estimated that there are over 60 million golfers worldwide with the United States of America accounting for 21.7 million players; Japan, 12 million; Germany, 300,000 and one million in Canada (Holder, 2003). In the United States in 1994, there were approximately 10.5 million golf travelers compared to eight million in 1989 (Petrick and Blackman, 2002) indicating the fast growth in the industry. Golf tourism is said to be worth approximately US$10 million (£5 million) annually representing the largest sports-related travel market (Readman, 2003). Golf course development, built around the tourism industry, is now regarded as one of the most viable ways of tourism diversification for many tourism dependent regions, particularly those with few other economic resources (Markwick, 2000).

The development of golf tourism is viable for a number of reasons. Besides being a lucrative market with an aggregate spend of over US$10 million (£5 million) a year, golf courses do not necessarily need to be built on beach front locations but can instead contribute to inland tourism development. The Sandy Lane Golf and Country Club, as well as the Royal Westmoreland and Apes Hill projects in Barbados are examples of attractive inland developments. The development of golf courses creates additional recreation facilities for visitors to enjoy at a destination. This can assist in rendering the destination more competitive. Golf attractions can also play a role in alleviating the problem of seasonality in tourism. Seasonality deals with the tendency of tourism business flows to be concentrated into a relatively short period of the year (Moutinho, 2000). In Barbados, the greatest demand tends to be concentrated in December through March when it is winter in North America, England and Europe. This period is referred to as the 'high season'; but as the summer months approach and the weather becomes warmer in these countries, there is the challenge of filling idle room capacity in many hotels, which is not sufficiently ameliorated by the lower accommodation rates and packages offered (Palmer, 1993). It is argued that golf facilities can attract visitors outside of the traditional 'high season', thereby either extending the tourists season or attracting visitors in the otherwise 'low season' helping to reduce idle capacity (Marwick, 2000).

Another reason golf tourism is considered a viable strategy in tourism development is because golf tourists are believed to spend more and stay longer than other types of tourists (Readman, 2003). They are also likely to visit the destination again with their relatives or acquaintances, making them viable return visit prospects (Kim, Chun and Petrick, 2005). In Barbados, those who support the development of golf courses contend that they are not only necessary for foreign exchange generation but also for the creation of new employment (Wilson, 1996). Wilson (1996) argues that golf tourism will provide Barbados with much needed free, up-market publicity that can position the island as part of the international golfing circuit. Golf tourism can also create an image enhancement opportunity for the golf course where a major golf tournament is played. Once a high profile golf championship has been held at a particular golf course, the course becomes known as a 'trophy course'. A trophy course is sought by individuals who wish to follow in the footsteps of their golfing heroes thereby fulfilling the ambition of playing on world famous courses frequented by the world's top players (Readman, 2003). These courses have the effect of ensuring long-term popularity among golf tourists and can play an integral role in attracting golfers to the islands or regions in which they are situated. However, those who oppose golf tourism in the Caribbean are of the view that golf courses require too much land which could be better utilised for agricultural purposes (Pattulo, 1996). Furthermore, golf tourism is sometimes rejected on the basis that golf course developments subscribe to an enclave type of tourism (Readman, 2003). The following sub-section examines the history and organisation of the Golf World Cup.

4.5.1.1 The Golf World Cup

The First World Cup of Golf was hosted in 1953 but it was not until the year 2000 that the event became part of the *World Golf Championships* when an agreement was reached between the International Federation of PGA Tours and the International Golf Association, the organization that initiated the World Cup in 1953. The Golf World Cup under the International Federation of Golf, was inaugurated in December 2000 in Buenos Aires, Argentina. Players qualify for the championship based on the Official World Golf Ranking. Twenty-four countries were represented in 2006 with each country's team comprising its two best players according to the official ranking. The competition is usually played in four rounds, two of which are played in foursomes and the other two as four-balls. Eighteen teams qualify according to the world ranking while the remaining six have to win their places in a competition. Since the event was hosted under the auspices of the World Championships in 2000, it has been played in Argentina, Japan, Mexico, the United States of America, Spain and Portugal (World Golf Championships, 2006). Barbados is the first Caribbean island to host the event under the auspices of the International Federation of Golf (PGA) tours.

As discussed in the introductory chapter, the Golf World Cup took place in Barbados from December 4-10, 2006. A total of 24 nations, including the host country, participated. The official name of the event was the *World Golf Championships - Barbados World Cup.* The winners were awarded £2,000,000 in prize money. The Golf World Cup was played at one of the three golf courses at the Sandy Lane Hotel in St. James, Barbados. The Sandy Lane facility is described and discussed in the next section.

4.6 THE SANDY LANE RESORT AND COUNTRY CLUB

A golf resort may be defined as a self-contained leisure complex, which as a minimum requirement includes accommodation facilities and one golf course, to which other golf courses and facilities may be added (Priestly and Ashworth, 1995:209). These resorts tend to be heavily secured with sophisticated security systems and perimeter walls and are associated with exclusive developments. The Sandy Lane Resort, where the Barbados World Cup was hosted, falls into this typology. The Sandy Lane Resort is one of Barbados' most luxurious hotels. It is outfitted with 122 luxury rooms and suites, a spa with a fitness centre and swimming pool, three golf courses, tennis courts and gourmet restaurants and bars. This type of facility appeals to golfers since it allows them to pursue the sport while their families can enjoy a range of other activities.

The Sandy Lane facility was given a US$350 million (£175 million) face-lift when the hotel closed in 2000/2001 and clearly caters to the luxury market, projecting an image of being glitzy and flashy, probably due to its clientèle of famous guests, celebrities and movie stars (Davies, 2006). Famous guests have included Tiger Woods who was married there in October 2004; Maria Callas, Aristotle Onassis and David Niven. During the hotel's high season, room rates range from US$2,800 (£1400.00) per night for an orchid suite to US$25,000 (£12,500) per night for a villa on the estate (sandylane.com). Sandy Lane hotel has a golfing tradition and with the new development there are now three golf courses on the estate. The original course, the Old Nine, was built in 1961 while the two new eighteen-hole courses were built during the renovation in 2000. Both courses are designed by Tom Fazio, an internationally renowned golf course designer. The Old Nine and the Country Club courses are open to visitors from outside the hotel, but the 7343-yard Green Monkey course is reserved strictly for hotel guests (Its Tee Time, 2006).

Barbados also has four other existing championship golf courses - Royal Westmoreland designed by Robert Trent Jones Jr. and the Barbados Golf Club designed by Ron Kirby as well as two additional nine-hole tracks at Rockley Resort on the south coast and at the now closed Almond Beach Village on the west coast. The Royal Westmoreland course is also located on the west coast, inland from the Holetown area. The development comprises not only the golf course but luxury villas and is a private club, with promotional material advising visitors that they must call in advance if they wish to reserve a tee-time (Royal Westmoreland Brochure, 2006). The Barbados Golf Club on the South Coast is a 18-hole PGA approved public course on the island's south coast. It is widely regarded as the home of local golf since it has an active local membership which is available at a reasonable cost (Its Tee Time, 2006). The course also caters to the many visitors who choose to stay in accommodations on the south coast and is open to the public at large.

For those visitors who just wish to 'putt' around, there is a nine-hole putting green at the Rockley Resort. The Rockley course, a public course, is described as a pay-as-you-play course with a 'friendly atmosphere' (Its Tee Time, 2006: 86). However, although golfers can play 18 holes twice, the course is not considered as challenging as those previously mentioned. Although Almond Beach Village in St. Peter had a nine – hole course, as an all-inclusive hotel this was a private course, which is available exclusively for the hotel's guests. The newest course at Apes Hill which was under construction at the time of this research is now opened. This consists of an 18-hole championship course on 470 acres of land, 200 single-family homes and 150 cluster units. In addition, it is expected that two other courses at Bushy Park and Westmoreland commenced construction in 2007. It is at this point that some caveats are raised about golf and up-market tourism. These issues form the basis of the next discussion.

4.7 GOLF EVENTS AND UPMARKET TOURISM

Although high profile events such as the Golf World Cup may have the propensity to enhance the image of the country as an up-market destination, caution should be exercised. Golf has a conservative image and is perceived by non-golfers to be the leisure pursuit of affluent, middle–aged men (Mintel.com). Some authors conclude that golf is a game that fosters social elitism (Lowerson, 1994; Palmer, 2004; Pattulo, 1996; Readman, 2003; Sinclair, 2006; Swarbrook, 1999). This attribute is also reinforced by the physical structures of many golf course developments. Readman (2003) observes that:

> ….segregation is often achieved through the erection of walls or security systems creating a separate, exclusive enclave that has little contact with the local population, causing a fragmentation of that community (Readman, 2003: 188).

In the Caribbean context, Sinclair (2006) drew attention to the view that golf is a past- time outside the purview of ordinary people. He comments that:

> The kinds of media analysis, investigation and debate that center upon other sports, where personalities and performances are scrutinized, discussed and evaluated seem foreign to golf reporting. This media aloofness further reinforces the sentiment that golf is a pastime that is outside the common gaze, beyond the pale of mass attention (Sinclair, 2006:7).

Ioannides and Holcombe (2003) raised other caveats about islands pursuing up-market tourism policies. They claim that during a crisis,

111

whether political or economic, up-market resorts tend to experience downturns in business. Their arguments are based on evidence collected from a number of Caribbean resorts after the events of September 11, 2001. They found that the luxury golf resort of Casa de Campo in the Dominican Republic had to cut its winter rates by 30% while the exclusive Varadero suffered a 40% decline in occupancy. The evidence suggested that affluent tourists tended to visit resorts that are closer and more familiar, or ones that are perceived to be safer, rather than long-haul exotic destinations. The authors also warned that up-market tourists tend to be culture vultures that constantly seek out new destinations and are unlikely to return to the same destination every year. Lessons can be learned from the island of Bermuda. Bermuda traditionally pursued an up-scale tourist market policy only to find that by 1990 the island had experienced a significant decline in tourist arrivals (Conlin, 1995). The Bermuda Planning Committee concluded that the affluent market is small and exclusive and it is a market sought after by many other destinations, including destinations in the United States of America. Thus, there is considerable competition for this niche markets. Marketers targeting up-market tourists may need to consider that although customers may be demanding better quality products, they may not be prepared to pay more for these upgraded services (Moutinho, 2000). If this is the case, extensive and costly upgrading of facilities and the up-market approach may prove futile. Therefore, the right balance must be found so that publicity does not deter future potential tourists from seeking more information due to a perceived exclusive image. The next section presents some concluding remarks.

4.8 CONCLUSION

The preceding chapter has addressed the historical forces that shaped the Barbados society and economy. The problems and challenges that small islands like Barbados face in the management and marketing of the tourism industry have also been expounded. This chapter has also enhanced the reader's knowledge of the events industry in Barbados and has provided some background to the Golf World Cup event. The main focus of this chapter was therefore to highlight and expound on the cultural and social context in which this event took place and to give a vivid account of the tourism environment in Barbados.

The tourism authorities in Barbados initially anticipated that approximately 8,000 foreign visitors would converge on Barbados for the Golf World Cup and these visitors were expected to be supplemented by local spectators. The success of the Golf World Cup was based on its effectiveness as an attractive 'pull' agent for foreign visitors. If events are to be successful there must therefore be an understanding of the perceptions and expectations that all tourists and local residents hold of these events. Without an understanding of these it is not clear how golf events should be designed and marketed for international and local markets. These questions therefore guided the fieldwork for this research. Hence, the field observations and interviews were aimed at getting to the 'heart' of the participants' expectations and perceptions so that there will be a systematic body of knowledge on event tourism in Barbados from the stakeholders' perspective. The following chapter presents the findings from interviews with the international tourists and the field observations on the island of Barbados.

5 -CHAPTER FIVE
IN THEIR OWN WORDS - THE INTERNATIONAL TOURISTS

5.1 INTRODUCTION

This chapter discusses the international tourists' perceptions and expectations of the Golf World Cup. The semi-structured interviews explore how individuals became aware of the event, their perceptions of the event in terms of enjoyment and entertainment quality and their recommendations for event tourism in Barbados.

A major finding from the international perspective is the lack of awareness of the Golf World Cup in international markets. This prompted a critique of the communications strategies employed by the tourism decision-makers. The experiential dimensions of event enjoyment are also discovered and addressed. Under this heading the concept of 'event atmosphere' is discussed thoroughly and is based around a discussion about how this event's atmosphere either contributed to, or hampered, the enjoyment of the event for those who attended. This theme provokes a discussion which examines many aspects of event marketing and design, particularly the practice of event augmentation. The final discussion explores the views of international tourists concerning the development of event tourism in Barbados. All discussions draw on the theories presented in the tourism, sport and event management literature.

5.2 RESPONDENT PROFILE

As stated in chapter two, the international perspective is based on semi-structured interviews conducted with international tourists. This study's international participants were visitors to Barbados during or around the time of the Golf World Cup. The majority attended the Golf World Cup for at least one day of their stay in Barbados. These participants came from a variety of countries including Sweden, the United States of America, the United Kingdom, Ireland, Sweden, Canada and the Caribbean islands of St. Lucia, Grenada, Trinidad and Tobago, and Jamaica.

The majority of the international visitors stayed on the island for periods of two to 14 days (two to four days for the Caribbean visitors and four to 14 days for the international visitors). Holiday activities included participation in a variety of events including beach and water activities such as swimming with the turtles, cruising and sun bathing. Other popular activities included shopping, clubbing, dining out, sightseeing and relaxing. The majority of these international participants described themselves as business people all of whom owned their own business. Many were repeat visitors who had visited Barbados many times before and had been coming to the island from as few as five years to as many as 26 years. Other professions represented were solicitors, professors and journalists. Thirty-one of the respondents were male and fourteen were female. The international participants stayed in a variety of accommodation on the west and south coasts of Barbados. These included the luxury resorts of Port St. Charles, Royal Pavilion Resorts, Tamarind Cove Hotel, and private villas on the west coast while others stayed in more modest accommodation like the 'Peach and Quiet' hotel and self-contained apartments on the south coast. The rest stayed in private residences with family or friends. Only one respondent said that they owned their own condominium on the island. Many of the individual respondents traveled in parties of two persons to six persons. Parties consisted of groups of friends who traveled together or families such as married couples and couples who traveled with their children. The first discussion addresses the role of the media in the individual's decision to visit Barbados.

5.3 THE ROLE OF THE MEDIA IN INFLUENCING TRAVEL

The narratives derived from the semi-structured interviews conducted with international visitors to the Golf World Cup, revealed a predominance of international media sources in influencing visitation to Barbados, but not necessarily to the Golf World Cup event. The narratives also illustrate the importance of the organic images in stimulating interest and building awareness of Barbados as a tourist destination. One male respondent, visiting with his children from the United States of America reported: "we first heard about the island when my daughter bought home a storybook about Barbados from school". Another male respondent who travelled from the United States of America stated: "my daughter had a book about pirates in Barbados, that's how we first heard about the island", while a Canadian visitor indicated that "I think I first heard about it on a television clip, but I can't remember where".

News stories about sport personalities and sporting events were also cited by two visitors from the United States as sources of information that raised awareness of Barbados. This American couple, on honeymoon in Barbados, reported that: "we first learned about the island when we saw on the news that Tiger Woods married here. Then we did an Internet search and thought that we would check it out". Tiger Woods, the American golfer, married at the Sandy Lane Country Club in October 2004. The wedding received substantial media coverage worldwide. This couple explained that these stories significantly influenced them to seek further information on the island and their subsequent visit. Other types of news stories identified by the visitors that influenced their interests in Barbados are stories about test match cricket, the Cricket World Cup and the Formula One car race, which are all events that take place on the island.

The movie *Pirates of the Caribbean,* was cited as a source of initial curiosity after which further information was sought on the Internet or from travel agents and brochures. As a couple from England explained: "we first knew about the island when we saw that movie, *Pirates of the Caribbean.* We then decided to do more research on the Internet". This finding is particularly interesting as the movie, *Pirates of the Caribbean* was not filmed in Barbados and it is not quite clear how these individuals came to associate the movie with Barbados. The movie theme was an on-going theme with tourists who participated in this research. Another movie cited was, *Island in the Sun,* which was made in Barbados in the 1960's (Totally Barbados, 2007). One participant said that they fell in love with the song sung by Harry Belafonte and from then on always wanted to take a vacation in Barbados.

The influence of the media in directing tourists' behaviour has been recognised by many authors (Butler, 1990; Grabowski and Wei Du, 2005; Mason Hanefors and Mossberg, 2001; Schofield, 1996; Wickens, 2002). Butler (1990) commented on the role of the media in shaping tourists' awareness of tourist destinations through, literary and visual forms of communication. He claims that the media is one of the ways in which people become aware of places beyond their immediate experience. This Barbados study supports this view. The findings from the qualitative data revealed several dimensions of the international media as sources through which visitors at the Golf World Cup first became aware of Barbados. Kim and Richardson (2003) posit that news coverage and popular culture such as films and television programmes can provide substantial information about a place over time. Schofield (1996) claims that tourists' organic images of places are shaped through the vicarious consumption of film and

116

television without the perceived bias of promotional tactics. They claim that because news and popular culture is so embedded in everyday life they can alter a place's image dramatically.

While movies are often regarded as effective destination marketing tools (Silverstone, 1999), this phenomenon is still not completely understood. A major weakness with movie research is that it does not indicate exactly how or why visitation was induced and there is a question as to whether increased visitation was due to some form of image change or other factors. In this research, however, the findings that emerged did not present any hint as to which dimensions of destination image were affected through the various media sources cited so it may be important that there be further investigations into how the media influences the choice of Barbados as a destination and what dimensions of destination image may be affected or exert the most influence.

Researchers in the travel and leisure industries recognise the value played by oral sources of communication in the shaping of destination awareness. Word-of-mouth is still considered to be a very effective and reliable form of communication (Butler, 1990; Gitelson and Kerstetter, 2000; Sealy and Wickens, 2008; Swarbrook and Horner, 2003) especially in the recommendation of tourism products. The fieldwork revealed that international tourists at the Golf World Cup were visiting Barbados based on recommendations from individuals who had previously visited the destination. Many of these recommendations came from primary group relationships such as friends, relatives or work colleagues. The following extracts from the semi-structured interviews with various international tourists visiting the Golf World Cup illustrate the prominence of word-of-mouth recommendations: "We are here visiting our friends who live here, and they suggested that we visit", reported a group of travellers from the United States of America. Similarly, other typical statements were: "Our friends have been here before and we decided to return with them"; "we are visiting together as a group, but our friends have been here before, this is our first time" and "our friends recommended it".

It is suggested that today's consumers are distrusting of institutionalised advertising and prefer instead to listen to the recommendations of other people for more reliable and trustworthy information (Hsu, Kang and Lam, 2006; Solomon, Bamossy, and Askergaard, 1999) since it is perceived to be less biased. An American participant commented: "the thing is that Americans talk about their good experiences. If they have a good time, they tell lots of people. But if they have a bad time they will tell more people". In the case of Barbados, the high financial risk associated with long haul travel means that word-of-mouth recommendations may be more powerful in generating tourists to the island than any other medium. Hsu, Kang and Lam (2006) noted that the greater the perceived risk of a purchase decision, the higher the degree of personal influence as consumers, who wish to decrease pre-choice uncertainty, may refer to other individuals who have experienced the services directly.

Although many studies have focussed on the decision-making process of tourists, the influence of word-of-mouth recommendations has been largely neglected (Gitelson and Kerstetter, 2000). Although a number of decision-making studies have dealt with tourism decision-making, the focus tends to be on the influence of spousal decision-making or the influence of various family members on decision-making behaviour (Decrop, 2006). Fewer studies have dealt with special events. Furthermore, based on documents inspected during the fieldwork, it was observed that the Barbados Stay-Over Visitor Survey does not attempt to measure the influence of word-of-mouth recommendations in the decision to visit Barbados. The Barbados Stay-Over Visitor Survey is compiled by the Ministry of Tourism in association with the Tourism Development Corporation, the Barbados Tourism Authority & the Barbados Statistical Service. It is a satisfaction and marketing survey, which is used to inform tourism decision-makers in Barbados. The stay-over survey questionnaire should be amended so that greater light can be shed on this phenomenon as it relates to Barbados.

The fieldwork observations and semi-structured interviews also show that group influences guided the decision by many of the respondents to visit the island and the Golf World Cup. There was a predominance of travelling groups at this event. There were families and friends who indicated that they were influenced by each other to visit Barbados or to attend the event. However, at the Golf World Cup, the semi-structured interviews and subsequent data analysis confirmed that for the participants the primary group was the main contextual group force influencing visitation. These groups were composed of friends, family and friends, work colleagues and housewives. Many individuals interviewed travelled with family or friends who influenced their vacation based on past experience with the destination. Masterman (2004) notes that attending a sporting event is a highly social affair, and the effects of group acceptance must thus be considered a determining factor in patronage intentions. The

Jamaicans who were interviewed came in a group of five, the Trinidadians claimed: "It's a group of six of us here. We came for the lime". Fieldwork observations noted that groups were made up of families with parents and children; couples on holiday or honeymoon; work colleagues; a group of housewives, girlfriends and teachers with students. Group members will also impact how each other perceived the quality of the arena, food, ticket value and overall satisfaction with the experience (Shank, 1999). Group typologies should be the focus of golf event research to determine the different combinations and characteristics of individuals who should be targeted as golf event tourists.

Another group phenomenon that requires further investigation is the impact of tour groups. The fieldwork confirmed the presence of a number of tour groups on the island. Although the Barbados Tourism Authority advised that the event did not attract many tour groups or package tour tourists, a hotel manager confirmed that they had a group of over 20 persons visiting from the United States of America especially for the Golf World Cup. Caribbean Dynamics, a company that provides ground and recreational services to international tourists, advised that they had a group of 100 persons in Barbados for the event. The influence, and the role played by the various groups needs to be explored further in terms of who functions as the group leaders, the main decision-makers, initiators of specific behaviour, and the 'opinion leaders' of primary and reference groups. The role played by both the availability of package tours and the opportunity to travel with a tour group in the decision to travel overseas to attend an event needs further exploration. These issues can be the focus of future research on the impact of groups on the decision to travel and to attend an event.

Other participants indicated that they first learned about the island after visiting previously on a cruise. The value of cruise tourism was highlighted during this study as participants indicated that they were impressed by what they saw of the island during the brief period spent while visiting on a cruise liner. A group of visitors from the United States commented:

> We first came on a cruise many years ago. We rented a taxi and drove around the island. We always knew that someday we would return. We were impressed by the greenery and the houses. The island was so clean and people polite. This time we came back and bought our friends with us.

119

The cruise industry is a controversial sector in Barbados, mainly because the industry is perceived to contribute very little to the economy. Nearly 50% of all visitors to Barbados visit off the cruise liners. Cruise liners are perceived to dump their garbage on the island, and the visitors that they bring are accused of injecting very little cash into the economy (Pattulo, 1996). However, these findings indicate that the authorities in Barbados should look at ways in which the cruise business could be harnessed to encourage more future long stay visitors to the island.

Although participants indicated that they used other sources for collecting information about the island, these were more for collecting basic or general information after the initial decision was made to travel. The Internet was mentioned as a frequently used source for collecting general information on the destination. Although the fieldwork revealed that many international visitors at the Golf World Cup became aware of Barbados from a variety of media sources, the semi-structured interviews also revealed that many of these visitors did not hear about the Golf World Cup until after their arrival in Barbados. The next section addresses the communications strategies employed for this event as experienced by the international visitors at the Golf World Cup.

5.3.1 AWARENESS OF THE GOLF WORLD CUP, MARKETING AND COMMUNICATIONS STRATEGIES

During the fieldwork and semi-structured interviews, a major marketing issue that arose was the lack of awareness of the Golf World Cup in international markets. Many international tourists who participated in this research reported that they knew nothing about the Golf World Cup taking place in Barbados prior to their arrival on the island. Some statements that illustrate such occurrences include: "we never saw this [the Golf World Cup] advertised", "we heard at our hotel", "we saw the billboard on the highway when we arrived, that's how we knew", "was this advertised?"; or, "we knew about it because we were here earlier this year…, no we did not see it advertised anywhere at home". These comments prompted an investigation into the international marketing and promotional strategies employed by the tourism authorities in Barbados to market the Golf World Cup. Details concerning the marketing of the Golf World Cup were obtained from semi-structured interviews with tourism officials and international tourists. Information was also compiled from the examination of promotional brochures and other materials.

According to the tourism officials at the Barbados Tourism Authority, the Golf World Cup was advertised overseas in various promotional and advertising campaigns. A major strategy was to promote the event to those who have a genuine interest in golf. This approach is also validated by academic researchers who claim that event visitation is linked to an interest in the theme of the event (Kim and Chalip, 2004; Light, 1996; Nicholson and Pearce, 2001). The Accenture Match Play Tournament in California, the Bridgestone Tournament in Ohio and the American Express Championship in England are some of the tournaments at which the Golf World Cup was promoted. This promotion involved contingents from the Barbados Tourism Authority and Sandy Lane travelling to these events to "spread the word and to promote Barbados". A tourism official explained:

> To advertise this event we tried to position ourselves with the high profile players in golf sponsorship. We aligned ourselves with Accenture and started the campaign at the Accenture Match Play Tournament in California in February looking to bring as many people as possible to the island when it is played. From there we attended two other international events to further push the cause ..... We displayed our banners and we had an information booth as well at all these events...handed out brochures etc.

Officials at the Sandy Lane hotel supported this approach claiming that the golf market requires an approach that is different from the strategies employed when targeting other types of tourists. According to a Sandy Lane official the golf market requires a more subtle approach than that used with other tourism products. They stated: "you go to one of the tournaments and try to convince the captain to come play at your facility. You don't put out an ad saying come play golf here".

Fieldwork observations revealed that information on the Golf World Cup could be found on golf web sites such as the World Golf Championships website and the PGA tours website. The information took the form of press releases but did not include any dates or details concerning the schedule of events, play offs or the names of competitors. Numerous advertisements were posted in the promotional

121

guide books and brochures advertising Barbados and details could also be found on the Barbados Tourism Authority and the Sandy Lane websites. However, the majority of foreign visitors interviewed reported that they found out about the event when they saw the billboards on the Adams, Barrow and Cummings (ABC) highway after their arrival in Barbados rather than in advertisements in their countries of origin. Other tourists heard by word-of-mouth at their respective hotels. Further fieldwork investigations revealed that the Golf World Cup was indeed publicised on the island's highways. During the field observations billboards were spotted as the researcher drove around the island. Many of these were positioned on the ABC highway, which runs from the Grantley Adams Airport to the west coast with exits to other parts of the island. Billboards were visible at all of the highway exits and in Bridgetown at the end of the Chamberlain Bridge, just in front of the parliament buildings. These billboards were also visible at the Grantley Adams Airport at the entrance to the arrivals hall. However, according to international visitors, the same level of awareness about the event was not present in their country of origin.

If global events are to attract international visitors these potential visitors must be aware of the event taking place. If a potential consumer has no awareness of a product that product is unlikely to be included in the consumer's 'consideration set'. A 'consideration set' is the set of, or range of, destinations that one considers when making travel choices. Although awareness may not always lead to a purchase, at best it may only lead to a further information search or at least curiosity and eventually to trial. Tourism officials then need to ensure that their events are publicised overseas in awareness building ways if they wish to attract foreign visitors. Awareness is the first stage in the travel decision-making process. For any tourism product to be successful, potential consumers must, therefore, have an awareness of the destination and its attributes. Furthermore, the awareness must constitute a positive image of the destination (Milman and Pizam, 1995). International visitors constantly commented about their lack of awareness of the golfing event prior to their arrival on the island. One visitor from the United States of America commented: "well it's not surprising that nobody knew...the problem with Barbados is that no one knows about it – there is no awareness. You hear about Aruba, you hear about the Bahamas, Jamaica but nothing about Barbados". An Irish visitor to the Golf World Cup expressed disappointment at not being aware of the

122

event prior to his visit, although they were travelling to Barbados at the same time. He explained:

> We did not know about the golf. It was not advertised anywhere in Ireland at all. It wasn't even advertised in the hotel. I only knew about it when I overheard a conversation at breakfast one morning.... I am leaving on the last day. If I had known about this I would have extended my stay. Damn!.

Similarly, a British businessman who owns a hotel on the west coast commented:

> I never knew about the golf. I didn't see it anywhere in England. Hamish, my General Manager, did not know either. I only found out when I ran into the minister and he asked me, 'so you gearing up for the golf'? and I said, 'what golf?', and you should see the look of horror on his face. I didn't see it advertised anywhere.

Two visitors from Philadelphia noted that although they had awareness of Barbados' tourism product and all the attractions available on the island, they did not see the Golf World Cup advertised despite being "avid followers of the sport". The male respondent claimed:

> I didn't see it anywhere at all. The attendance is very poor, you should aim for at least 1500 persons per hole and this definitely is way below that. I have been to golf tournaments in Jamaica and Cancun with lots more people and much better advertised. Not having a good crowd takes away from the atmosphere. It should have been better advertised.

Similarly, a visitor from Ireland commented: "I think many more people would have come had they been aware, but I don't think many people knew.... you should have advertised better".

According to the authorities at the Barbados Tourism Authority, the Golf World Cup was advertised on American television during the staging of the qualifying tournaments for the event. "Yes, we advertised the event. You know the qualifying matches leading up to this event? Well, during those programmes, it was advertised.... There are also advertisements in all of our promotional materials and brochures". An American solicitor at the Golf World Cup mentioned

123

that he saw the advertisement on the 'Golf Channel' in the United States but argued that this would have been insufficient to build effective awareness of this event. He commented:

> I know that the event was advertised on the golf channel but I don't think anywhere else. Not everybody has access to the golf channel and other people would have been attracted to other channels. There should have been ads elsewhere.

Footage of the television advertisement shown in the United States of America was not available to the researcher; however, the advertisement that was posted in promotional brochures was obtained from the Barbados Tourism Authority office and this was analysed. This advertisement was also featured on the Barbados Tourism Authority's website, 'Visit Barbados' (visitbarbados.org). The advertisement was informative, advising potential visitors of the date and place of the Golf World Cup and the fact that the event was taking place in Barbados. Besides the official logo and an aerial shot of the Sandy Lane Golf and Country Club, no other symbols or additional pictorials were part of the advertisement campaign. This highlighted a major flaw in that the advertisement did not promote the experiential nature of the event. Advertisements must promote the tangible and intangible benefits of attending an event in order to stimulate the emotional responses necessary for the advertisement to work. Vacation decision making is as much affective as it is cognitive. Failure to promote the experience aspect of the Golf World Cup probably explains why many people were not attracted to it. A Barbados tourism official explained the development of the advertisement for the Golf World Cup. "It is difficult to conduct research for an event like this due to time and financial constraints; once the men say it's a go we go into action with whatever we have. We have a library of pictures that we use and we just take whatever we need from there". This statement re- emphasises the tendency of Barbados' tourism officials to make decisions haphazardly and without the benefit of research.

This statement also confirms MacKay and Fesenmaier's (1997) view that often pictorial images for promotional materials are chosen by national tourism organisation's staff who tend to perceive what is and is not important to the potential tourist based on their own familiarity with the destination. However, such images may be interpreted differently by potential tourists who have no prior experience of the product. This appears to be the case in this study.

The exclusion of experiential visuals in the brochure also puts the destination at risk of conveying a negative message. For instance, Williams (2006) notes that people respond more positively to advertisements that convey the feelings of fantasy, fun and excitement in the pictorials portrayed, so advertisements must include visuals that play the role of animator. The inclusion of people enjoying the experience in the advertisement would therefore have animated the event by making the destination product come alive and thus tapping favourable psychological responses from potential customers. Event managers must ensure that they sell the experience of attending the event and stress the benefits of attending (Getz, 1998).

Another notable flaw in the Golf World Cup's advertisement is that it ignored the emotional responses that advertisers will particularly attempt to arouse. Emotion can be defined as a state of arousal involving conscious experiences and visceral or psychological changes (Mullen and Johnson, 1990:75). Since tourism is an experiential product tourism marketers must recognise that its consumption would be associated, not only with cognitive or rational information processing, but also in accordance with feelings of fantasy and fun. Sport products also obtain power through the emotional associations they facilitate (Chalip, 1992). Sport marketers need to become more creative at tapping that emotion in their advertisements and this is exactly what this advertisement failed to do. International tourists who were visiting Barbados during the Golf World Cup but who chose not to attend commented about the lack of excitement surrounding the event. They commented: "It seems boring", "golf is not an exciting game", or "it doesn't seem special". These types of remarks are likely to be a consequence of the advertisement's failure to tap the emotions of prospective visitors. Stimulating emotional responses in advertising is particularly important since consumers tend to be increasingly sophisticated and sceptical about advertising, they know that they are being influenced and will only likely respond to advertisements that demonstrate some tangible or emotional benefits (Wilmshurst and Macay, 1999). In event tourism advertising it is suggested that visuals include imagery that show something tangible such as conveying a message of variety, activity and sophistication (Getz, 1997). Photographs used in tourism advertising are only successful if they make a link between the individual's motivations, goals and preferences and the destination (Jenkins, 2003).

However, advertising alone tends to be problematic because it addresses several individuals at once and the message in a single advertisement cannot always be adjusted to suit individual tastes and interests (Wilmshurst and Macay, 1999). What was evident in this research is that the international participants interviewed at the Golf World Cup had a series of complex motives for attending all of which could not be tapped with a single advertisement. Many indicated that they came 'to socialise', 'to entertain friends', 'to be seen', 'to see the stars' or to be part of a 'once in a life time event'. This multiplicity of motivations is difficult for a single advertisement to convey. The advertisement for the Golf World Cup would have failed to capture all these motives due to its lack of an experiential component. This explains why many international participants described their perception of the Golf World Cup as' boring' or 'lacking in appeal'.

Brochure advertising in itself is particularly restrictive in building initial awareness since a potential tourist may only be exposed to the brochure if they make a conscious effort to do so. Travel decision-making models suggest that potential travelers must first have an awareness of a place before they seek out further information (Fakeye and Crompton, 1991; Mansfeld, 1992; Matheson and Wall, 1982; Um and Crompton, 1990). Brochures tend to be consulted at the evaluative stage after the decision has been made to travel and the destination is actually being considered (Fakeye and Crompton, 1991). This was illustrated by the comments of a British businessman:

> We never heard about the golf at all before coming out to Barbados. It was only after we had booked our flight and decided to consult a travel brochure on things to do in Barbados that we realized that the golf was being held here. We called the Barbados Tourism Authority office in London and they sent us an 'Ins and Outs', and that is where we saw it, so although before that we were coming out to Barbados, we never knew.

Conveying the right message is important in advertising as sport events compete with other leisure activities for the consumer's attention and time (Getz, 1997; Shilbury Quick and Westerbeek, 2003). Advertising is one of the most important and sometimes most expensive choices to be made by marketing managers when planning communications campaigns, but it requires justification (Van Der Veen, 2006). Hence, advertising decisions should be based on the results of reliable research in order to minimize the potential risks.

126

Consumers are not passive receivers of advertising, but instead they interact with, respond to and interpret advertising, and they can choose to embrace or reject a message, particularly if the perceived benefits are not illustrated. However, it is not always possible to carry out full-scale investigations when advertising decisions have to be made. A Barbados tourism authority official explained:

> The truth is that we have to use whatever information that we have at the time to make the decisions that we need to make. Not everything can be researched with the use of a survey; when we have to make decisions fast we work with what we have. There is just no time!!

The lack of the appropriate research retards the tourism and event planner's ability to convey in advertisements the messages that would stimulate travel to an event by particular market segments. This again draws attention to the view that very often decisions go ahead to stage events without the relevant *a priori e*valuations. Advertising campaigns need to be targeted to specific individuals and the right groups. Messages must tap into the cognitive and affective components of the event visitors' motivations. This can only be achieved if the event planner has thorough knowledge of the event visitor and the benefits that they seek from attending. Barbados' inexperience with large-scaled event tourism means that such evaluations are even more critical to the proper marketing of events in Barbados.

There is evidence to suggest that the advertising strategies for the Golf World Cup were insufficient to block the 'noise' caused by the advertisements for the Cricket World Cup. As stated in chapter one, major emphasis was being placed on the staging of the Cricket World Cup in March and April 2007. 'Noise' in advertising occurs when the receiver of is no inundated with advertising messages that they can only pay attention to a selective number of messages and block out the others. A promotional brochure entitled "Barbados – the Heart of the World Cup" devoted one (the back page) out of twenty-three pages to the golf event. The remainder of the brochure promoted the Cricket World Cup with editorials, profiles of famous players, the history of the game and the match schedule. Much of the promotional literature on Barbados was inundated with information on the Cricket World Cup while less coverage was given to the Golf World Cup. There were numerous press releases, match schedules, stories about

127

famous cricketers and an array of other stories, competitions and narratives that related to the Cricket World Cup. The attention paid to the cricket by the tourism authorities probably explains why the cricket event was more salient in the minds of the individuals who participated in this research.

Comments made by international tourists interviewed during the Golf World Cup illustrate how advertising messages can become 'blocked' by other similar promotions. For instance, a visiting British visitor commented: "I know about the Cricket World Cup but didn't hear about the golf". Similarly, a German tourist reported: "I knew about the Cricket World Cup but not the golf. My friend called me from Germany to tell me he saw the golf on television, that's how I knew". The fieldwork therefore revealed that tourists were affected by selective attention. Selective attention can occur because people are exposed to a tremendous amount of daily stimuli. The average person may be exposed to over 1500 advertisements per day but cannot possibly attend to all of these (Van Der Veen, 2006). Selective attention is a state of consciousness which involves focusing on a specific aspect of a phenomenon while ignoring other aspects. Selective attention can be conscious as when one chooses to attend to an interesting object, such as a television programme versus a radio programme. In this case, the television programme may attain more attention if the programme is perceived to be more interesting to the individual. Often, people believe they have taken in all aspects of a phenomenon when, in reality, they have only processed the area they were attending to.

Evidence from the fieldwork suggests that the Golf World Cup advertising could also have been drowned out by the advertising of not only the Cricket World Cup, but the advertising for other prominent tourist and media driven events on the island. It was observed, from information provided on the Barbados Tourism Authority's website, that Barbados was hosting five large events in a space of four months - the Run Barbados Marathon, the Golf World Cup, the Barbados Jazz Festival, the Sandy Lane Gold Cup (horseracing event) and the Cricket World Cup. The Golf World Cup might have therefore suffered from 'event saturation'. Event saturation occurs when they are too many events of a similar, or even a different, nature all occurring at the same time or in the same place (Getz, 2000b). Events compete with all other entertainment and leisure products including movies, festivals, concerts and sports events, amongst others. The wisdom of hosting so many events at the same time was questioned by participants. For instance, a visitor at the Golf World Cup on the Sunday commented:

> I feel that the poor turnout was due to the other things going on in Barbados and people were not expressing much interest in the game because the Cricket World Cup is coming up ….and now people are concentrating their efforts on Christmas.

Similarly, a hotel manager, commenting on the poor international turnout, argued:

> The Run Barbados Marathon is also slated for early December. I think that the sport authorities at the BTA are trying very hard to create a shot in the arm for tourism by using that period for major sports events but they may just be having too many things going on so soon after each other.

The hosting of so many key events in such a short space of time means that the Golf World Cup might have been competing for, not only the advertising attention of individuals, but also for the individual's time and money. Having too many events means that marketers have to work even harder to attract attention to their own or a single event. Event saturation is one of the reasons that events fail and hosting too many events at the same time can affect demand (See Getz, 2000b). At the time of the Golf World Cup, not only was Barbados saturated with events, but the Golf World Cup dates also fell at the end of the United States' Thanksgiving celebrations and just before the Christmas holiday. It is not known how this might have affected international visitors from the United States of America, but it is surely something that planners will have to consider when planning major events. This study suggests that event planners need to be aware of all the other leisure and entertainment products that may provide competition for their event in local and international markets. Timing is a critical component of proper planning and evaluation in event tourism.

The semi-structured interviews and fieldwork observations also revealed a lack of enthusiasm within the local hotels to advertise the Golf World Cup to international tourists. A group of four visitors at the Golf World Cup reported that they had not seen the Golf World Cup advertised anywhere at their luxurious Port St. Charles hotel. They commented: "we only knew because we overheard a conversation at breakfast". These comments prompted field visits to

129

hotels on the south and west coasts to observe how the event was advertised in the hotels. Visits to the Bougainvillea Beach Resort, the Butterfly Hotel, Golden Sands Hotel, Southwinds Hotel and the Hilton Hotel on the South Coast revealed limited enthusiasm in promoting the Golf World Cup to tourists. Only one hotel, the Bougainvillea Beach Resort, displayed a small poster. Staff at this hotel commented: "we have a group of 20 people staying here for golf but most of their arrangements are pre-arranged... besides this event is not really something for our guests, it seems to benefit more the west coast hotels and villas". Similarly, a tour representative at this hotel who arranges recreational activities for visitors from the United States commented: "I find it hard to get anybody to play golf.... For me the thing that I find sells the most is the Bajan Roots and Rhythms show[4]... that's where my people go". The Bajan Roots and Rhythms show, before its cancellation, continued to be popular with visitors but has been criticized on the grounds that it resembles more of a Las Vegas cabaret show than a genuine representation of local culture. The show resembles what many scholars have termed 'staged authenticity' in that it was simply choreographed and commoditized to suit tourists taste and perceptions of the islands and bore no relevance to Barbadian culture.

At the Hilton Hotel, a conversation with the 'Island Magic' tour desk operator revealed even less enthusiasm for promoting the golf to international visitors. The tour representative at this desk commented: "the people who are here for golf have nothing to do with us. They have their own arrangements". Visits to the Almond Beach Club on the west coast did not reveal one single piece of promotional material for the Golf World Cup. When questioned about the Golf World Cup, the guest services representative at this hotel advised: "that is not really our market". Hotel tour representatives are the 'gatekeepers' of the recreational activities in which international tourists participate. They are in a position to promote and recommend a wide variety of events to their visiting clients. The fieldwork suggests that their importance in the promotional programme for the Golf World Cup might have been overlooked by the local tourism authorities. Evidently, the Golf World Cup seemed to have taken place in a social

---

[4]   Bajan Roots & Rhythms, held at The Plantation Theatre, at that time was the only dinner and stage show in Barbados designed to offer visitors a genuine representation of West Indian culture. Bajan Roots & Rhythms, uniquely known for its interactive segments and party atmosphere, affords its guests plenty of opportunities to join in the fun. The show has since been cancelled.

vacuum on its own with many international visitors totally oblivious to its presence prior to arrival in Barbados. For those that attended the Golf World Cup, the event was an avenue to derive a variety of benefits and to satisfy divergent needs. The next section discusses the motivations of those who attended the Golf World Cup.

5.4 MOTIVES AND BENEFITS SOUGHT

Tourist attractions are the core of the tourism product (Gunn, 1988; Miller, 1989; Swarbrook, 2002). Dann (1977) contends that tourists are motivated based on two factors, which he describes as the 'push', and 'pull' factors. The 'push' concept deals with the need to 'get away from it all', the desire to take a holiday, to relax or experience something unique and different, while the 'pull' concept deals with the actual attributes or attractiveness of a particular destination that induces travel to a specific place. Attractions are the major component of what makes people motivated to travel and they can contribute to the overall attractiveness of a tourist destination because they can act as a 'lure' or a 'pull' that attracts potential tourists. For some visitors at the Golf World Cup, the golf was the major 'pull' factor. This Jamaican visitor explained:

> We came because of the golf. The golf for me is a 'once in a lifetime' event, we don't know when this will even happen again in the Caribbean... It's the first time in the Caribbean so I probably won't get to see such a thing again.

Likewise, a Swedish couple at the Golf World Cup commented: "we came especially for the golf and to support the Swedish players", while two Caribbean male respondents travelling together, one from Trinidad and the other from St. Lucia, reported: "I really made the trip for the golf, I just want to see the golf!". The Trinidad contingent reported:" we are here to support Steven Ames[5]" and a visitor from the United Kingdom on his second trip to Barbados in less than a year, explained: "I learned about the golf through the promotions in the local press earlier this year when we were here ......so we came back again specifically for the golf". In this case, the Golf World Cup was not only a primary attraction for this visitor but it stimulated an extra visit to the island by this golf fan. This is significant since these trips might not have otherwise occurred if the event had not taken place.

---

[5] Steven Ames represented the island of Trinidad in the Golf World Cup of 2006.

These findings suggest that tourism planners can leverage the marketing of an event to stimulate repeat visitation and should research ways to do this effectively (see Getz, 1997; Gitelson and Kerstetter, 2000).

Although some respondents indicated that they were attracted by the golf, they also stressed that: "the golf alone was not the only attraction", but was a secondary attraction in the sense that they did not come for the golf alone but were "attracted to the experience of the event" in the context of a visit to Barbados. These visitors also took part in other tourist activities. The semi-structured interviews revealed that the Caribbean visitors seemed to be interested in the nightlife, through their visits to nightclubs and bars. The international visitors were also attracted to the warm weather, beach, water and cultural activities as well as dining out at night. A group of four American visitors at the Golf World Cup on the last day, revealed: "when we are here we always go to the Independence Day celebrations and enjoy going to church with the locals". These narratives illustrate the importance of bundling the appropriate set of activities and packages into the event promotional strategies in order to attract visitors. An emerging challenge in sport event tourism is to incorporate events more strategically into the host destination's overall mix of tourism products and services. An effective procedure is to bundle event elements with the host destination's attractions using a mixed bundling strategy. However, different market segments may be attracted to different combinations of attractions. Further work will be required to identify the elements that would attract the different market segments in order to initiate optimal procedures for bundling sport event elements with activities and attractions at host destinations (Chalip and McGuirty, 2004). Perhaps this approach provides the key to the marketing of events in Barbados and should be further explored.

There was no evidence to suggest that the golf event attracted 'sport junkies' (Getz, 2003) who are sports tourists who are mainly interested in consuming the sport rather than participating in any other holiday activities. However, Jones (2001) notes how sport junkies are probably more typical of day-trippers than stay-over tourists. The tendency for Barbados to attract 'sport junkies' is minimized due to its distance from key tourist markets like the United Kingdom, Canada and the United States of America (see chapter four) making it almost impractical to visit the island, attend the golf and leave on the same day, This highlights the likelihood that golf visitors would most probably combine a golf event with a long stay holiday.

The fieldwork revealed some evidence of 'time shifting'. The semi-structured interviews revealed that some international respondents shifted the dates of their vacation to accommodate the event. For instance, a British visitor traveling with his two sons advised: "I was always planning to come here but I knew about the golf so I just arranged this trip around it". Likewise, two Canadian visitors who were interviewed on the third day of the event reported: "we were going to come in January but came now so that we could take in the golf". This finding supports Crompton, Lee and Shuster's (2001) view that planners need to be aware that events do not always attract new visitors who are attracted specifically by the event, but also those visitors who were already planning to visit the destination but just shifted their dates to accommodate the event. These visits should not be included in any evaluative economic impacts study as this would distort the actual economic value of this event since these visits were not in any way stimulated by the Golf World Cup.

Many international visitors reported that the event was a pleasant surprise. For instance, an American visitor who was travelling with his wife and children exclaimed: "wow! I couldn't believe my luck that I am here during this event. This is the highlight of our stay here". Similarly, a British visitor expounded: "this is by far the best thing that has happened to us to be able to see an event like this... I just wished we could stay longer"; and likewise, two visitors from Philadelphia exclaimed: "This is good for Barbados, we are so glad that we can experience this during our stay". This evidence is indicative of how mega events can act as animators and make the destination come alive thus adding value to the entire vacation experience (Getz, 1997).

The semi-structured interviews revealed that one of the reasons why individuals attended the Golf World Cup was because they were affiliated to the sport in one way or another. For instance, some international tourists were associated with a family member or a friend who played the game. Others came because they played golf themselves. For example, two businessmen revealed: "oh!, we play golf here", while a British manager of a west coast hotel commented: "well, you know I am a golfer so I gotta be here". Wives attended because their husbands played the game. Other visitors came to support their national teams or specific players. The Jamaicans reported that: "we are here to see the Jamaicans of course", while the Swedish visitors revealed: "we came to see the Swedish golfers".

The narratives in this section give credence to Krohn and Clark's (1998) argument that people who are connected with a sport develop a fondness for the intricacies of the game and are more likely to choose to further their own participation in the sport by becoming spectators. They claim that spectators fulfil their enjoyment by casually viewing the sport and not getting caught up in the logistics of the event. While there are many ways of developing an interest in a sport, one of the principal methods of developing deep knowledge of a sport is through participation, either as a player or as a spectator (Brokaw, Stone and Jones, 2006). In addition, as this study on Barbados indicates, there were some spectators who travelled to support their national golf teams and this suggests that this is a market segment that event marketers could pursue in the countries which the competitors represent. However, more research is needed to further illuminate the characteristics of these individuals.

5.4.1 Favourable experiential dimensions

The Golf World Cup provided an avenue for participants to socialise with family and friends. Fieldwork observations and the semi-structured interviews revealed that socialization was a primary expectation; however, the social incentive varied from spectator to spectator. An American couple, who reported that they were on honeymoon, said that they visited the golf event because: "we thought it would be a nice way to enjoy our time together". The Trinidadian visitors, who were traveling in a group of six, described their motive as follows: "we came for the lime[6]. One respondent who is originally from North America but now lives in Barbados commented: "I am entertaining my friends here from North America and thought that they would like the atmosphere here where we can have some drinks and enjoy the golf". Another informant who was traveling in a group of six from North America commented: "We are all traveling in a group and thought that it would be nice to get off the beach and this would be a nice way to spend the time together". Based on this data, it is evident that some spectators came as couples to spend time together and to enjoy the golf while others came to spend time with family and friends.

---

[6]   'Lime' in colloquial terms refers to a gathering of individuals with the sole purpose of socialising.

134

Some visitors described the event as a 'once in a life time experience'. For example, an American tourist visiting the event on the second day described his experience as "I cannot believe that this is happening here during my stay". For two Canadian tourists the thrill of seeing the golfers up-close was a major factor of the 'fun and enjoyment' derived from the event. "It's a thrill to see Jim Rutledge and Mike Weir up close" was how these spectators described their feelings. One Jamaican woman traveling with her young son commented that she was enjoying the "awesome shots". Funk, Mahony, Nakazawa and Hirakawa (2001) conceptualize shot making in sport as an appreciation for the aesthetics of the game. Hansen and Gauthier (1994) also note that shot making is an integral part of the golf spectators' enjoyment. Another factor contributing to the enjoyment of the event was the landscape. Many foreign visitors commented on the "beautifully landscaped grounds" or the "beautiful gardens" at Sandy Lane as a highlight of their visit. Other comments related to this theme included: "this place is beautiful!", "this is a very pretty golf course" or "I like the flowers".

Many dimensions of event enjoyment identified are consistent with the work in the tourism and sports literature. Studies in tourism have pointed to the relationship between destination and the destination's 'atmospherics' (Etchner and Richie, 1993; Gartner, 1989, 1993). Most of these atmospheric dimensions have related to hotel accommodations, scenery and landscaping (Mansfeld, 1992). However, with regards to sport events, Chalip (1992) and Kim and Chalip (2004) have noted that event atmospherics is an essential component of event enjoyment and that this should be given special attention by sport event marketers. These findings also corroborate the work of Hansen and Gauthier (1994), which identified five dimensions of golf spectator's enjoyment. These included prestige, fun, great players, shot making, the course setting (scenic) and the atmosphere (relaxing and social atmosphere). However, although the atmosphere played a contextual role in the level of enjoyment experienced by the international tourists, the role of 'atmospherics' arose in a totally different context in this study. This is discussed in the next section.

5.4.2   Unfavourable Experiential Dimensions

One of the major fieldwork observations made in this study was the poor attendance at the Golf World Cup. The attendance was way below the typical attendance that is associated with similar PGA events. The PGA, FDR open in Scottsdale, Arizona attracted 537,767 spectators in 2006 (pgatour.com/story/9210547/) while events like the Open Championship at St. Andrews, Scotland in 2000 attracted 230,000 spectators within the eight-day period of the competition (Bowdin, McDonnell, Allen and O'Toole, 1999). Even small-scale, less prestigious events like the 2000 Buy.com in Louisiana attracted 59,750 visitors. Early press reports had confirmed that tourism officials expected at least 8000 visitors to Barbados for the Golf World Cup (The US$3m golf question, 2006). However, shortly before the event the authorities said that they anticipated approximately 3500 to travel to Barbados. An official the Barbados Tourism Authority explained: "we are expecting about 3500 will come from overseas, mainly from the USA and England. There will be others too from European countries where the game is popular, Scotland, Germany and Sweden as well". However, a follow up interview in September of 2007 with an official at the Barbados Tourism Authority confirmed that:

> The event was a disaster in terms of attendance. You can quote me or you can quote the minister.... the fact is that the minister is saying that 2000 tourists flew in from overseas, but that's for the newspapers. The truth is that the figure is more like 200 and most of that is press.

This source explained that because of the poor attendance an economic impact study would not make economic sense but that a guesstimate of 200 persons is close to the actual attendance by international visitors. This source explained:

> No, there is no post impact study and I do not expect one either. That event is history and we have more important things to take care of for the future. At this stage an impact study would be difficult and in any event it is difficult to count and estimate visitors to these events with the risk of counting the same persons twice and separating locals from visitors and other problems.

Because of the small number of visitors, many of the participants in this research commented about the small crowd and the 'lack of atmosphere' at the golf course. Evidently, this lack of atmosphere affected the enjoyment and satisfaction levels of the visitors, many of whom had come "to party", "to lime", "to mingle

136

with other fans" and to "enjoy the atmosphere". In this study, the environmental setting, the layout and design of the event's environment and the ability to socially interact was a recurring theme among the participants. The need for social interaction as a travel motivator was identified by Wickens (2002). Congruent with these findings Wickens found that the pleasure vacation served as a medium through which relationships could be enhanced or enriched through socialisation.

International tourists attending the Golf World Cup constantly commented about the small crowd. A Philadelphia visitor noted: "Not having a good crowd takes away from the atmosphere". This comment draws attention to the argument that people are an essential part of the event tourism product since the presence of people contributes to the ambiance and atmosphere of the physical surroundings (Getz, 1997; Masterman, 2004; Westerbeek, Turner and Ingerson, 2002). Funk, Mahony, Nakazawa and Hirakawa (2001) note how spectators like to talk to other spectators sitting near them at soccer games. The Trinidadian group was constantly looking for a group of people to start a party or a conversation but was hindered because the people needed to create the psychological impact conducive to parting were not there. As a result, they were repeatedly asking: "where the party man, where the party?". On each occasion that they confronted the researcher, they kept trying to push her into the bar with comments like: "come have a gin and tonic, come and start the party man". A Canadian visitor was surprised at the small crowd. He noted: "I have been to these events before but this one though is not crowded, all the others that we have watched seem to be really crowded", while the Jamaicans exclaimed: "but I am amazed that the crowd is so small. When we go to tournaments in Jamaica there are so many more people".

From the foregoing comments it is evident that people are an integral part of the event product and must not be overlooked. They can create the ambiance needed to make an event meaningful for all participants without the need for any additional props. (See Shone and Parry, 2001 and Westerbeek, Turner and Ingerson, 2002). The findings from the semi-structured interviews and observations show that an atmosphere conducive to socializing was a primary expectation of many spectators. With socialization as a major incentive respondents continued to be particularly expressive about the 'lack of atmosphere' at the event with statements like: "there is nobody here", "was this thing advertised"? or "why are there so few people?" or "the place is lacking in atmosphere". One visitor from the United States of

America, travelling with a group of friends, commented: "we go to these PGA events all the time, but this is not like other PGA events at all. There is hardly anybody here".

The concept of 'atmosphere' or 'atmospherics' is most prominent in the retail industry but it is now gaining some credence in the tourism industry, particularly as it relates to heritage and cultural attractions (Bonn, Joseph-Mathews, Dai, Hayes and Cave, 2007). The concept of atmospherics usually refers to the factors that may be designed into or manipulated within spaces in order to produce emotional and in turn behavioral responses in consumers (Foxall, Goldsmith and Brown, 1998). Kotler (1973) points out that consumers purchase a total product, consisting not only of the physical item but of the packaging, after sales deals, advertising, image and most importantly the atmosphere of the place in which the transaction takes place. The atmosphere at an event can affect the visitor's perception of enjoyment and service quality, value for money and ultimate customer satisfaction. 'Atmospherics' is therefore not necessarily concerned with the objective and physical factors but with the subjective feelings that these factors engender in the consumer. Whereas retailers can arrange the visual, aural, olfactory and tactile dimensions of a store's atmosphere, designers of events can draw on the use of entertainment and other activities, services and facilities to create an atmosphere conducive to the visitors' enjoyment. Many authors have commented about the social atmosphere as an underlying reason for attending a sport event (Crompton and Mckay, 1997; Funk, Mahony, Nakazawa and Hirakawa, 2001; Gibson, Willming and Holdnak, 2003; Melnick, 1993; Neirotti, Bosetti and Teed, 1996; Nogawa, Yamaguchi and Hagi, 1996). Some researchers contend that social interaction may be more important than the competition itself (Chalip, 2000; Sullivan, 2004).

The fieldwork observations and semi-structured interviews, conducted at the Golf World Cup, provide evidence that not only did the small crowd hampered visitors' enjoyment, but the layout of services and facilities at the golf course also fell below the respondents' expectations. The interviews revealed that visitors were expecting specially designated arenas to congregate and socialize. Participants kept on asking about "somewhere to sit", "shade from the sun", "where is the arena". One American visitor was particularly vocal about the atmosphere and facilities at the event. He noted: "my friends and I would like to relax but there are no bleachers or stands

138

where people can congregate and talk about the competition. This is very disappointing".

It should be recognized that a sport event is not just about providing good sport (Garcia, 2001; Green, 2001; Shank, 1999). The sports marketing literature notes that spectators purchase not only the sport, but also the benefits that spectatorship is perceived to provide (Shank, 1999). The Olympic Games for example provides consumers with the benefits of entertainment, the ability to socialise and feelings of identification with their countries' teams and athletes (Chalip, 2000). When considering the unique nature of golf it is understandable why many of the spectators interviewed expected to experience more than just 'awesome shots'. Whereas at most sport events spectators are confined to a seat in a potentially crowded environment so that they can watch all of the action on the field of play, in golf this is not the case. Golf is a unique sport in that the playing field covers several acres of land so that spectators do not see all of the action at the same time. Spectators wishing to follow the progress of their favourite players must be prepared to 'walk the course' along the specially designated roped-off walking areas as the player plays each hold. In Barbados spectators not only had to endure walking several miles to see their favourite player in action but also had to endure the elements. This meant enduring temperatures of around 32 degrees Celsius, risking sunburn due to the scorching sun and being soaked by the rain. Considering the nature of this environment it is easy to comprehend why spectators expected to be accommodated in covered marquees.

The absence of seating at a golf event of this level is unusual. Shank (1999) drew attention to the importance of the 'sports-scape' in sports marketing. 'Sports-scape' refers to the physical surroundings of the arena that impact spectators' desire to stay or return to the stadium. Shank (1999) notes that facility aesthetics such as layout, scoreboard quality or seating comfort will impact on a spectator's affective response or judgment as to pleasure or displeasure, which in turn will affect satisfaction. The Open Championship, organized by the Royal and Ancient Golf Club at St. Andrews, Scotland, provides 21,000 grandstand seats as well as a tented village where patrons can enjoy a meal and follow the competition via giant television screens (Bowdin, McDonnell, Allen and O'Toole, 2001). These type of facilities were absent from this event making it difficult for disabled persons and families with small children to be comfortably accommodated. Furthermore, even those who were contented to follow their favorite player from hole to hole wanted somewhere to rest and relax periodically. In the absence of a tented arena spectators tended to sit on the grass near the 18th hole while trying to find shade from any piece of overhanging shrubbery. Two visitors from New York thought that it was a bad reflection on Barbados not to provide certain services. They cited the newspaper notice that stated that certain items were banned from the golf course. These banned items included cell phones, folding chairs, cameras and food amongst other things. They commented that a lot was taken away through the restrictions but that the authorities should have compensated by providing seats for patrons. They exclaimed: "wait, you can't bring in no chairs but they have no seats in here?.....I can't get a good meal and a place to sit". They further commented that the only thing that brought them out was their love of golf. The only seating provided was in an exclusively roped off, tented area but this was for corporate sponsors' hospitality and for their guests. Entrance was by special invitation only. Spectators at the Golf World Cup were expecting an arena with good food and drink, plasma screen televisions so that they could follow the game and scoreboards but these facilities were not included for regular patrons. This study confirms Shank's view that event layout and design is an important component of event design. The design of the sports-scape is an area that event organizers in Barbados will have to consider when planning future events.

The findings from the qualitative data suggest, therefore, that consumers of the Golf World Cup were looking for more than just good golf and facilities. A golf fan from St. Lucia explained the poor attendance in the following terms:

> Golf is not a spectator sport, so you will not find many people here. Personally I would not travel to watch golf, because you get better coverage on the TV. On the TV you get a better overall coverage. You know what is going on the entire course and you have all the access to the statistics and inside information. I don't know, you will probably need some side activities to get the people to come out.

Another St. Lucian tourist commented: "it just seemed boring. I did not attend the golf because it is boring to watch. I know about golf. I used to play the game when I worked in St. Lucia and I understand it, but it is just a boring game to watch. I prefer to play it". A sense of festival surrounding the event would have made the Golf World Cup more exciting and encourage more participation from a variety of segments in the market place. It was evident that no cultural activities were planned or organized around the event, neither at the golf course nor outside the course. Many of the spectators expressed surprise at this, calling for a forum to interact with "the stars" and "Tiger Woods and Phil Mickelson should have been here doing free clinics" and, "activities for children" and 'where the party'. One American visitor commented:

> Not many people are going to travel this far just to see golf, there would have to be another attraction.....There are golf events all over the USA so people would need a reason to come.

Another golf visitor commented: "People not gonna come just for golf. I can get that in the US". It is important then to recognise that if the investment in time, money and long-haul travel is to be made, the event should be perceived as a worthwhile investment and this would have to be communicated in the communications strategy. Not measuring up to what is usually offered at other PGA events would be a cause for concern since those who have attended previous events will refer to past experience to create their own expectations in terms of service quality at future events. With the mirage of PGA events worldwide it was evident that events of this nature in Barbados must offer an additional value component through fringe events and other activities. A United Kingdom resident and a lover of golf commented that they would not have made the trip to Barbados for the Golf World Cup because: "It did not offer anything that I cannot get in Berkshire. If I want to watch golf, I'll just wait for the next tournament there". Another United Kingdom based informant argued: "I wouldn't travel all the way to Barbados just to watch golf... these people need to understand that they need to offer something really special....like maybe I would have gone if I could mingle with celebrities there...", whereas another international participant noted: "I wouldn't travel to watch golf... it's not a spectator sport... you get a better perspective on TV". The inclusion of fringe events and cultural activities is consistent with PGA events in the United States. For example at the FBR open, there is an open concert/party held in the Scottsdale area called the 'Bird's Nest', in which music artistes, like Huey Lewis and the News, perform (www. en.wikipedia.org/wiki/FDR_open). The 'Bird's Nest' is the hot spot for the golf spectators during this tournament so it is easy to understand why these golf visitors were expecting more activities to be associated with the Golf World Cup.

These narratives corroborate the views in the sports marketing literature that organizers of sport events need to think beyond the sporting competition when marketing and designing a sporting competition. Event organizers need to invent ways to make events more appealing to wider audiences. Where necessary organizers must augment the product to fit in with the needs and desires of the consumers by providing a number of extra activities and services in order to enhance the event's attractiveness and to appeal to a variety of market segments. Planners must recognize that in the sports industry the 'core product' is largely intangible (Sullivan, 2004). In the case of the Golf World Cup the 'core product' is likely to have been the emotional experience. A major component of the 'core product' for many of the visitors interviewed appeared to be the gratification derived from social interaction. Researchers (Chalip, Green and Vander Velden, 2000; Garcia, 2001 and Green, 2001) note that several organisations are adding benefits and features to their products to ensure that their products offer a differential advantage from their competitors. This is known as the augmented product.

The concept of the augmented product assumes that often the consumer has complex motivations and needs, which extend beyond the basic satisfaction of attendance at an event (Garcia, 2001). Findings from this study indicate that Barbados organisers of special events need to augment their product around the 'core' so that more buying motivations can be tapped (Green and Chalip, 1998). Event augmentation strategies could have broadened the range of market segments for which the event could have appeared attractive. Through event augmentation sport organizers can increase the attention paid to events and the diversity of event audiences by incorporating non-sport activities and experiences through cultural activities and other side attractions as part of the event programming. The narratives highlight how augmentation strategies could have provided the facilities to cater to the complex and heterogeneous needs of the spectators at the Golf World Cup. Augmentation could have provided the party atmosphere and an environment more conducive to socializing that the participants in this study expected.

There is agreement in the literature that 'festivals' can play an integral part in the event augmentation process (Chalip, 1992; Chalip, Green and Vander Velden, 2000; Green, 2001). At events designed to attract participants, the opportunity to parade and celebrate the sub-

142

culture that participants share has been found to be important, particularly where a shared subculture or fan-ship may be a significant source of attraction for attendees (Gibson, Green and Chalip, 1998; Willming and Holdnak, 2003). This may be particularly important in golf tourism events since followers of golf tend to follow and support individual players as a type of fan-ship sub-culture. Hall and Selwood (1989) note how the Australian Tourism Commission increased the marketing thrusts for the America's Cup by organizing a wide range of events to be held in conjunction with this event. Organizers of future golf events in Barbados should not discount the need for side attractions at golf events and would be wise to research augmentation strategies employed at other PGA and similar competitions. It is imperative that such initiatives be included in the bid contract before authorities decide to go ahead with an event.

The Golf World Cup was well organized from an operational and logistical standpoint but the organizers failed to develop a strong experiential component and USP. Fieldwork observations revealed a lack of cultural or celebratory activities organized around the golf event. When questioned about the absence of cultural activities, an official at the Barbados Tourism Authority was of the view that cultural activities were not necessary for this event since they thought "those types of people wouldn't be interested in that sort of thing". When interviewing tourism officials, there was the constant referral to "those people" or "those types of people". For example, statements like: "those people may feel harassed", "those people may not want to talk", and "that type of people may want their privacy". Another typical statement came from a local car rental manager, who supplied the transportation for PGA officials. She stated that:

> I don't think that having cultural activities will make a difference and I think that it has been over-looked because of the Sandy Lane element. After all, such cultural activities and Sandy Lane don't go together. I mean everyone is supposed to be posh so I can't see 'those people' would want to take part in our of culture.

This statement is illustrative of the perception within tourism organizations that visitors to the Caribbean are not interested in things local but want what they can get at home (Pattulo, 1996). As a result local tourism authorities operate under the assumption that the 'feeding' of things local – food, music and the arts is an inappropriate diet for the foreign tourist (see chapter 4). One only has to dine out at a Barbados hotel to experience the diet of Continental and American cuisine that is fed to tourists because it is generally believed that this is what the visitors want. As one hotelier explained when asked why there were no local delicacies on the menu: "They just won't eat it". However, contrary to these views, a tour operator who handles recreational arrangements for American visitors was of the opinion that: "If Barbados wants to attract tourists I think we need to go back to basics. The Americans want unique experiences – they want culture, not things that they can get elsewhere". However, despite the lack of cultural events surrounding the golf, the Cricket World Cup was being promoted as "more than just cricket" by highlighting the cultural element. A promotional narrative for the Cricket World Cup stated:

> The Barbadian love of sport is matched equally by our love of life, which is why we will ensure that these events are more than just wonderful sporting occasions. Around each we will be putting on special entertainment for all the family, ranging from concerts featuring world famous orchestras to festivals of local music - all done with a passionate Barbados spirit (Barbados, the Heart of the World Cup, 2006:1).

Promotional material advertising the Cricket World Cup described the event as "The Greatest Caribbean Party" or "Come for the Cricket Stay for the Party". The following extract from the Cricket World Cup brochure emphasised the party and cultural element of this event:

> If you've never been to cricket in the Caribbean, you can expect to experience sizzling excitement both on and off the field, whilst up-tempo rhythms keep the crowd going all day long. Where else can you find a dedicated party stand? Come celebrate cricket with thousands of fans from around the world and see why so many love this game. The West Indies aims to host the best Cricket World Cup ever and we're doing it with a Caribbean flavour.

Unlike the brochure promoting the Golf World Cup, the Cricket World Cup brochure was filled with images portraying the party, the costumes, the festival and carnival-like atmosphere. This evidence suggests that the Barbadian authorities were aware of the practice of staging cultural activities with sporting events; however,

144

what it also suggests is that they might have made decisions about the golf based on preconceived notions about the needs and expectations of golf tourists versus cricket tourists. The narratives indicate that the Barbados authorities might not have been aware of the motives and expectations of the golf spectator but instead made decisions based on their own values and preconceived ideas and without the benefit of research. It should be noted here that the tourism industry in Barbados is dominated by mainly middle-class individuals many of whom play golf and preside over the more senior positions. The middle-classes in Barbados tend to reject the African folk culture and gravitate towards a more affluent American lifestyle and values which reflect the way that the tourism industry is organized. This, along with the fact that golf is perceived to be a conservative sport in the Caribbean might have guided the decision not to have any cultural events attached to the Golf World Cup. The Barbados organizers did not associate the golf with cultural activities but instead with cocktail parties, receptions and corporate hospitality. When asked what events were being planned around the Golf World Cup, a Barbados Tourism Authority official responded: "we have a cocktail party on Friday night planned at Holders Hill. Many of the PGA people will be attending. We also have a special tent at the golf course but there is a list of special people who are invited to that – everybody cannot go". It should be noted here that Holders Hill is a very upscale residential district on the west coast of Barbados.

During the Golf World Cup there was only one cultural activity that took place on the island. The activity was called "Bridgetown Alive" and it was held on Thursday, December 7 from 9.00am to 6.00 pm. Fieldwork notes from this event noted that this event took the form of a street parade in the main shopping center of Broad Street in the city of Bridgetown. It included appearances by many of Barbados' cultural performers including a golf cart parade, the police band, poetry tellers, steel bands, folk singing and other forms of entertainment. The parade was part of an annual event, which is sponsored by the Barbados Tourism Authority to celebrate its 30th anniversary and 'Tourism Week'. The parade was advertised in the daily newspaper but did not in any way seem connected to golf. Additionally, this activity was staged in Bridgetown in the middle of the day conflicting with the golf, which was being held seven miles away at Sandy Lane. At no time during the observation, which took place between 9.00am and 2.30pm, did the master of ceremonies mention the golf. Many of the tourists at this event also seemed to be visiting off the cruise ship 'Destiny' which was docked in the Bridgetown harbour that day but the majority of people attending this event appeared to be locals conducting business in Bridgetown. With no cultural fringe events organized around the golf the foreign visitors tended to make their own parties in the evening. The Trinidadian and Jamaican contingent indicated that they attended the golf during the day and "… we go to nightspots in the evening" while the Jamaicans said "we travel to the 'Gap[7]', and we have done the Harbour Master and partied at the Boatyard".

Fieldwork observations at the golf course also revealed that this event did not display the 'spectacle' usually associated with mega events, such as an opening or closing ceremony. There was no opening ceremony and the closing ceremony involved a few brief remarks by the Barbados Prime Minister, the Minister of Tourism and Jack Warfield, Vice President of the PGA Tour. The omission of a closing and opening ceremony seemed rather strange since one of the major justifications for staging these events is the opportunity to showcase the host location's culture to the television viewers and to entertain the visitors who choose to view the event in its live setting. The event's marketing strategy thus appeared to lack the many meanings associated with sport consumption: spectacle, culture, fanship and celebration.

Further evidence led the researcher to conclude that the Golf World Cup might have been downplayed as the Cricket World Cup was due to be hosted a few months later. For instance much of the promotional material on Barbados at the time highlighted the Cricket World Cup with pages of slogans, press reports and advertisements. A twenty-three page brochure devoted twenty-two pages to promoting the Cricket World Cup and only one page was devoted to the Golf World Cup. During a semi-structured interview, a tourism official downplayed the importance of the Golf World Cup by commenting: "I don't think that the golf will really do much for us. But the Cricket World Cup, well, that will be the biggest event that we will ever have in this place". Hence, much of the promotional material on Barbados was overwhelmed with information on the Cricket World Cup whereas information on the Golf World Cup was less emphasized. At the World Travel Market in November 2006, just three weeks before the Golf World Cup, the Barbados stand, which was designed to depict a cricket pavilion, was inundated with information on the Cricket World

---

[7]   The 'Gap' is an abbreviated term for St. Lawrence Gap, Barbados'
nightclub district on the south coast.

Cup. There were guide books, numerous brochures, publications, match schedules and souvenirs on display. Former West Indies cricket players, Gordon Greenidge, Joel Garner and Sir Garfield Sobers hovered around the stand encouraging people to visit for the Cricket World Cup. There was much less enthusiasm in promoting the Golf World Cup at World Travel Market in 2006, and if one was interested in this event, one had to ask for the information as there was no information on display. The attendant at World Travel Market therefore had to dig into her many boxes to come up with a brochure that promoted the Golf World Cup for the prospective tourist. Local residents also noted that the importance of the event was not emphasized in the press. As a local resident pointed out: "they just did not emphasize its importance". Even the local press was quick to stress that the significance of the Golf World Cup did not hit home until it had started. For instance, the Nation of December 9, 2006 noted:

> The golf championship was talked about for more than a year; but the magnitude of the event, we suspect, only dawned on many when it teed off this week and images of Barbados were being viewed by millions of people live from the Country Club Course at Sandy Lane, St James, via major television networks, ESPN, ABC and Sky, with delayed coverage in Europe and more than 100 countries worldwide (World class future, 2006: 29A).

Masterman (2004) notes that the timing of an event is an important part of the product. This view draws attention to the realization that Barbados was hosting too many important events all in the space of four months and this may have contributed to the low-keyed nature of the advertising campaign. Tourism authorities were concentrating their efforts on marketing the Cricket World Cup to international tourists with less attention being paid to the golf. The following chapter deals with the issue of event saturation in more detail, however, attention is now given to the opinions of international tourists with regards to the development of event tourism in Barbados.

5.5 THE CASE FOR EVENT TOURISM IN BARBADOS – THE INTERNATIONAL PERSPECTIVE

All international tourists interviewed were asked what type of events they would like to see in Barbados. Consistent with the Barbados survey the majority of tourists said that they came to Barbados for the "weather", "the relaxing atmosphere" and "the people".   During the field research many visitors stressed the view that cultural and historical events are what make Barbados attractive. In terms of events, this couple attending the Golf World Cup explained:

> When we are here we like to go to church with the locals, yes we go to St. Matthias. We attended the Independence Day celebrations at the Garrison but we did not like it this year when they moved it to the National Stadium. The Golf World Cup is a great event and we are enjoying it but it is not the reason why we come here. We like dining out at night but in Barbados you can hardly find mid-range restaurants. You have the low-end or the high-end but you need some good mid-range restaurants.

A couple from Berkshire in England commented:
> We just love Barbados, we have been coming here for many years…we love the people, we have a friend who lives in the St. James area, he's a carpenter and as soon as we arrive we call him up and he would say, let's meet for a drink. And we love to go to Rocky's Bar, in St. James, Rocky is so great and the people that come would take pictures and next time you go back you would see them on the wall. We like to go to the Gold Cup at the Garrison, we just love the parades before the horses run and the Crop-Over festival parade…and we go to the Holetown Festival all the time. One time we went to the cricket when England was playing and we won.

A female English visitor, interviewed at St. Lawrence gap, explained her reason for visiting Barbados:

> I have been visiting now for five years and I come now to see my many friends on the island. I feel very comfortable and safe

148

here and I am considering moving to Barbados. I have already been to the employment office and they have told me what I need to do to get a job.

A married couple, at Accra Beach, noted that the Golf World Cup was a great addition to the holiday experience but stressed that: "we have been coming here for many years because, well, there is no place like it…it's civilized… we wanted to do the Golf World Cup … But did not make it, but it's a good event that we would have appreciated seeing". A group of tourists at Miami Beach, visiting from Germany and England, felt that the Golf World Cup was:

> Only good for those who are interested in golf. We come here mainly for the weather, the sea and the people, the pace of life. This island is very good for families and couples. We like the horseracing, we usually go on Boxing Day but for us it's shopping at Pricesmart, but the shopping is better for women than it is for men.

A Canadian visitor also explained her reason for visiting Barbados in the following terms:

> I have been visiting for 25 years. I come every winter. I keep returning for the weather. I know about the golf cup but did not care to attend. If you ask me about events in Barbados well then that would have to be the Jazz Festival. I attend every year but I feel it has gotten a bit too expensive. I am not surprised that the golf was poorly attended; it is not just a popular sport, period. People just don't understand it.

Some international visitors felt that the Oistins Fish Fry was the best thing that the island had to offer. According to one English visitor: "well there isn't anything like it anywhere", while another visitor thought: "the dancers were really great and we like the atmosphere". Likewise, a Canadian visitor added: "Oistins is the thing to do, I go every weekend". Many of the visitors interviewed also indicated that they were attracted to the water activities available in Barbados. If they were not lying at the beach they spent time "swimming with the turtles", driving around in jeeps, sailing and snorkeling.

149

A group of visitors from the United States, who were visiting friends on the island, were of the opinion that Barbados' tourism objective should be concentrated more on improving the service levels in the country rather than staging mega events. One of the male visitors at the Golf World Cup explained that:

> Staging events like this are good and I am enjoying this {golf} but Barbados has more pressing matters such as service. The service here is very inconsistent. If you go to Sandy Lane, Royal Pavilion and Tides, Daphney's, you are treated very well and then if you go to the supermarkets or Chefette it is not so good. St. Lucia has been able to embrace a service culture; it engulfs the whole island whether you are in the hotels or in Castries. Barbados needs lessons from St. Lucia if you really want to develop your tourism. For Americans service is important. Americans tell a lot of people about a good experience but more about a bad experience. Your Prime Minister needs to get into the ads and welcome visitors.

This evidence suggests that there is scope for the further development of cultural events in Barbados. The participants from abroad highlighted preferences for events that involve cultural presentations or parades. Interestingly, none of the international visitors expressed a desire for more sporting events except perhaps horseracing but this ironically is preceded by a week of cultural activities and a colourful parade on the day of the race.

5.6 CONCLUSION

This chapter provided valuable insights into the reasons individuals consume events and provided many clues as to how authorities can leverage events in order to encourage international travel. It is interesting to note the synergies that exist between the event and the destination as a tourist attraction. Foreign visitors therefore did not purchase the golf tournament but purchased instead a bundle of benefits that contributed to the overall vacation experience. While many visitors expressed satisfaction at their holiday in Barbados others expressed disappointment with the Golf World Cup in terms of the low spectator turn out, the 'lack of atmosphere' and the perception that the event did not offer anything 'special' or different from other PGA events. Another key issue is that many of the tourists interviewed indicated that they did not see the event advertised in their home countries. This lack of awareness occurred although many of these visitors described themselves as followers of the game. This was a significant finding as it highlighted flaws in the advertising and communications campaign. This was further compounded due to the fact that the authorities failed to promote the experiential dimensions of the golf event in the advertisements. The narratives also bought into question the timing of the Golf World Cup so close to the Cricket World Cup and the view that much of the advertising for the Golf World Cup was blocked by the advertising for the Cricket World Cup. Many visitors noted that they appreciated cultural and heritage events as activities during their stay, while others said that the climate and beaches were the major attractions.

When engaging in participant observation at a golf event it is acknowledged that it is not always possible to record every phenomenon. The Sandy Lane golf course is located on several acres of land so it was not possible to engage in observations on the entire 18-hole expanse of this facility. As explained in chapter two, at the Golf World Cup many spectators tended to follow their favourite player as they played 'hole' to 'hole' so this meant that many of them were not in any one place for more than ten minutes at a time. Once the ball was played they moved on to the next hole and consequently it was not always possible to explore all of the themes in the interview guide with these participants, particularly on the first day of the Golf World Cup. On subsequent days, as the researcher became more familiar with the surroundings at Sandy Lane, she was able to 'pin down' international participants at the Golf World Cup for more in-depth interviews while they were socialising at one of the bars or sitting for extended periods at the 18th hole (see chapter three). The views expressed in this chapter are limited to the individuals who participated in the interviews as seen through the eyes of this researcher. These views however do provide us with many conceptual issues that need to be addressed in relation to event tourism in Barbados. The next section is concerned with the local perspective and it deals with many issues that arose in the semi-structured interviews with local residents.

6 -CHAPTER SIX
IN THEIR OWN WORDS - THE LOCAL STAKEHOLDERS

6.1 INTRODUCTION

Many salient themes emerged from semi-structured interviews with local residents and tourism industry stakeholders. The logic behind hosting this event is addressed by the local tourism decision-makers. The analysis of the qualitative data suggests that both the perceptions held by local residents of the Golf World Cup and the non-appearance of golf's top international stars negatively affected local participation and support for this event. The narratives suggest that Sandy Lane's association with the Golf World Cup and the associated advertising and promotion in the local media projected an image of the event as a socially exclusive occasion. Furthermore, the fieldwork revealed that local residents felt alienated from the event due to its nature and their lack of involvement in the planning and decision-making process. Some participants expressed the view that since golf was not a popular sport in Barbados, this accounted for the lack of interest and subsequent poor participation by local residents. On the positive side, some local residents felt that the media coverage of the Golf World Cup did much to enhance the image of the island and to promote tourism. The discussion in this section commences with the views of the local authorities with emphasis on why the Golf World Cup was held in Barbados.

6.2 THE LOGIC BEHIND THE GOLF WORLD CUP

The authorities in Barbados selected the Golf World Cup mainly because it was perceived to fit well with Barbados' upmarket tourism profile. This event was also deemed to fit well with Barbados' tourism diversification strategies and it was felt that it would generate much needed publicity for the island and launch Barbados as a premier golfing destination. The authorities stressed that special events must conform to the tourism policy in that they must target the up-market visitor. A tourism official explained:

> Barbados is embarking on new marketing strategies to attract more tourism dollars and so has entered a partnership with IMG which is the largest sports and lifestyle consulting group

in the world. They have been contracted to examine the potential of developing a series of world-class events for Barbados and the Golf World Cup is one of the first that they have recommended due to its up- market nature.

IMG is the world's largest company dedicated to the marketing and management of sport, leisure and lifestyle. It represents performing artistes, writers, and fashion models, broadcasters, leading corporations, cultural institutions and recreational resorts. The company has worked with some of the world's best known sporting icons, like Tiger Woods, Brian Lara, Venus Williams, John McEnroe, Joe Montana and Pete Sampras. IMG identified the Golf World Cup as the ideal brand match for Barbados.

Special events must not only fit the up-market profile but they should also have a high estimated revenue value to the island in terms of immediate returns and media exposure. According to this tourism official:

> Events must be valuable to Barbados, I am looking at many event proposals here on my desk but not every event would qualify. This volleyball event for instance, I don't think caters to the market that we would want to attract. In order for events to qualify, they must fit in with our target markets and we must get at least a 20% ROI (return on investments) as well....For instance with the golf the international attention would be of enormous benefit to the island. The tournament will be seen in more than 140 countries, reaching over 200 million viewers on ESPN, ABC, and the event will also be seen on Sky Sports in Britain and NHK in Asia.

In accordance with the policy of attracting up-market tourists, golf has been identified as one of the areas that fit the profile of the Barbados tourism product. The tourism official explained:

> The planners saw those who play golf as fitting perfectly within the island's tourism strategy and the golf championship was a perfect target. If you look at the Barbados tourism you will see that golf fits well with the middle-class profile of people who visit Barbados.

In addition, this Barbados Tourism Authority official advised that:

> Golf is one of the many niches we are pursuing in diversifying the tourism product and in catering to an upper class clientele. It is also one of the recreational activities that have been identified as very viable since many people travel to play golf. Although we have had golf courses in Barbados before we have not actually pursued the market. We are still behind our Caribbean counterparts, like Bermuda, in the golf tourism business.

The tourism officials felt that golf could provide Barbados with the high yield tourists that are required to increase tourism expenditure. However, as will be discussed later in this chapter, this event did not result in any high-yielding tourists visiting the island. In fact, it is acknowledged that the attendance was very poor at the Golf World Cup. A tourism official guesstimated that the event only attracted about 200 overseas visitors and they stressed that the majority of them were press. Many of the international visitors interviewed at the event were found to be 'casuals' who were attending the event because they just happened to be in Barbados at the time. With no post impact study available it is still not clear what type of tourists were attracted to Barbados for the Golf World Cup and how many visits were actually inspired by the event.

A major argument put forward by the authorities for the staging of the Golf World Cup was its publicity value. A government official argued that the total media value from the championship would be approximately US$24 million (£12 million). He claimed that the tournament would bring exposure to a high-end market, which the island could not pay for. He said:

> The evidence shows that the profile of people who play and follow golf are an ideal match for Barbados' visitor profile...you realise the game is played by a set of people in a particular socio-economic bracket. The publicity that we will get from this we could not buy it, we don't have that money to.

The media has played a significant role in making events such as the Olympic Games profitable for host cities. It is continuously argued that television coverage and the value of the exposure that they bring can reap lucrative rewards for host countries. However, as discussed in chapter three, many of these assertions are not empirically verified. Chalip, Green and Hill (2003) argue that the value of event media has to be determined not by the number of individuals exposed to it or its related commercial value but by the actual effects that it has on travel to the destination. So far research has been unable to identify any link between event media and destination choice. Nevertheless, the tourism authorities seemed satisfied at the media outcome of this event.

Another reason the Golf World Cup was seen as an obvious choice for Barbados is because the infrastructure was already in place. Many mega events require large financial inputs, particularly from the public purse, in order to provide the necessary infrastructure (Kang and Perdue, 1994). In this case, the Sandy Lane Golf and Country Club where this event was held, was already in place and as a private sector investment it required no influx of public capital. The Sandy Lane facility was also the obvious choice for this competition because, as a tourism official explained:

> The course is challenging enough for a competition at this level. In golf you play the course, you have to beat the landscape, the wind and other elements and the layout of Sandy Lane was thought to provide a sufficient challenge that would attract the world's top golfers and provide a worthwhile competition.

Although this event failed to attract a significant number of tourists and was deemed a failure by the local press in terms of tourists numbers, the tourism authorities in Barbados considered the Golf World Cup to be a success. A follow up interview with a Barbados Tourism Authority official confirmed:

> The event was a success. You do not host these events to attract a million people. The event was well organised and its execution went as planned. The event was staged to build awareness of Barbados to an up-market clientele, which is the type of visitor that we attract anyway. We are satisfied that we have achieved this.

While the Barbados authorities continued to preach the up-market dictum, the tourists to Barbados remain generally 'mass' tourists who come on package tours booked through tour operators. As this south coast hotelier pointed out: "90% of our visitors book through tour operators, especially from the United Kingdom. If you are not in the tour operator brochure you are as good as dead". Pattulo (2005) notes how many summer visitors to Barbados, particularly those from North America, are anything but up-market or wealthy and many are uneducated. The next section concentrates on the views of local resident and local tourism entrepreneurs.

6.3 THE IMAGE OF SANDY LANE AND GOLF

The Golf World Cup was also poorly attended by local residents. Local participants attributed the poor attendance to the event's image of being socially exclusive. The perception held of the Sandy Lane Hotel by members of the host community negatively affected their attitudes and the lack of interest in attending the Golf World Cup. As stated earlier, Sandy Lane as a resort has an up-market profile. It is projected as a facility that caters to the social elite, mainly famous sports and movie stars, royalty and the very wealthy. Local residents concluded that non-attendance was attributed to the perception that the event was 'posh' or was for 'certain types of people' or 'was for celebrities' and was thus socially exclusive. The high profile and up-market image of the Sandy Lane Resort thus acted as a major turn-off from attending. When trying to explain the poor turnout, a local resident in the car rental business concluded: "I think a lot of people didn't go because of the Sandy Lane element". Likewise, a taxi driver exclaimed: "The golf at Sandy Lane, I certainly won't be going in there, not even if they pay me. That for rich people".

A male respondent, admitted:

> Well yes, I knew that we were hosting this golf thing, but never thought of going...I thought that was for Tiger Woods type people and celebrities...It didn't seem like something that Bajans would go to....I didn't even know that the general public was invited to the exclusive Sandy Lane.

An official at the National Sports Council indicated that he did not attend because: "that thing design for west coast people not the mass of the population". The reference to the west coast means that it was perceived as a posh affair since many of the luxury hotels, including Sandy Lane and expensive villas, are located on the island's western shoreline. As was explained in chapter five, tourism

156

development is concentrated on the coastline areas of the west and south coast and to a lesser extent the east coast. The west coast is promoted as the most affluent area and the south coast as less affluent with budget hotels. The east coast is known more for its historical sites and scenic attractions.

Therefore, perceptions held of west coast tourism and Sandy Lane as a hotel affected the way that potential local consumers perceived the Golf World Cup. Reports in the local and international media also reinforced Sandy Lane's image as a place for the international 'glitterati'. For instance, Tiger Woods' wedding at Sandy Lane in October 2004 received substantial international and local media coverage. In addition, stories of celebrities holidaying at Sandy Lane are a constant feature in celebrity magazines such as *Hello, OK* and *People*. Recently the London 'Times' of January 6 2007, in an extract titled "Why I love Barbados", printed comments made by British celebrities Jemma Kidd, Michael Vaughan and Luke Donald, all of whom have houses on the Sandy Lane estate. These constant re-enforcements of Sandy Lane's glamorous image affected how locals perceived the Golf World Cup.

The exclusive and the glamorous image of the Golf World Cup was also enforced by the perception of golf as an elite sport. As one local resident explained: "I think the poor turnout among locals is that golf is treated as an 'elite' sport and not an event for 'John Public', so 'John Public' did not attend and there are not enough 'elite' people to attend". In Barbados golf is not perceived by the local residents as a 'mass sport' and consequently does not stimulate much interest among the local population. One local resident, who attended the Golf World Cup on the Sunday, was quick to note: "golf here is not a 'mass sport'. People here just see it as a tourist thing or a game that rich people play". As shown in chapter four, golf resorts in the Caribbean are perceived negatively due to their enclave nature and this affects how individuals react towards the sport. Reports of segregation facilitated by high walls and sophisticated security systems dominate the literature on golf tourism (Lowerson, 1994; Pattulo, 1996; Readman, 2003; Sinclair, 2006; Swarbrooke, 1999. The fieldwork visits confirm that this description accurately describes Sandy Lane.

When this researcher visited the Sandy Lane hotel during the fieldwork, she was first scrutinized by the security guard positioned outside the iron gates at the entrance. The security guard tried to turn her away by telling her that the hotel was closed to the public until Monday and that she would have to make an appointment. At the

157

insistence of the researcher, the security guard instructed the researcher that she should drive through and go directly to the front desk. Once on the inside, she was met by a member of management who advised her that she could not walk around the resort un-escorted and that if she wanted to view the hotel she would have to make an appointment. When she questioned why she could not walk around on her own, the response from the Sandy Lane representative was: "we have to protect the privacy of our guests. We do tours of the hotel Monday to Friday between 9.00am and 4.00pm. You will need to call to make an appointment". Consequently, the researcher had to return the following week to get a glimpse of the hotel. This time there was no trouble getting inside the 'iron gates' as the guard was expecting her to arrive. She was greeted by a doorman and her car was valet parked.

Sandy Lane is owned by two Irish businessmen named John McManus and Dermond Desmond. The Sandy Lane which the researcher experienced on this occasion was different to the Sandy Lane which she patronized during her years working in Barbados and prior to the redevelopment and the ownership takeover. First of all, locals are not necessarily welcomed. The Sandy Lane representative during the tour pointed out:

> I have been working at Sandy Lane for over 16 years but I prefer the old Sandy Lane. Before the redevelopment, it was a friendlier, more welcoming hotel and you were able to enter without any appointment. Before, we used to get a lot of locals coming through for lunch and as a member of staff you were more relaxed, now you have to watch your P's and Q's. Locals can use the beach but they cannot pass through the hotel to do so. The closed-door policy was implemented because this is how the new owners want the hotel to be run.

The tour guide rightly described the hotel as 'super luxury'. There were marble columns and floors in the main lobby and corridors. Guests came in and out in their beach and resort wear, some wearing large diamond rings. Women wore their swimsuits as they came through the lobby dressed in high-heeled shoes. On the beach guests shaded from the sun under green cabana umbrellas and were told to place the yellow flag into the ground if they needed service. Security guards hovered discreetly on the beach while guests soaked up the sun or read a book in the shade of a palm tree.

The hotel room that was shown to the researcher smelled of luxury potpourri. All rooms have plasma, wide-screen televisions, an interactive entertainment system, stereo, private bar, personal in-room safe, and a convenient telephone system with direct dial access. Averaging 900 square feet, rooms at Sandy Lane are spacious and uniquely feature a large private veranda overlooking the Caribbean Sea. Large bathrooms are complimented by an oval shaped jacuzzi tub and marble finishes. All bathrooms have specially designed multi-spray showers and heated mirrors. The bedroom drapes are remote controlled.

Sandy Lane guests come from all over the world with the majority coming from the United Kingdom. The female representative explained:

> Our guests are 80% repeat business. Many of them have been coming since the hotel opened in the early 1960's. 75% of all our visitors are from the United Kingdom while the rest come from the United States, Europe, South America and the Caribbean, mainly Trinidad. Our guests belong to the super rich and many are over 50 years. We have had Pavarotti who came with a large entourage and took over the entire west wing.

She also noted that despite the publicity, Sandy Lane did not reap many benefits from the Golf World Cup. She explained:

> The Golf World Cup was a special event that had nothing to do with Sandy Lane, except that they used our golf course for the event. I can't really say that anyone stayed with us because of the golf. The only guests we had were nine of the top golfers who were invited by the owners to stay with us. The other golfers stayed, at, I believe, the Hilton; so contrary to public belief, the golf did not have any impact on Sandy Lane at all.

Enclave tourism seems to be the norm in Barbados in recent times. Visits to other golf developments on the island also projected this picture of exclusivity and super luxury. Entrance to the Royal Westmoreland facility, located five miles from Sandy Lane, is facilitated through large iron gates only on the condition that you are a member, a resident at the resort or have an appointment with a member of management[8]. Royal Westmoreland is a 72, 6870 yards-long course. The golfing complex has a club house and pro-shop surrounded by spectacular properties representing some of the most beautiful homes in Barbados. British entertainer Sir Cliff Richards owns a property on the estate and his home has been the vacation retreat of British Prime Minister, Tony Blair on several occasions. Further observations revealed that newer golf developments, such as the Apes Hill project to be completed in 2008, promote an enclave type of environment. The promotional material indicates that the Apes Hill project comprises a private gated community with 200 single-family homes on 470 acres of land and an 18-hole golf course (Par Ful Stuff, 2008).

The perception of exclusivity associated with golf in Barbados is understood after a comparison is made between Sandy Lane and other golf and tourist establishments in Barbados. Traditionally, the Barbadian public is not used to this type of enclave tourism, which promotes snobbery and exclusiveness. For example, there is open access for local or foreign persons to enter hotel premises in Barbados. During fieldwork, the researcher had free access to the Bougainvillea Beach Resort, the Butterfly Hotel, the Southern Palms hotel, the Crane Resort Hotel, the Hilton Hotel and the Almond Beach Club without the scrutiny of security guards. Free and open access to the Barbados Golf and Country Club was also obtained. The Barbados Golf and Country Club is a golf development located on the less affluent south coast. The Barbados Golf Club is located just ½ mile inland from the southern coastline in an area called Durants. According to the promotional material offered to the researcher during a visit on December 12, 2006, it was evident that the Barbados Golf Club differentiates itself from its west coast counterparts by stressing its open accessibility as a 'pay as you play' establishment with a 'friendly atmosphere'. As the promotional narrative explains:

> The Barbados Golf Club has become the soul of Barbados golf with its friendly atmosphere, coaching programmes and charming terraced clubhouse, which opens onto an expansive and unique triple green... The Barbados golf club is the island's first public 18th hole course. The links-style 6705 yard par 72 course features gently rolling hills, wide open fairways

---

[8] The researcher is familiar with the environment at Royal Westmoreland due to her work experience in Barbados which involved interaction with management and guests at this establishment.

and a series of coral waste bunkers add character to several holes. A large central lake adds intrigue on 3 holes and mature mile tress bends and beckon in the cooling coastal breezes... The Barbados Golf Club is a championship course officially sanctioned by the European PGA tour.

The green fees at the Barbados Golf Club were also considerably cheaper than Sandy Lane with 18 holes costing US$135.00 (£80.50) per person compared with US$400.00 (£300.00) at Sandy Lane's 'Old Nine' and US$1000.00 (£700.00) at the 'Green Monkey'. It was further revealed that many south coast hotels were partners with the Barbados Golf Club. These partnerships allowed preferential access and green fees to guests at these hotels who wished to play golf but also provided a quality facility that allowed access to a course to those who did not have access to Sandy Lane. South coast hotels with partnerships in the Barbados Golf Club include Almond Casuarina, Amaryllis, Barbados Beach Club, Blue Horizon Hotel, Bougainvillea Beach Resort and others. In fact there are a total of 20 south coast hotels with partnerships in the Barbados Golf Club. Although it is not conclusive, it is possible that these partnership arrangements could explain why many south coast hotels did not promote the Golf World Cup with more enthusiasm.

With free access the norm at other hotels in Barbados it is easy to understand why locals would associate the Golf World Cup with the same aloofness and snobbery that is perceived to be associated with the Sandy Lane Resort and other golfing resorts on the island. The perception of golf as an exclusive pastime is illustrated in this quote from two local businessmen:

> We used to be members at Sandy Lane, yes, the 'Old Nine', which is not so expensive but since the renovation and the country club, the membership fees are very expensive, even just to play a round they want BDS$800.00 [£500.00], and they make a caddy compulsory. Since we have so many golf courses it is even more difficult to play golf. They want a lot of money and don't talk about Westmoreland, they want not only a membership fee but a joining fee as well which you only get back when you terminate your membership. That means that you'll be giving them an interest free loan. By the time you get it back you would only be able to buy smarties.

A promotional narrative on the Sandy Lane golf course confirms the reflections of these two businessmen. This extract in Sporting Barbados (2006) states:

> Nothing comes cheap at Sandy Lane, but it is a pay-as-you-play course and you certainly get quality for your dollar! The same may not be said though for the Green Monkey course given that you have to stay at Sandy Lane Hotel to be permitted to play and pay over US$400.00 [£300.00] a round if some rare tee-times are available (Its tee time, 2008: 80).

These narratives illustrate the exclusive nature of golf at the Sandy Lane Hotel. Having to be resident at the resort in order to play at the 'Green Monkey' course is not considered ideal for local persons who may find it inconvenient to check into a hotel just to play a round of golf. This could be construed as a deliberate attempt to exclude the local market from participating in the golfing experience offered at this resort. The narrative continues: The holes around the lake are stunning but unfortunately most normal golfing mortals are unlikely to share the experience unless the owners adopt a much more open policy on playing" (Its tee time, 2006: 80). However, it should be noted here that Sandy Lane has a total of three golf courses and it is only the 'Green Monkey' course that is exclusive to hotel guests. The general public has access to the two other courses on the development, but the green fees are still considered expensive. Two local golfers revealed that along with meeting the cost of the green fees "you have to have money to pay for a caddy because a caddy is compulsory at the 'Country Club' [Sandy Lane].

` A local cultural activist expressed concern about this type of tourism. He noted:

> Barbados has not been able to attract 600,000 long-stay visitors this year because of snobbishness in its marketing campaign. We are promoting snobbishness in our tourism marketing strategy. We are just looking at the people with the big bucks, we are even asking tourists to meet each other on the golf course, rather than interact with the local people in the villages, in the rum shops and other areas. And we are not promoting community tourism, which would bring tourists into the homes

162

and villages and have a spending pattern with a multiplier effect on the economy.

Similarly, a Barbadian who now lives in New York expressed concern about Barbados' marketing strategy. She argued:

> In the process of modernizing the island to please an up-market client, ordinary sights that gave the island its charm and colour have disappeared: the indigenous vendors along the streets and the byways of Bridgetown; the small bands of black belly sheep roaming the byways outside the city… has government recognized that having pushed aside-banished- the very elements that originally lured visitors to the island, the fickle tourists will move onto another unspoiled place and leave Barbados holding the bag?

Likewise, a south coast hotel manager expressed the view that:

> … all I can see these golf courses doing is creating more and more areas in this island that are off-limits to locals. Areas where I used to play as a child have now been developed and fenced in for only those who can afford it. I can't even look in, why would I want to pay to go in?

The political activist was of the opinion that potential international tourists will be "turned off" traveling to Barbados if the island is perceived to be too exclusive in much the same way that Barbadians have been "turned off" attending the Golf World Cup. In another instance it was thought that Barbados might be destroying the very attributes that are most appealing to visitors. This issue was discussed at length in chapter four where concern was raised about Barbados appearing to be too exclusive and expensive a destination for ordinary tourists as a result of golf tourism. It was argued that this may foster the perception of social exclusion which may have a negative impact on future tourist arrivals.

Academics in the field of tourism development and planning have cautioned that excessive tourism development can destroy the very elements that made a destination popular in the initial phases and that extensive development can tend to displace and alienate local residents (Doxey, 1975; Butler, 1980). These narratives corroborate the views in the literature about golf being a sport that fosters social exclusion. Beall and Piron (2005: 9) defined social exclusion as:

> a process and a state that prevents individuals or groups from full participation in social, economic and political life and from asserting their rights. It derives from exclusionary relationships based on power.

Beall and Piron (2005) explain social exclusion as a concept that can describe, on the one hand, a condition or outcome and, on the other hand, a dynamic process. As a condition or outcome, social exclusion is a state which excludes individuals from fully participating in their society due to their social identity such as race, gender, ethnicity, caste, religion, or social location. As a multidimensional and dynamic process, social exclusion refers to the social relations and organizational barriers that block the attainment of livelihoods, human development and equal citizenship. It can create or sustain poverty and inequality, and can restrict social participation. As a dynamic process, social exclusion is governed by social and political relations and access to organizations and institutional sites of power. What is evident is that golf developments such as Sandy Lane have developed institutional barriers to ensure that only a few select people can qualify to use the facilities. This is certainly illustrated in how Sandy Lane promotes itself. The promotional material for Sandy Lane indicates that not only is it expensive to play golf at the resort's Green Monkey Course but visitors also have to be able to afford the minimum US$2800.00 (£2000) per night accommodation fee and be a registered guest to qualify. What is clear is that Sandy Lane is not only shutting out locals but other tourists visiting the island who may be desirous of playing a round of golf but are either unable to afford, or do not wish to stay at, Sandy Lane. Further institutional barriers are imposed at the Royal Westmoreland, through both excessive membership and joining fees. This situation was highlighted by two local golfers who commented: "They want not only a membership fee but a joining fee as well which you only get back when you terminate your membership. They making sure that only certain people can play there".

A local historian was of the view that the Golf World Cup would not have been well attended because it bore images of the island's colonial past. She commented:

164

It is obvious that people would not want to go. They promoting the snobbery and social divisions of the past by hosting it at Sandy Lane. They need to remember that they are still old people living in their 100s or 90s whose grandparents or even parents would have told them tales of slavery or hardships. That is still our recent history and the hotel is reminiscent of that. Golf too is seen as a white man sport and they promoted it as high end. My husband even says that they could never get him to go even if they pay him. People were calling into the call-in programmes saying that they did not want that bout here.

The foregoing narrative reinforces the view that has been long posited by historians and scholars in the Caribbean in that the tourism industry continues to reflect and perpetuate the old social structures of the colonial past. The educator stressed that this was a grave cause for concern and urged the authorities to reverse this pattern with urgency.

The perception of the Golf World Cup as a socially exclusive event represents a paradoxical state. On one hand, a major justification for staging events is that they can act as catalysts for the encouragement of participation in sport and the reduction of social exclusion (Horner and Manzenreiter, 2006). On the other hand, the Golf World Cup seems to have bought to the fore the tendency of certain forms of tourism development to do the opposite by perpetuating the social divisions of the past and discouraging local participating. Much of the work on social exclusion in sport tends to focus on social exclusion as a result of poverty, or on the basis of gender, disability and social class (Collins and Kay, 2003). Unfortunately, the findings of this study do not present an in-depth understanding of social exclusion due to perceptions of exclusivity and/or how it works in relation to tourism, hospitality or sports marketing. This is evidently an area that requires further study.

Many residents who participated in this study claimed that they did not perceive golf as a pastime for local or ordinary people. For instance, a taxi driver when asked if he would be attending the Golf World Cup, responded: "me, not me, I ain't going to that. I will drop people there but that is not for folks like me". Some local residents were also of the view that the promotions in the local environment painted a picture of exclusivity. As one sport official at the National Sports Council pointed out: "They get bout here and pitch this thing as if they only wanted rich and famous". Similarly, some residents thought that the event was designed to specifically attract celebrities. As one local resident revealed: "I thought that was for Tiger Woods type people and celebrities", while a similar comment was: "I didn't know that the general public was invited to the exclusive Sandy Lane". Examination of local press reports found that editorials often referred to the Golf World Cup as 'high end', 'star studded', 'prestigious', or 'five diamond'. A Nation newspaper report of September 20, 2006 illustrates these themes:

> When the prestigious World Cup Golf Championships is hosted at Sandy Lane in December, the coaches and champions (management and staff) of the resort will be well prepared. The five-diamond property has implemented a "Sandy Lane World Cup Champion" series of events aimed to ensure this, and Michael Pownall, chief executive of the hotel, said it started on a high with enthusiastic participation by employees (Sandy Lane gets world golf ready, 2006: 46A).

Similarly, the December 28, 2005 issue of the Nation reported:

> Minister of Tourism, Noel Lynch said the tournament will bring exposure to a high-end market, which the island could not pay for. "When you look at the profile of people who play golf and stack that up against what we want to do, you would realise the game is played by a set of people in a particular socio-economic bracket, which profiles well with Barbados (Spooner, 2005: 10).

A further report in the Nation of December 7, 2006 was also consistent in the use of these words:

> Star-studded. ...Other favourites include the Irish pair of Padraig Harrington and Paul McGinley, Luke Donald and David Howell of England, and defending champions Stephen Dodd and Bradley Dredge of Wales.....Tickets for the prestigious event have been going well, bringing a smile to the faces of organisers. Jack Warfield, the PGA Tour's vice-president of championship management, said there was "tremendous interest" in the event and tickets were going quickly (Spooner, 2006c:20A).

And finally, an editorial in the Nation of September 21, 2006 reported:

> The windfall surrounding the tournament is expected to come as over 5000 <u>high-end visitors</u>, most from the United States, are expected for the event (Spooner, 2006d: 25).

A local tour representative also commented that in her business it is very difficult to sell golf packages to tourists. She commented:

> I find it hard to convince anybody to play golf. The tourists think that golf is for the old, rich and retired or just is boring...the people that I deal with prefer cultural activities rather than playing golf.

She attributed this difficulty to the perception that her clients have of golf. She claims that even when dealing with international clients that golf is perceived to be very elitist. Media reports about golf on the island, especially in recent times, continue to portray exclusivity. A local sports administrator commented about the publicity from the Tiger Woods wedding. They claimed that: "when Tiger got married, man you could not even drive down the road outside Sandy Lane. They block-off the entire road and made the people divert. It was so hush, hush, so exclusive that you could not even go into the area". Tiger Woods , the American golfer married at Sandy Lane in 2004 on the same golf course on which the Golf World Cup was played.

People attach meanings to media messages, which interact with other media messages, experiences, predispositions and individual characteristics to create an impression directed at a particular object. These messages are then subject to interpretation. A person will base their interpretation on what is familiar and the knowledge already stored in their memory (Dibb, Simkin, Pride and Ferrell, 1994). Once people develop a set of beliefs and impressions about a product or event, it is difficult to change them (Crompton, 1996). This permanency exists because if people have a certain image about a product/event they become selective perceivers of future data. Selective perception means that individuals are orientated towards seeing what they expect or want to see. Selective perception from a psychological standpoint is how we view our world to create or justify our own reality (de Mooij, 2004). This means that what we wish to see in this world we will see in this world. Information received is

167

processed in a manner that harmonizes with and supports the individual's current beliefs. So although leading up to and during the event there were advertisements and various press reports encouraging locals to attend the Golf World Cup, the existing or current perceptions held by individuals of the Sandy Lane Hotel remained fixed in their minds and this overshadowed the advertisements encouraging locals to attend. What is evident is that the social divisions of the past are so etched in the minds of average Barbadians that it continues to affect how locals perceive tourism development even if social-exclusion is not the intention of planners.

During the fieldwork the advertisements in the local press which encouraged locals to attend the Golf World Cup were observed. The Golf World Cup was not exclusive to 'Tiger Woods type people and celebrities" but was instead a public event, open to the public at a charge. Special efforts were made by local authorities to stimulate local attendance. The special price of US$30.00 (£20.00) per person, per day, was exclusive to local residents on presentation of their Barbados identification card and was considered reasonable. Those interviewed thought that this price was "cheap" considering the high profile nature of the event. Children age 16 and under were admitted free when accompanied by a parent. In addition, all of the warm up rounds were free to local residents. Jack Warfield, the PGA tour's Vice-President of championship management publicly invited local residents to attend the Golf World Cup. In the Nation of December 7 (2006: 1) he was quoted: "we would like those people living here to come and watch and experience this wonderful experience (Tee Time, 2006:1)". However, despite this, because of the Sandy Lane element individuals perceived it as expensive and did not even bother to check prices. A couple who were interviewed on Accra Beach, advised: "we knew that it was at Sandy Lane, so we just thought that it would be expensive". Likewise, a local taxi driver noted: "That thing at Sandy Lane so I wouldn't waste my time checking prices". A government official, attached to the Ministry of Youth Affairs and Sport, agreed that many locals would not have attended because of the way that golf is generally promoted on the island. He argued that:

> The Golf World Cup was promoted in the local press and it is now catching on in Barbados but golf facilities are more perceived as tourist attractions. Although we have more golf courses, they seem more semi-upscale catering to the up market tourists. To get more people involve in golf they would

need to shed their image as just a thing that tourists do. I never felt encouraged to use any facility.

What this study has demonstrated is that some social exclusion can also be self-imposed. Some local residents withdrew from the desire to attend the Golf World Cup in what could be described as a self-imposed exclusion syndrome which occurred due to their perception of the event and its association with Sandy Lane despite the fact that the event was opened to the public and that the price was considered reasonable. The reasons for this self-imposition are not all clear but could include the belief that the social setting might not have been congruent with the individuals' personality or social status; or, it could even be construed as a form of protest against the establishment. Social exclusion is broadly seen as the impossibility of an individual or a social group to participate actively in the economic, cultural, political or institutional spheres of society (Loury, 2000). The concept has proved a useful tool for analysing many societies because it includes notions of 'marginality', 'poverty' and 'invisibility'. It also includes the lack of access to services, amenities, infrastructure and social cohesion. However, as this study has shown, social exclusion in sport is not always about the lack of money or access to services since the Golf World Cup was opened to the public at a reasonable price.

It is questionable whether attitudes towards the Golf World Cup would have been different had this event been hosted at the Barbados Golf and Country Club on the south coast instead of Sandy Lane on the west coast. Some local participants were of the opinion that more people might have been encouraged to attend the Golf World Cup had it been held at the Barbados Golf and Country Club because it might have been perceived as 'less intimidating'. As explained by an 18 year old male resident:

> hmmm ......I think it might have been less intimidating to some so some might have been less reluctant ....but if they didn't do more ads to invite people to it, I doubt anybody would have gone ....

A local south coast hotel manager felt that a different location would have been less intimidating but was also of the view that people would still have stayed away due to a lack of interest. She commented:

169

There is the possibility that more local people would have been more inclined to attend the event if it had been held at the Barbados Golf Club simply because it would have been a less intimidating venue. However, golf is one of the sports that you are either interested in it or you are not. If you are, then you will go where ever it goes and pay whatever price is being asked, the venue would not be a deterrent.

What is clear is that the phenomenon of social exclusion exists in the context of sport event tourism and event planners need to introduce measures to counteract this if golf events are to be successful on the island. Had there been a strategic local marketing programme some of these perceptions might have been dispelled and more locals might have been encouraged to attend. The foregoing views also draw attention to the theory of self-perception. Studies have shown that individuals withdraw from purchasing products that they are not totally comfortable with regardless of cost. Hence, an individual will resist purchasing a product that does not conform to his or her sense of self. The concept of self- perception is discussed in the next section.

6.3.1   The role of self-perception

The image that is projected of any product is important in marketing. Consumers tend to buy products that are consistent with their own perceived self-image. The theoretical background underlying self-perception argues that consumers′ sense of self can be inferred from the brands they use. It is further argued that consumers prefer products that are congruent to and reinforce the way they think about themselves or the brand with an image most like their own self-concept (Dibb, Simkin, Pride and Ferrell, 1994; Sirgy; 1982). Attitudes towards different brands influence brand decisions, in that ownership or usage of a particular brand with a particular image, appears to be consistent with consumers' own self-concept. Malhotra (1998:7) defines self-concept as the totality of individual's thoughts and feelings having reference to themselves as subjects or objects. The self-concept theory focuses on how an individual perceives him or herself. This consists of what he/she knows about her/himself; what he/she thinks about her/himself; how he/she values her/himself; and how he/she intends to enhance or defend her/himself (O'Brien, Tapia and Brown, 1997: 65). The self-concept is multidimensional as there are many possible concepts that individuals have of themselves. The self-concept includes the 'actual self', which is concerned with how

170

individuals view themselves in terms of an honest appraisal of the qualities they have or lack (Solomon, Bamossy and Askergaard 1999); the 'ideal self' which is the way that they ideally want to be; the 'social self' which represents the way that individuals perceive others in society view them; and the 'expected self' which refers to that image that falls between the actual and the ideal self-concept (Sirgy, 1982).

Collins and Kay (2003) note that social psychological factors such as how the individual perceives certain activities can also be construed as a form of social exclusion. They claim that individuals may perceive certain activities as "not for me" due to feelings of powerlessness or for the lack of certain skills such as the social, cultural or educational capital required for access to certain sports, other activities or events. Hence, the individual may tend to exclude themselves from attending golf events due to these perceptions of self. It was evident that since the golf was perceived as an event for up-market tourists, local residents thought that they would be out of place or would not fit in with the environment or atmosphere at the Golf World Cup. This conclusion can be inferred from these quotations from local residents: "It did not seem like something that locals would attend" or "it appeared more like something for west coast tourists". Similarly, "I did not feel like going. I thought that was for Tiger Woods type people and celebrities" and "my husband wanted to go but it is not the type of thing that you would go to those rich tourists".

It is argued in the marketing literature that the products purchased by consumers serve as symbols that communicate meanings to others as to how the individuals want others to see them and how they see themselves (O'Brien, Tapia and Brown, 1997). de Mooij, (2004) points out how humans value an object more favorably if it readily resembles who they are or what or where they wish to belong. This idea supports how consumers to an increasing degree give commitment to the brand if its image represents what she/he wishes to be their "ideal-self". The theoretical base of this concept thus suggests that consumers purchase products that are congruent with or reinforce the way that the consumer views his or her 'self', or the brand that conforms to the image of his or her 'self-concept', instead of consideration of the practical value of the products (Todd, 2001).

In Barbados this concept of 'self' is still likely to persist due to the colonial history and history of race relations on the island. Golf is still very much perceived as a white man's game and in the Caribbean, event today, tourists are usually perceived as coming from a more

171

powerful, relevant place thus providing the perception that things local are inferior and will not be accepted within the tourists' domain. What is clear from the narratives above is that the phenomenon of social exclusion exists in the context of sport event tourism and event planners need to introduce measures to counteract this if golf events are to be successful on the island. Had there been a strategic local communications programme that addressed these issues some of these perceptions might have been dispelled and more locals might have been encouraged to attend. Another reason why many local participants felt that the Golf World Cup was poorly attended was due to the fact that it did not attract the world's top golfers. This issue forms the basis of the next discussion.

6.4 THE ABSENCE OF SPORT ICONS

According to a Sandy Lane official it is important that the world's best golfers patronize your golf courses if you want to be recognized as a golfing destination. She explained that: "You go to one of the tournaments and try to convince the captain to come play at your facility. You don't put out an ad saying come play golf here". While it was acknowledged that the presence of major golfing stars can enhance the image of a golf course, the Golf World Cup failed to attract the top players in the golfing arena. As will be discussed later many local and international informants were of the view that the standard and the prestige of the event were diminished due to the non-appearance of Tiger Woods and other golfing stars. Informants who participated in this research felt that the poor attendance was attributed to this.

Many local residents expressed disappointment at the non-appearance of Tiger Woods and felt that the event lost its status as the showcase of world golf because of his absence. Reports in the Nation of December 7, 2006 expressed concern at the absence of top golfers. Spooner in his article 'Full Monty Ahead' notes:

> The absence of several of the world's top ranked players has been a topic for discussion. World No.1 Tiger Woods, Phil Mickelson and Jim Furyk turned down the chance to represent the United States while Els and Retief Goosen opted not to play for South Africa. This means Stewart Cink and J.J. Henry will fly the Stars and Stripes of the United States and Rory Sabbatini and Richard Sterne will team up for the Proteas. Luke Donald, the high-flying England player, said something

was taken away from the event when the leading players from the United States did not accept the invitation (Spooner, 2006e: 29).

Tiger Woods' name was mentioned in many interviews with local informants. Those who had no particular interest or affiliation to golf stated that if Woods was appearing that they might have considered attending. One local spectator, who was of the opinion that the presence of Tiger Woods would have drawn the crowd, stated: "I came to see what the event was all about but I think that if Tiger were here that a lot more people would have come out".

Belch and Belch (1999) argue that a popular celebrity will favorably influence consumers' feelings, attitudes and purchase intentions. They believe that the influence of a celebrity can enhance audience perceptions of a product. As a result, people are more likely to consume products associated with sport heroes, particularly if they believe that through consumption their own performance or lifestyle will be enhanced or their curiosity fulfilled. It was evident that Tiger Woods was an iconic symbol through which many of the local residents identified with golf as a sport. In a country where golf is not considered a mass sport, it is through Tiger Woods that locals felt some sort of affiliation or attachment to the game. A local spectator explained the poor turnout by locals: "I think that if Tiger were here that a lot more people would have come out…you know he got married here". A local sports administrator, commenting on the small crowd, felt that the poor attendance was due to the non-appearance of Tiger Woods. He commented: "I think things would have been different if Tiger Woods was appearing. You would certainly have gotten more people. To not have Tiger Woods is like having a test match at Kensington without Lara, Gale, Chanderpaul and Sarwan". A local female educator also attributed the poor turnout to the absence of the 'big names'. She claimed:

There was an expectation that some of the big names would participate, and at the last minute we were told that they were not coming - those persons who were interested (local and international), changed their minds.

Instead of the Tiger Woods and Phil Mickelson, the United States was represented by Stewart Cink and J.J. Henry. Luke Donald, one of the competing golfers, in reaction to the absence of Mickelson and Woods, commented:

173

Nothing against Stewart Cink or J.J. Henry. They are very strong players…, But to have to go that far down on the list, it weakens the overall feel of the tournament just a little bit because they could potentially field a much stronger team (Spooner, 2006e: 29).

The presence of the game's top players at any sporting event is important because it raises the profile and maintains the prestigious image of the event (Gwinner, 1997). In the Barbados market the presence of the game's most popular players might have held even more importance considering that Barbados does not have a golfing tradition. Belch and Belch (1999) argue that celebrities have "stopping power" in that they can draw attention to a product. It is recognized that Tiger Woods has done much to raise the profile, and has drawn attention to the game of golf in a way that no other golfer has (Farrell, Karels, Monfort, and McClatchey, 2000). Similarly, by getting married in Barbados, Woods has done much to stimulate attention to the sport on the island. Consequently, Tiger Woods has become the iconic symbol of golf in Barbados in much the same way that David Beckham has become the iconic symbol of football in many parts of the world (see Bolsmann and Parker, 2007). As a local sports administrator explained: "I feel people here would have gone to see Tiger Woods. Barbadians are curious people and many did not get to see him when he married here".

The concept of iconic symbols is particularly important when promoting tourism and sport events especially in environments where the game is not popular among the residents. In this case residents may only identify with the game through its iconic personalities. The presence of the iconic symbols can be used as a 'magnet' drawing people to the sport so that it is the iconic personality that people may want to see rather than the sport itself. In Barbados numerous local residents said that they "really wanted to see Tiger Woods" or that "if Tiger Woods were here, I would have gone". The concept of iconic symbols may be more relevant in Barbados, since the island does not have a golfing tradition. As a result, the Barbadian public cannot draw on any local golfing icons in order to identify with the sport. Consequently they turn instead to the international icons of golf with whom they are familiar in order to gain any attachment or affiliation with the sport. Basil (1996) notes that individuals, who are exposed to personalities over time through the media, even if not in person, are expected to develop a sense of intimacy and identification with that

174

celebrity. People not only consume movies, television programmes or sports they also consume the 'stars' (Pringle, 2004). The point is that people also consume celebrity since celebrity, consumption, and identification with a celebrity, can be a form of vicarious escape (McCutcheon, Lange and Houran, 2002). Many local participants kept making reference to Tiger Woods with statements like. "I not going …Well Tiger Woods ain't there", "Tiger Woods would have made a difference" or "I would have gone to see Tiger Woods".

Sports performers become famous for their physical and cognitive abilities, their off field exploits, their charismatic demeanour. However, much of the sports literature suggests that visitors to sport events are more interested in teams rather than individual players (Chalip, 2000). Only one study (Funk, Mahonhony, Nakazawa and Hirakara, 2001) addressed the issue of individual sport starts and how they affect attendance at a sporting event. Qualitative data in their study of attendance at the FIFA Women's World Cup suggests that sports stars could be catalysts for stimulating interest in a sport event. They suggest that spectators may associate players with the function that they serve rather than as individual personalities on the field, but also recognised that further research is required in order to shed more light on this area. The absence of golf's most prominent icons at the Golf World Cup meant that for some individuals there was no incentive to attend. In golf the presence of individual players rather than teams is more significant due to the nature of the competition. The authorities in Barbados neglected to recognise that golf is an individual sport (Nicholls, Roslow and Dublish, 1999) so spectators are oriented towards supporting individual players rather than teams. Because it is an individual sport, it is easy to segregate an individual athlete's performance. For instance, during golf tournaments when a golfer is in contention to win a major tournament they receive increased media coverage (Farrell, Karels, Monfort and McClatchney, 2000). This explains why at the Golf World Cup spectators kept on making reference to the absence of individual players rather than teams.

A local golf enthusiast was keen to explain why the presence of specific performers was important. He claimed that individual golfers have their followings, so people would travel to see individual players perform rather than national teams. The Golf World Cup is unique in the sense that it is a team competition, unlike other PGA tours or golf tournaments, which are individually contested. This Barbadian golf fan explained:

175

People are not going to come from America just to see American golfers. They want to see the stars. If the stars are not performing they are not going to bother. Tiger has a special gathering. He has 50/50 fans. 50% will travel anywhere to see him succeed and the other 50% want to see him fail.

Two local ladies agreed that the presence of Tiger Woods would have made a difference. They claimed: "If Tiger were here, he would have attracted more locals and international people". Local spectators and non-spectators were constantly asking for Tiger Woods: "Tiger Woods…. should be here doing clinics"; " Tiger Woods not being here has taken away from the event" and "I came all this way to see Tiger Woods, this is very disappointing". A local tourism official agreed, claiming: "Tiger Woods would have attracted more people". A local professor was of the view: "They needed to have Tiger Woods, because as a black man many Barbadians would have identified with him".

One of the competitors in the tournament offered a possible explanation for the non-appearance of the Americans. Padraig Harrington was quoted in the Nation of December 7, 2006:

> I would defend the Americans…The Europeans, we're all playing in season now but it's out of season for the United States, so this date is particularly penal for them. This tournament needs a better date, and possibly every four years (Spooner, 2006e: 29).

A report in the Nation of September 27, 2006 confirmed that Woods would not be appearing. Instead, it was revealed that Woods had accepted an offer to travel to Dubai. The report stated:

> Tiger Woods, the world No.1 and the most popular player in the history of the game, was expected to be part of the tournament. Organisers however announced on Monday that the legend, who was married at Sandy Lane almost two years ago, accepted a more lucrative offer to play in Dubai, and was skipping the US$4 million World Cup show-piece (Spooner, 2006f: 43A).

176

Although the exact cost of Tiger Woods' non-appearance in Barbados is not known, it has drawn attention to an important issue - the importance of sports stars in influencing attendance at a golfing event. According to commentators, having the top golfers perform at your event is significant for marketing. This point was also raised by a local resident in a letter published by the Nation on May 11, 2006. The letter stated:

> Permit me a few lines in your publication to address the tourism bosses regarding the Golf World Cup scheduled for Barbados in December. Mr Minister, I know a thing or two about golf and I put it to you that if the big names like Tiger Woods, Mickleson, Vijay Singh and so on do not come to Barbados for this event, as they have avoided it in recent years, Barbados will be left holding a bag of meaningless advertising value and a bill of much more than $3 million! (The $3m golf question, 2007: 10).

Similarly, a Sandy Lane official commented:

> If you hold an international event where you attract some of the very best players in that particular sport, it gives credibility to the destination, it gives credibility to the course. We might have always said in our publicity, in our brochures, how wonderful the golf experience at Sandy Lane is, but that is just us saying it. The testimony really to powerful public relations is when you get some of the world's top players playing at your facility and the exposure that will give.

It was clear that local residents felt that the absence of stars like Tiger Woods, lowered the importance, prestige and credibility ordinarily attached to PGA events and this significantly affected local support for the Gold World Cup.

This study has also clearly demonstrated the importance of local involvement in the planning and decision-making processes involved in staging a mega event. Local residents were of the view that their desires were not considered by the authorities and that the Golf World Cup bore no cultural relevance to the local community. These themes are now discussed at length.

177

6.5 LOCAL INVOLVEMENT

The sustainable tourism plan for Barbados (2002: 10) states that planners and policy makers must recognize the role of local communities in the planning, development and operation of tourism if the industry is to be successful. It acknowledges that local communities are becoming more aware of their rights and are prepared to express their views in the media and through public demonstrations. Hiller (2000:449) acknowledges that:

> One of the hallmarks of good development programmes is that they involve the community in an on-going way. Ideally, the community affected has determined independently that a course of action is desirable, and then it is a matter of consultation to decide how, when and at what pace to institute changes.

Local residents felt that the reason many locals did not attend the Golf World Cup was because authorities ignored the local market in the planning, decision-making and marketing. As a local female educator explained: "I did not go because…well there was not a local thrust to the marketing". Other local respondents were of the opinion that the authorities neglected the local market in their marketing campaigns. As one male resident explained: "I found that they only started advertising about two to three days before. The ad was weird with a voice over by an American. Thought that was weird, it didn't seem like a local ad for local people". Similarly, another resident commented: "They should have advertised it earlier. Most Bajans did not know about it…it wasn't ringing in your ears…"

Local residents just like the international tourists, reported limited or no awareness of the Golf World Cup. While there was no firm local dimension to the marketing thrust, what little advertising that was done in the local market failed to break through the 'noise' and 'clutter' caused by the advertisements for the Cricket World Cup. Several local participants indicated that they knew about the Cricket World Cup and were aware of the advertisements for cricket but not the golf. A Christ Church resident noted:

> It did not seem to be very important. They did not emphasize its importance. When I saw the billboard across the bridge, I thought they were promoting the cricket, but, when I looked closely the second time, I realized it was the golf. I saw World

Cup and I thought, cricket, since the cricket was being emphasized for over a year. Locally, it wasn't hyped. 80% of Bajans did not know about the golf until four days before.

Likewise, a local spectator who visited the Golf World Cup event on the last day reported that:

We did not know about this event...It came outta nowhere....we only found out yesterday when they were begging locals to come out and support the event. Me and my wife thought that they were talking about the cricket but later realized that there was something big going on at Sandy Lane so I came to see what it was all about.

Similarly, a resident in Bridgetown noted: "We have been hearing about the World Cup [cricket] for over a year now, but the golf, it isn't ringing in your ears".

Getz (1997) warned of the danger of alienating local communities in the staging of an event as it may create the perception that community needs are being ignored or that residents are not valued as much as the tourists. Some of the local participants felt that locals were deliberately excluded from the event and that their importance as spectators was only recognised when the expected tourists turnout was not realised. A local resident thought that: "they did not emphasise its importance... They should have advertised it here earlier so that people would have been talking about it, encouraging other people to go". One local resident from the south coast felt that the value of the local market was only realised because of the poor turnout by international tourists. They commented: "I realised that after the bad turnout there was a mad rush to get local people to turn up". Similarly, another local resident noted: "They were giving away tickets and all then, trying to get locals to come". In addition, a local sport administrator commented: "they get bout here and pitch this thing as if they only wanted rich and famous and then when nobody ain't come now they trying to get the locals to come". This was the common view held by local informants. Many felt that the event was never meant for local consumption but when the poor spectator turnout was realized there was a mad rush in the media to get locals to come out and support the tournament. A female customs officer commented: "they only advertised it for locals to attend as volunteers...not spectators". A local tour operator was of the view

179

that more emphasis should have been placed on getting locals to come and that the small crowd was noted in the international media. They commented: "I heard about the poor turn out on ESPN and felt embarrassed. To have such a poor crowd sends a bad message in that the island is not worth visiting. They should have considered the local market more".

Many local residents also expressed the view that the Golf World Cup was not culturally relevant to Barbados as golf is not a sport that is popular amongst the masses. As a local visitor to the Golf World Cup noted.

> That is not our culture. The Barbadian people are not going to find this attractive (referring to the golf). Golf is not the culture here, they do not understand it. You have to develop cricket; football and road tennis. I guess the golf is good for those who are interested in golf but not much else.

Likewise, a local hotel manager stated:

> It puzzles me that they would bring an event like this to Barbados and expect it to be financially viable. I mean it doesn't make sense considering that 99% of Bajans[9] don't play golf, don't know two hoots about the game and have probably never even seen inside a golf course.

Ritchie (1984: 9) cautioned against developing events that encourage activities, which contradict the cultural values of the society. He claims that events which try to impose lifestyles or behaviours, which alienate significant segments of the population, will not leave the expected and desirable legacies. Consistent with Ritchie's position, an official at the National Sports Council felt that the government's approach in developing sports tourism was wrong and that sports tourism needs to develop so that the whole population can participate and benefit. He stated:

> That event designed for west coast people... Now the Cricket World Cup is a good event because it will bring people and the whole country can participate... They need to look at sports tourism holistically and work closely with the national

---

9   Bajan is a colloquial term for Barbadian.

180

associations. Get football, basketball, hockey so that low-end hotels can also benefit.

Similarly, an official at the Ministry of Sport thought that:

> Sport is a multi-million dollar business but our cricket and football facilities are no way near world class standards. They need to promote netball, volleyball, cricket, basketball, football, car racing, horse racing, these are mass sports.... Golf and lawn tennis are not mass sports here. ...there is a need to develop other facilities... at the micro level there is a need for playing fields and pavilions...

The issue of cultural relevance draws attention to Fredline's (2000) work. She notes that unless imported events are perceived to embody the values that are consistent with the socio-cultural values of residents; and unless they meet the expectations of the host community, they are unlikely to be supported. This study supports the view that when residents feel that an event has been imposed upon them by external forces they are least likely to lend their support to the event (Getz, 1991a).

Residents complained about not being involved in the decision to host the Golf World Cup. According to the legacy document, a committee of 75 individuals from all walks of life came together to craft a legacy vision for Barbados (Legacy Barbados, 2006). As stated by one local resident involved in the legacy planning for Barbados:

> A legacy sub-committee to the Board of World Cup Barbados (WCB) was formed, together with a series of teams totalling about 75 persons, representing a wide cross-section of Barbados. These teams have worked to craft the Legacy Vision, select the Target Areas, and identify what are the likely Strategic Objectives for us to focus on to deliver the legacy. The next step is for all persons with an interest in Barbados to share their thoughts and make the plans the best that we can make them, as we strive to make Barbados the number one place for all of us to live, work, play and invest!

The legacy document indicates plans for *Junior Think Tanks* involving schoolchildren and a *National Think Tank* and makes a plea for all individuals to contribute to legacy by forwarding their ideas to *Legacy*

181

Barbados and to participate in the open forums. However, although the Legacy Barbados document makes claims about community participation there was no evidence that suggested the actual level of awareness among the local population of such forums; or, how individuals or community groups were selected to take part, for instance, in the *National Think Tank* or the *Junior Think Tank*.

Local participants seemed oblivious to any community consultation programmes. The findings support Hall's (2006) claims that mega sport events are developed by undemocratic processes often with anarchic decision-making processes and a lack of transparency. The findings in this study support this view and are further exemplified by this narrative from a local customs officer:

> Authorities here tend to make decisions without doing proper research or public consultation. Everything seems to be secretive. These events are high-risk events and to this day no studies have shown any tangible rate of return. These people always keep the public in the dark about these things. Not surprised that nobody came. Locals were not encouraged to attend. They promoted it in the press but it was more for locals to attend as volunteers not as spectators.

Similarly, a sports official noted:

> Man, the Prime Minister doing as he like. They don't consult the people about nothing; they just get in they big houses and think up these things without any thought of how they will affect the people. When I think of all the money they wasting without proper consultation as to what the people want.

Commentators (Hall, 2006; Horne and Manzenreiter, 2006; Lenskyj, 2000) also contend that governments develop mega sport events in the interests of global flows rather than the local communities. These commentators contend that in this respect they represent a shift of public funds to satisfy private interests. Consistent with this view, many of the local residents felt that Golf World Cup was designed for the wealthy Sandy Lane and west coast enterprises. A car rental agency manager expressed the view that the Golf World Cup was mainly a Sandy Lane event that benefited only Sandy Lane. They claimed: "Barbados does not need any promotion, it is already well known, this event is a Sandy Lane event geared towards Sandy

Lane guests and it promotes Sandy Lane and no one else". A local hotel manager was of the same opinion:

> …. it was beneficial to the upscale hotels like Sandy Lane and Royal Pavilion and some of the west coast villas but in terms of guests who would spend money visiting local attractions and restaurants etc. that was not the kind of crowd that came into the island.

A local owner of a south coast hotel expressed the same sentiment:

> Well I don't know who is supposed to benefit from this golf but I can tell you who ain't benefiting. My hotel running at 50%. The golf event is evidently for just the luxury west coast properties. I think they will be the ones to benefit along with the west coast restaurants and transportation services. If we are going to try to attract events to Barbados, I really think that they need to go after events that have a wide market base so that all entities can benefit, not just a few – it sends the wrong message.

Similarly, another hotel manager criticized the Golf World Cup on the basis that:

> There may be the claim that 'world-class' events held on the island offer some long-term benefit to the people as a whole. But I believe that as with so many other ventures undertaken here, they are designed to benefit only the 'affluent few' that can afford the initial investment. When I think about the people who accepted the offer from government to build home accommodation for Cricket World Cup that never got used (which incidentally they are now paying for and desperately trying to rent out to recoup monies to pay back the loans), it is clear that no serious, long-term thought is given to these ventures and how they impact society as a whole.

Clearly, and as the above narratives illustrate, in Barbados, questions were posed about for whom and why are these events held. As demonstrated, the views of the participants held consistent with the views in the literature that these events are often staged to support the wealthy and the affluent few while ignoring the impacts that they have

183

on the rest of the community. One of the themes that arose from the local perspective was that the event lacked a local flavor and this theme is discussed in the section that follows.

6.6 LACK OF LOCAL FLAVOUR

A number of residents drew attention to the view that the Golf World Cup held little relevance to them for a variety of reasons. Many commented about the event's 'lack of appeal' and that the event bore no cultural relevance to Barbados. A local sport administrator, attached to the National Sports Council, commented about the lack of appeal associated with the Golf World Cup. He commented:

> This golf just don't appeal to me....the government went about this thing all wrong. If they want to develop sport tourism in this country they need to do so holistically.... At football for instance, we get people involved by providing a range of attractions to get the people out. We have the dancers and cheerleaders, the DJ and you know one time we even had 'Crossfire' perform[10], but this event is bland, real bland.

Fieldwork observations and semi-structured interviews with local residents revealed that many other aspects of the Golf World Cup lacked a local flavour. Not only was Sandy Lane awarded the event but the contract for other services. For example, the contract for the provision of souvenirs was awarded to Sandy Lane, but none of the souvenirs were of an indigenous nature. Sandy Lane Hotel was responsible for providing the souvenirs available to visitors at the Golf World Cup. The souvenir shop was located at the entrance to the event and provided a wide range of memorabilia with the events' logo. This included golf shirts and t-shirts, golf balls, miniature golf clubs, mugs, short pants, key rings and clocks. The attendant confirmed that the merchandise was imported and there was no sign of any Barbados made memorabilia.

When questioned on the sources of origin of the souvenirs, the shop attendant advised proudly: "this is all imported stuff, they are from all over the world. New York, China, Japan, all over. Oh no, there is no stuff here from Barbados"! The prices of these souvenirs were exorbitant, a point that was highlighted in a local newspaper. The

---

[10]   'Crossfire' is a popular 'soca' band from Barbados. 'Soca' is the traditional music of Barbados.

local press was of the view that the prices were only what the affluent could afford and that what was on offer was way beyond what the average person would be prepared to pay. The Nation of December 14, 2006 reported:

> ....I had a look around the pro-shop... I wasn't looking for Sandy Lane items, but something with the golf championship logo that I could keep. Well, unless I wanted to spend my whole Christmas budget on one item, I declined. An insulated drinking tumbler with a patch of the logo on the inside was at least BDS$45 [£15.25]. A set of four small tumblers was BDS$200 [£75.00]. Yes, these were duty-paid prices and as a local that's what I'm told I had to pay. But the worst was a golf cap and T-shirt bundle for children. Looked really nice and I thought I might get these to give to my children (who were with me at the time), but when I finally looked at the price the set was US$95 [£30.74] duty-free, BDS$180 [£65.00] duty-free and a whopping BDS$450 [£180.50] duty-paid price. This price for a golf cap and a T-shirt for a child? Okay, I know some unsuspecting foreigners will pay the US$95 [£30.74] duty-free price for the set to take home for their children, but I've lost out on being able to give my children something special to remind them of this event. Trust me when I tell you, either plan on having deep pockets for souvenirs of the Cricket World Cup, or plan on going home empty-handed (Golf souvenirs way beyond one's pocket, 2007: 18).

While it is understandable that Sandy Lane would have wanted a stake in the event, it appears as though no consideration was made for community entrepreneurs to ply their trade at the golf course. There was no vendors' market for souvenirs or local snacks. This is surprising considering that while some visitors might have been able to afford Sandy Lane prices for souvenirs other individuals might have welcomed the opportunity to select from more budget options. Instead, Sandy Lane Hotel provided the souvenirs while a local catering company provided the food.

Even the food lacked the local flavour. Although a local concessionaire provided the food, the menu at the snack counter was not illustrative of the local cuisine. This extract from the observation diary recorded the menu options:

185

The menu consisted of mainly cold snacks including sandwiches. There were ham and cheese sandwiches and tuna sandwiches. The only hot food was grilled hamburgers and hot dogs. There was an assortment of both alcoholic and non-alcoholic drinks including soft drinks, local and foreign beer, rum, wine, gin and tonic. There was no sign of local delicacies such as peas and rice, fish cakes, flying fish cutters, rice and stew, mauby or ginger beer. The snacks on offer were Walker's crisps. No local snacks such as plantain chips or breadfruit chips were on offer and sweets included Cadbury chocolate bars rather than the local sugar or nut cakes.

When the researcher questioned the nature of the menu on offer, the attendant at the 'Café 66', the local catering concessionaires for the event responded: "Oh! the PGA set the menu and prices".

This was an alarming revelation that raised the issue concerning residents' power and control over tourism development. In this research it is clearly demonstrated that transnational organisations still maintain some dominance over the tourism industry in small island states. Lewis (2002) drew attention to this when she alluded to the view that the locus of control over the Caribbean tourism industry continues to shift from the local people to foreign interest. Moreover, this occurrence gives credence to the views that event tourism must have a local focus. Why would the PGA, a foreign and independent organisation, dictate the menu and prices of a locally owned and private catering firm? The answer is simple. Considering the menu on offer, it is clear that the catering was designed to cater for a more European/American customer and was not for local palates.

Lenskyj (2000: 195) draws attention to the power of international mega event organisations and claims that they have become more like transnational corporations that have increasingly exploited young athletes and labour for corporate aggrandisement and profit. Barbados, for instance, had reportedly paid US$3 million (£1.5 million) to the PGA to bring this event to Barbados, but did the local organisers have any power or say in how the event would be run and organised and how the local community will be accommodated? According to a Barbados Tourism Authority official, as the major sponsor, they were forced to comply with many restrictions.

We had to comply with all sorts of rules and regulations, even despite being a sponsor. We had to put our welcome booth in a specific space as dictated by the PGA, we were restricted as to where we could display our promotional materials, signs and banners and we could not even conduct a survey with visitors.

A Sandy Lane official explained: "This event belongs to the PGA and that means that everyone has to comply with PGA regulations. This event is only being held at our golf course, so there are certain things that we cannot permit without conferring with the PGA". Likewise, an official at the Barbados Tourism Authority commented:

> I know that the event did not have a Caribbean flavour but there are restrictions that prevented us from doing more than we did...I mean you even have rules as to where you can put a banner so any entertainment, cultural events would have been outta the question.

The continued domination of Caribbean tourism by external entities is a cause for concern. It is one thing when these entities pay for the right to set up business on the islands through taxes and other levies but it is certainly another when Caribbean people pay them to come. With the Barbados government paying the PGA US$3 million to host this event, it is alarming that the tourism authorities did not have much say in how the event was to be organized. Another reason suggested for the poor local turnout was the lack of knowledge about golf in the local market. These views are discussed next.

6.7 THE NEED FOR EDUCATION

The findings from the semi-structured interviews with local residents show that respondents believed that the reason why local patrons were poorly represented at the event was because golf is not a popular sport on the island. As a local spectator explained: "golf is not in the top ten sports in Barbados. Cricket, soccer, basketball and paddle tennis are popular". Spectators were of the view that more effort was required to get locals interested in the game. A group of four golf resort employees commented:

> We are landscapers and caddies and therefore have knowledge of the game. We tried to encourage our peers to come but the concern was they wouldn't understand what's going on. There needs to be more education and knowledge about the game if

locals are to participate. Locals are not going to spend that money when you are not going to understand anything.

Many local spectators and other residents, recognising the need for more education among local people, expressed the view that the authorities must target the schools if more people in Barbados are to become interested in golf. For instance, a local spectator noted: "they would need junior clinics for kids", while another was of the view that free tickets should have been made available to school children so that they could experience the event and learn about golf at the same time. Others commented that golfing stars like Tiger Woods and Phil Mickelson should have been present conducting clinics for school children. This resident argued:

> Golf facilities are at resorts with no access for locals. They need to start a driving range and they need to start promoting golf in the schools. Have inter-school competitions for youngsters. How they are promoted gives you the impression that they are just for tourists. They are not promoted for locals.

The Barbadian competitor at the Golf World Cup also expressed the view that the key to stimulating interest in golf is through education, particularly the youth. He stressed:

> I believe that the growth of golf in the Caribbean depends on the implementation of golf programmes in the school system. If students could experience golf at a young age, and their skills could be honed and their minds trained, golf will grow quickly. More driving ranges and golf courses are also needed, but without the young people of the region being given the opportunity to learn to play, these facilities will not have enough support (Select Barbados, 2006: 40).

One of the positive impacts of mega sport events is that they can initiate activities and behaviours which would contribute to the overall wellbeing of the community. One such activity is the increased participation in sport (Ritchie, 1984). The legacy vision of Barbados states that one of the major objectives of the legacy programme would be to encourage participation and excellence in sport among the population. At the end of the tournament it was announced that the Barbadian competitor in the Golf World Cup would be donating his earnings to construct a driving range on the island. Peter Johnson who represented the island in the Golf World Cup, was quoted in the Nation of December 9, 2006: "I have no problem with giving back and I hope it goes a long way in helping to produce more golfers on the island. There are a lot of people here with a passion for the game and I hope I can be of help in this regard" (Spooner, 2006h). The report went on to explain that the donation will act as part of a public outreach programme by the Barbados Golfing Association which will be used to establish the driving range so "that 278,000 Bajans can become involved in the sport" (Spooner, 2006h) The driving range was subsequently opened on 26 March 2010. The following section discusses the benefits that the event is perceived to have bought Barbados.

6.8 PERCEIVED COMMUNITY BENEFITS

Data from the semi-structured interviews showed that residents had mixed views about the benefits of the Golf World Cup to the community. Those who supported the event expressed views that were consistent with the work of Waitt (2003) who identified civic pride amongst local communities as one of the positive outcomes of hosting events. Others comment on their effectiveness in building awareness and in promoting tourism in specific markets (Getz, 1991b; Hall, 1992a; 1997; Moutinho and Witt, 1994; Westerbeek, Turner and Ingerson, 2002). It is on this basis that the majority of local participants gave their support to Barbados hosting the Golf World Cup. The majority of those interviewed, despite their lack of interest in the event, were of the opinion that the Golf World Cup was good for Barbados in terms of the publicity that the island was getting in the international media. For example, a female sales clerk employed at a west coast pharmacy, noted that: "The island looks really nice and they have been showing you Harrison's Cave and other island attractions. This is really good for Barbados because of the media promotion". Another resident, a college student, said that although they were not interested in attending the event they supported Barbados hosting the event based on the coverage that the island was receiving in the media. He commented:

> Hopefully all this attention would dispel the myth about us being a third world country. Many tourists come here thinking that we are primitive but now they can see for themselves that we can work hard and be like everybody else.

A taxi driver mentioned that it was particularly pleasing to see Barbados being the focus of international attention: "now they will see that this is a modern country". Three local ladies who attended the Golf World Cup on the Sunday said: "this is a modern country, it's well developed, people overseas will see that now". Two other female residents supported this type of promotion stating that: "we prefer this to the type of promotion when the Barbados Tourism Authority brought travel agents to Barbados a few years ago and gave them spending money. We didn't like that at all". Similarly, an official in the Ministry of Sport was of the view that: "the three million spent to bring the event here is nothing, you will make that back in no time, just from the promotion alone". Some residents said that they would rather watch the event on television so that they could observe how the island was being showcased in the international media. Reports from local residents indicated that many of the island's tourist attractions were the focus of attention, including the beaches, gardens, the landscaped grounds at Sandy Lane and Harrison's Cave. According to one respondent: "commentators spoke about the beauty of the golf course and the green monkey; and they also promoted the other islands – Trinidad". A taxi driver was particularly pleased at the media outcome. He stated: "This and now Rihanna[11], man his is the best place in the world". In the local media, editorials in the national newspaper continuously made comments about the event boosting the island's image.

However, some residents expressed ambivalent views about the benefits derived from hosting the Golf World Cup. For instance, a local resident of English origin questioned the value of all this publicity. He commented:

> Hosting these things is good for the Caribbean but I question the money. Will we see the benefits? It is nice seeing Barbados promoted, it promotes Barbados and the Caribbean but at the end of the day what will we gain in the long-term? For instance, if the Indians watch it will they then visit Barbados?

---

[11]   'Rihanna' is an international pop star that was born and educated in Barbados. At the time of the Golf World Cup 'Rihanna' was named Billboard magazine's best female artist, becoming the first Barbadian artist to claim the award.

Other local participants thought that hosting the Golf World Cup on the basis of promoting Barbados was unnecessary. A local car rental supplier was of the view that "Barbados does not need any promotion, it is already well known". Another local resident thought: "Barbados needs to be careful with all this promotion if not the island would become common. The beauty of Barbados is, it is a little secret to be discovered".

A Front Desk clerk at a major hotel felt that the hosting of events was a good excuse to beautify the island, particularly Bridgetown. He claimed that:

> Although the publicity is good on ESPN the major benefit would be in the infrastructure projects. The river bus terminal, the roads, beautification of Bridgetown, these are things that should have been done long time but are now being done. The stench at the Constitution River is bad though but the work to the Swing Bridge is good.

Scholars (Emery, 2002) have noted how the finances used to host mega sport events is often money that is redirected from social services including housing and education. In Barbados, some of the participants felt that the money being directed to host events needed to be spent on social services or providing sport facilities for local communities. An official in the Ministry of Sport expressed the following concern:

> They need to realise that Barbados is still a third world country. We have other areas that need special attention where money could be better spent. Public transport for instance, we need more buses on the road. There are too many bad roads, potholes. We need another hospital, three hospitals not enough on this island; the Queen Elizabeth [hospital] has outgrown its usefulness. We need better accommodation for public servants, the offices of the library, drug service and attorney general. There is a need for adequate facilities for children with behavioural disorders and the need for trained professionals in preparing children for employment.

This official further explained:

Even if they want to develop sport tourism they need to build cricket and football pavilions in communities where there is a need. Many pavilions are in a state of disrepair, playing fields are needed. They need to develop cycling and basketball facilities and facilities for track and field and athletics. They keep talking about world-class facilities but many of our facilities are not world-class standards. They need to stop using so much land for golf and concentrate in using the land for other sport facilities for locals.

Similarly, this sports official argued:

They are spending a lot of unnecessary money, they just getting bout here and wasting taxpayers' well-earned dollars. There is nothing wrong spending money for development but it should be spent where it is most needed. For instance the Barbados Football Association need a new stadium so that we can develop football which is the sport of the majority of people but instead they promoting Sandy Lane. Sandy Lane could look after itself.

The views of this hotel manager were congruent with the views expressed in the preceding narratives:

I do not believe that there were any extraordinary benefits realised by Barbados from hosting the World Cup in December 2006. Maybe it was beneficial to the up-scale hotels like Sandy Lane and Royal Pavilion and some of the West Coast Villas but in terms of guests who would spend money visiting local attractions and restaurants etc. that was not the kind of crowd that came into the island.

These comments indicate that the staging of mega events will generate perceived benefits along three dimensions – those that are positive, those that are negative and those that are ambivalent (Fredline, 2000). The challenge for the planners would be to ensure that harmony is achieved between the needs of the visitor and the local stakeholder while at the same time ensuring the sustainability of the tourism product within the destination. There must be a proper balance between the economic, cultural and human objectives. Public consultation programmes must be grounded in good public relations

192

programmes in order to build awareness of the event and the public forums. Civic society must be aware of the channels of participation even though there will always be the difficulty of obtaining consensus on controversial issues.

6.9   A CASE FOR EVENT TOURISM IN BARBADOS – THE LOCAL PERSPECTIVE

Local residents expressed opposing views about the type of events that they would like to see hosted in Barbados. Some respondents felt that if Barbados were to host events, they should fit in with the country's infrastructure and the whole country should be able to benefit. For instance, this Barbados Community College student felt that the tropical weather should be the impetus from which events can develop. He commented:

> in any case....tennis would be cool, can't happen though, but water sports, surfing, anything cool like that are fun beach stuff ...beach volleyball if possible too was my fancy because it would fit with the tropics… surfing as well ... it would make sense to hold them here ....so I guess yea ...we wouldn't have to create resources for that stuff ...we already have them ....and just utilise our resources rather than make new ones...and don't host another one any time soon ....we need time to recover ...plus we don't have the infrastructure for it and they are unpredictable and you don't know what gonna happen...well golf wasn't that impactful ...so it didn't make a difference.

A local sports official commented that events should have mass appeal:

> Get football, basketball, hockey so that low-end hotels can also benefit. Football is a global sport and would attract fans from all over the world. For winter breaks especially like training. They need to develop facilities for other sports where money can be made. They need to stage events so that the whole country can participate.

A female hotel manager agreed:

> I think the general public in Barbados is entirely more supportive of events like Special Olympics and International

193

Senior games...Again, these events are not too intimidating. You don't have to have special knowledge of them in order to enjoy them and they are events that are very relatable to the everyday person as all of us may in some way be close to or know of someone with disabilities or that are elderly. Cricket is also one of the events that will always have a wide appeal so we can't go wrong there when it comes to attracting local and overseas audiences.

Opposition to the staging of mega events was expressed by some of the residents interviewed. For instance a female educator commented: "I don't want any of them here because then next year I gonna have to pay". A sports administrator was of the view that:

> The government needs to deal with pressing issues. I think they need to deal with poverty. They keep saying that we are a first world country and that we ain't have no poverty but the truth is that the poverty there, they hiding it. O.K, so what, it may not be much but still they need to deal with things like that before they think of entertaining mega events.

A resident from Christ Church expressed agitation at the hosting of events on the island. He stated: "All these events doing is making me miserable. All the road dig up, you can't pass, and the dust – can't wait till it's all over".

Construction work was evident all over the island during the period of the Golf World Cup. The fieldwork diary noted extensive road works taking place. The ABC highway was being widened from two lanes to four lanes from the exit at Wildey, Christ Church to the Warrens exit in St. Michael. In the Fontabelle area, the road was being repaired resulting in so much dust that the researcher had to close her car windows when travelling in the area. From here one could see the construction taking place at the new Kensington Oval for the Cricket World Cup in March and April 2007. In addition, during the dates of the Golf World Cup, major road closures and diversions were enforced. Newspaper notices advised motorists of closures in the St. James area on Bennetts Road from Norwoods to the Ronald Mapp Highway. These closures took place during rush hour from 6.00am to 6.00pm from Tuesday, December 5 to Sunday, December 10, 2006. It seemed rather strange that the Barbados authorities would add to the inconveniences caused by construction works by staging the Golf

World Cup. In addition, when travelling out of Bridgetown during the rush hour periods, there were traffic build-ups on the highways out of the city as the police gave the right-of-way to the large construction vehicles engaged in the regeneration process.

6.10 CONCLUSION

This chapter has presented the findings from a local perspective. It was particularly concerned with the reasons why the authorities hosted this event and why many local visitors did not attend the Golf World Cup. One of the major themes discussed was the impact of perception on decision-making. Perception of the Sandy Lane Resort and golf as a sport had an impact on how local residents perceived the event and their subsequent attitude towards the Golf World Cup. Consistent with the work of Gwinner (1997) the findings provided evidence to show that an event's image was not only a prerequisite for attaining sponsorship but it also affects attendance and the willingness of potential visitors to participate.

A major finding from the local perspective is that residents felt that the event was socially exclusive. Some residents described the event as 'intimidating' and felt that had the venue been different that there might have been more interest. This led to the conclusion that local residents might have suffered from a self-imposed social exclusion syndrome due to the impression that the event did not conform to the way individuals perceived themselves. This perception was on the basis that the event was designed for wealthy tourists and did not conform to the cultural values and traditions of the majority of Barbadians.

The absence of major international golfing stars from the competition was also identified as an issue that negatively impacted visitation among local spectators. Furthermore, local residents felt that the absence of stars like Tiger Woods, lowered the importance and prestige ordinarily attached to PGA events. Many of them thought that local input was lacking from the event due to the non-participation of the community in the decision process. Consistent with the literature on mega events, locals supported the event on the basis of the international media coverage received, particularly from a tourism perspective.

Chapters five and six have shown the importance of stakeholders' support in the successful staging of a mega event in Barbados. The evidence shows that diverse perceptions and

195

expectations exist between the stakeholder groups studied. Perceptions exist on three levels: Negative, positive and ambivalent. This study proves that event organisers must ensure that there is an appropriate match between the objectives of the tourism authorities, the expectations of tourists visiting for the event and the desire of the host community if events are to reap the maximum benefits for all those concerned. The next chapter presents a summary of this study and recommendations are made for event tourism in Barbados.

7 - CHAPTER SEVEN
SU MMARY & THE WAY FORWARD

7.1.1 THE INTERNATIONAL PERSPECTIVE

Through semi-structured interviews, participant observation and the examination of documents a number of important contextual issues related to the Golf World Cup, 2006 and event tourism in Barbados were identified. The issues therein will now be discussed as conclusions are drawn and recommendations made.

A significant finding from the international perspective was that many participants thought that the event was 'lacking in atmosphere'. Although this may have been part of the consequence of the poor spectator turn-out, event visitors were constantly asking for side attractions. Many commented that the "event was boring". The semi-structured interviews with international visitors at the Golf World Cup showed that many spectators attended the event not only to enjoy good golf, but to 'socialise', or to 'mingle with the stars'. Many were asking for more things to do such as cultural activities or golf clinics. Many participants felt that the event's poor spectator turnout was due to the event's 'lack of appeal' and lack of side attractions and fringe activities. The findings suggest that event organisers in Barbados will need to think beyond the sports product if they wish to appeal to a wide audience and to yield high customer satisfaction. This finding supports the views in the literature that special events may need to be augmented to cater to a variety of audiences (Garcia, 2001; Green, 2001). In fact, sports marketers claim that sport events that only cater to the 'fans' will not be financially viable due to the different levels and types of fandom that exists. For instance, some fans watch the sport on television but will not go to the arena to see the event in its live setting; some follow the scores in the press and others are content to purchase memorabilia. So, many of those who came to the Golf World Cup to watch golf came looking for more than just good golf but for an array of attractions combined with a holiday.

This raises questions about sport consumption and what it is that the consumer actually consumes. Evidently event organizers need to think beyond the nature and quality of sport provided by inventing ways to make events more appealing to a wider range of people (Green, 2001). Event organizers must, thus, augment the sports product to fit in with the needs and desires of the consumers.

Augmentation is necessary to provide a number of extra activities and services in order to enhance the event's attractiveness and to appeal to a variety of market segments. Augmentation strategies should be informed by the 'core' product when promoting an event. The 'core product' is the emotional experience and gratification that participants get from consuming the 'actual product' (Sullivan, 2004). At the Golf World Cup, a major component of the 'core product' for many of the visitors interviewed at the event appeared to be the emotional gratification from social interaction. Consumers of sport events have complex motivations and needs, which extend beyond the basic satisfaction of attendance at an event. Building in extra activities helps to secure customers who are interested in obtaining more than just the basic product or service (Chisnal, 1985: 13). Sports organisers in Barbados therefore need to develop sport events around the 'core' product in order to tap more buying motivations. This can be achieved through *apriori* investigations into the needs, expectations and motivations that potential customers have. This study clearly suggests that investigations into tourists' perceptions need to be grounded in the realities tourists themselves describe. Only when the range of expectations and perceptions are known can event managers augment these products to cater to their needs. Research is therefore needed to explore the specific combination of attractions that attract the golf visitor across the different market segments so that golf events can be appropriately augmented and designed in line with the potential visitors' expectations for gratification and satisfaction.

Events imported into Barbados need to be choreographed and packaged to fit into the island environment. They must be perceived as special so that people will make the extra effort to come. Tourists traveling to Barbados for an event need to be motivated by the opportunity to be part of an event that is distinctly Barbadian and provides benefits that could not be obtained elsewhere while perceiving that all of their other expectations will be met. One point that was noted by many international participants was that the event did not convey anything 'special'. This suggests that future PGA events in Barbados must have a 'Unique Selling Proposition' which is that distinct and appealing attribute that sets a tourism product or service favourably apart from every other generic competitor. A viable USP could have been accomplished through augmentation to include various festivals and other cultural activities that would have given the event a unique twist.

198

Another major issue that arose from the international participants is that international participants were not aware of the event taking place until they had actually arrived in Barbados. This certainly bought to the fore the importance of stimulating international awareness of the golf event taking place in Barbados in order to maximize on foreign visitation. While many overseas visitors became aware of this event after arrival in Barbados the seemingly lack of awareness of this event in international markets might have been due to the marketing and promotional strategy employed by the tourism authorities in Barbados. This issue is the focus of the following discussion.

7.1.2 Marketing and Promoting Golf Events in Barbados

The hosting of the Golf World Cup illustrated the potential of sports and tourism to reap mutually beneficial rewards if marketed adequately. However, the marketing of the Golf World Cup was plagued by many issues. One of the major concerns is that international visitors who participated in this study admitted having no awareness of the event before they embarked on their journey to Barbados. Many revealed that they became aware of the event only after arrival on the island. Event marketing is a critical component of event management but stimulating awareness of an event in international markets can be a challenging undertaking, particularly for an island state like Barbados with a small advertising budget. As noted from the semi-structured interviews with tourism authorities, the Golf World Cup was advertised on television in the United States and in Barbados' promotional literature which is distributed in Barbados' key markets. However, advertising is not the most effective way to build awareness of a destination since tourists are not passive receivers of advertising (Milman and Pizam, 1995). One-off advertising or advertising that is not part of a carefully orchestrated and strategic promotional campaign will most likely fail.

Consequently, scholars agree that the establishment of a strategic public relations and media programme is essential to the leveraging of an event for tourism benefits (Coathup, 1999; Laws, 1991; Morse, 2001). Public relation programmes are effective because they can target a wider and enthusiastic audience through a diversity of communications channels and programmes that cater to the interests of different market segments (Hsu and Powers, 2002). When promoting events in the international market, lessons can be learned from the

199

Australian experience. Australia launched massive public relations programmes, over a five-year period in tourism generating countries, in order to effectively promote the 2000 Olympic Games. The authorities worked with major international magazines and television networks to develop news stories, documentaries and other programmes about the Sydney Olympics. This programme included visiting journalists before and during the event, which generated an estimated AUS$2.3 billion (£1 billion) worth of exposure in the period 1998 to 2000 (Morse, 2001). Event organisers and destination managers must therefore synergise their efforts and work together with television broadcasters to negotiate for airtime and exposure for the destination in a way that would effectively attract the target audience. These are issues that will have to be written into the bid proposal and subsequent final agreement. Working with the producers and broadcasters of major television networks and publications, destination managers can develop programme ideas and decide on the appropriate news items, stories and images that will attract the viewer in the market that the destination wishes to target (Sealy and Wickens, 2006, 2008). This should be done in the lead up to the event and programmes should present images that would demonstrate the benefits of attendance. It should be noted here that the decision to host the Gold World Cup was made only the previous December which would not have allowed sufficient time for the tourism staff to develop a well-researched and effective promotional campaign and this would have contributed somewhat to the failed communications strategy. This demonstrates the importance of having sufficient lead-in time between the time that the decision is made to host and the actual date of the event.

Promotional programmes need to include travel agents, travel wholesalers and other trade partners. In Barbados the travel trade, particularly tour operators, could be instrumental in promoting an event. As explained in chapter four, Barbados, like other island destinations in the Caribbean, is dependent on trans-national tour operators for business. The competitive advantage of the trans-national operators lies in their strategic position between all principal suppliers and consumers. They derive their power from the volumes that they generate and their capacity to shift large tourist flows from one destination to another (Lewis, 2002). Tour operators have a vested interest in promoting tourism to the destinations featured in their brochure. They invest a substantial amount of time and effort in active publicity through the production of colourful brochures which are distributed to members of the travel trade where person to person contact is made with potential tourists. Their input is crucial to the development and survival of tourism in Barbados and their input should be solicited due to the power that they command in overseas markets. Tactical programmes with tour wholesalers and hotel operators should also form part of the promotional strategies but sufficient lead-in time is essential so that tour operators can include these events in their brochures. The one year lead-in time for the Gold World Cup would have been insufficient as tour operator brochures are produced up to 18 months in advance. In tourism the visitors do not make these decisions overnight. It has already been established that the decision to travel involves a very lengthy decision-making process which is mediated by multiple variables including available time, money and complex motives over a long period of time. Thus, it is essential that there is sufficient leeway for travel decisions to be made. Promotional campaigns need to be preceded by more robust demand analysis in order to identify and accommodate the decision-making behavior of potentially viable markets.

7.1.3 Motivational Factors from an International Perspective

This research identified a number of contextual issues related to the motivation to attend the event by international visitors. One finding in this area relates to the importance of the sporting stars to world class events such as the Golf World Cup. Many international visitors were desirous of being able to see some of the world's top golfers perform. Many expressed disappointment at the absence of Tiger Woods and other international golfing icons. Some visitors felt that more people would have travelled to Barbados for this event had Tiger Woods been in attendance. This finding certainly highlights the importance of ensuring that world renowned competitors in the sporting discipline are present at sporting events of world cup status. Participants who granted interviews for this research were of the opinion that internationally recognized golf icons like Vijay Singh and Tiger Woods should have been available for golf clinics or to compete for the trophy. Other participants expressed the desire for an opportunity to meet and mingle with these individuals as part of the event experience. It was felt that the absence of these players meant that the event lost its credibility. World Cup events must attract the world's top competitors. Organizers would need to make accommodation for competitors to be accessible to fans so that they can 'mingle with the stars' to satisfy their complex affiliation motives.

The need to socialize with family and friends drew attention to the issue of the social atmosphere at the event. The social atmosphere could be enhanced through the design and layout of the event arena in order to stimulate an enhanced perception of enjoyment. Participants in particular wished to be able to congregate in specially designated areas for conversations with other fans and to eat and drink. Arena design and layout issues need to be an integral part of the event planning process in order to optimize customer satisfaction. This issue was discussed at length in chapter five where it was recognized that events of this nature may have to be augmented to create the social atmosphere that customers expect through the implementation of suitable social and other cultural activities and the manipulation of the layout of the event environment. Special attention needs to be given to the placement of bars, food stalls and large television screens . Participants at this event expressed the desire to be able to sit while enjoying a meal and still keep abreast of the competition. Future design considerations could also involve the addition of accessories such as headphones so that patrons can follow radio or television commentary and close circuit television can be installed at strategic locations on the golf course.

Aligned to the need for friends and family to socialize is the realization that attendance at a sporting event will be influenced by the individual's reference group. Research in the social sciences, particularly consumer behavior has highlighted the tendency for peer groups to create a sense of identity and belonging. As Wakefield (1995) pointed out attendance at a sporting event is a highly social affair and thus the effects of reference group acceptance could be a determining factor in predicting attendance. As mentioned earlier, researchers will need to explore this area in more detail and use their marketing and promotional strategies in such a way that would inspire group attendance. This is where alliances with tour operators, sporting associations, sport clubs and other social groups will need to be harnessed.

Participants will also be motivated to attend a golf event based on their enjoyment for the sport itself. Appreciation for the technical skills displayed by competitors of golf events have been identified by Hansen and Gauthier (1993). Participants at the Golf World Cup also spoke of their enjoyment of the event in terms of the 'great shots'. Spectators attending a sporting event of world cup standards would expect a high level of competition from the competitors. The appearance of international sporting icons can instill a level of confidence among spectators that the quality of competition would be enhanced. This is equally as important for the competitors who expect a high level of competition. International golfing competitors at the Golf World Cup, 2006 also expressed concerned about the absence of Tiger Woods and other international golfing stars from the competition. It was felt that their absence lowered the standard of the competition. The failure of international sporting organizations to attract the top competitors at a sporting event of world cup standards is a cause for concern. This issue is elaborated in the section that follows.

7.2 THE LOCAL PERSPECTIVE

The final objective was to explore the expectations and perceptions of the local residents. The success of any event is embedded in its ability to stimulate community support and participation. If the perceptions of an event within a community are negative, community residents may be less enthusiastic about the event. As the findings indicate, the local participants perceived the Golf World Cup as an elitist event, catering to an exclusive, mainly wealthy international clientele and therefore perceived it as socially exclusive. Many narratives from local participants referred to the event not being advertised in the local market and lack of awareness among locals. Some participants drew attention to the perception that the local authorities were only interested in inviting locals to participate as volunteers rather than as spectators. This resulted in the perception that the Golf World Cup was designed for an exclusive clientele.

A major perception was that the community was excluded from the decision-making process. Participants expressed the view that public consultation should be part of the decision-making process for event tourism. Some participants highlighted the view that the lack of public consultation results in a lack of transparency and secrecy. The findings illustrate the need for tourism planners to involve the local community in all aspects of tourism development. This is a critical issue because local people are part of the tourism product (Murphy, 1985; Wickens, 2002). Events do not take place in a vacuum but within a particular social, economic and cultural context. As stated by Ryan (1991: 2) "tourism is about an experience of place…The tourists interact with other tourists, with people serving the tourism industry and with others of the host community". Therefore tourism development that does not have a local focus will probably fail. The failure of tourism authorities to focus their promotional efforts on the local market resulted in a poor spectator turnout by residents.

Many local residents stressed the view that the Golf World Cup held no cultural relevance to the local society. They highlighted the fact that Barbados does not have a golfing tradition and that golf is more perceived as a tourist activity. In addition, there was no local food, souvenirs or cultural activities that reflected the local flare. Many participants spoke about the custom of including cultural entertainment at sporting events in Barbados as part of the attraction and expressed surprise that cultural events were not part of the Golf World Cup experience. It is evident that although sport is often tooted as a global commodity the way that it is consumed in one community may be distinctly different to how it is consumed in another. Local and overseas organizers need to consider the 'culture of sport consumption' in the host area when planning special events and try to incorporate local customs and traditions into the event design and programme. Policies aimed at sports development should take into account the wider social, economic and cultural influences within the host community.

Where events alien to host communities are staged then there needs to be a public education programme to educate the host community about the intricacies of the sport. Some residents drew attention to the fact that golf was not a popular sport on the island and therefore many residents did not understand the game. It was felt that this lack of understanding would have kept spectators away since they would not be able to enjoy themselves if they were not aware of the competitive side of the sport. It is clear that in such a case the local authorities needed to launch a public education programme about the game. In the future this could include complimentary golf clinics, newspaper and television campaigns in the form of editorials, TV shows and competitions. These forums can also be used to stimulate more hype about the event in the host area.

Many locals thought that there would have been a better spectator turnout, both local and international, had Tiger Woods been competing. This draws attention to the realization that the event lost some of its attractiveness and credibility due to Woods' non-appearance. This should serve as a lesson for local organizing committees. Event organizers need to ensure that organizations like the PGA deliver the 'goods' by ensuring that the best performers are competing in their event. It is unacceptable that the Minister of Tourism in Barbados had to travel abroad to try to sell the event to

Tiger Woods and other internationally renowned golfers who then decided to play elsewhere. This is the job of those who are charged with organizing the sport event – in this case the PGA. It is the principle role of sport organizations to market their event to the best competitors (Masterman, 2004). In the future clauses to this effect will have to the written into the bid contract.

When dealing with international event owners, the local organizing committees should be more assertive about how the event will be organized and designed. The discovery that the PGA exerted much influence and authority over how the event was delivered is alarming considering that the host authorities paid US$ 3 million to the PGA to host the event. Local organizing committees should impose a 'if we pay then we must have some say' approach to dealing with these often autocratic international organizations. Policy should dictate that local organizers only work with international event owners who demonstrate a desire to engage with the destination ethos and provide the impetus for the host destination to achieve its social and economic objectives. Hede and Kellett's (2008) research into the relationship of local organizing committees and international event owners revealed a shift in power where event owners have to become move savvy in selling their events due to the plethora of events that can be bid for. Many of these alternate events are of the size and scope that can be better leveraged to enhance the host's capabilities to achieve its goals. Local authorities need to appreciate that international event organizations need to sell the licensing rights to their event to a host authority in order to offset the costs that they incur. This gives local organizing committees a considerable amount of bargaining power. It is on this basis that local authorities need to assert their influence on international event organizations in order to ensure that host communities are compensated adequately for their investment (Hede and Kellett, 2008). International events should only be chosen on the basis that their objectives are in alignment with the local agenda and the owners of these events should be sensitive to local needs and customs. Otherwise they should be told to take their event elsewhere.

Furthermore, local authorities should ensure that the correct training programmes are put in place for local businesses so that they too would know how to leverage their businesses to reap the rewards that these events are claimed to bring. Bringing a major event to a city or town is pointless if the people and organizations who are supposed to benefit are not properly trained and educated in the tactics and other leveraging techniques that they can utilize to reap the rewards. This may require a legacy organization being established to ensure that all of the training requirements are executed.

Those who supported this event did so on the basis that the event enhanced Barbados' international image. Participants indicated that they felt a degree of civic pride from the attention that Barbados was receiving in the international press. Others were supportive on the basis that event tourism had stimulated much needed beatification of the Bridgetown area, the roads and other infrastructural development. This provides evidence that event tourism authorities must continue to leverage events to achieve these aims. More important, the impacts derived from the media coverage and the infrastructural developments can be used to stimulate residents' 'buy in' and support for events which is necessary to ensure their success.

From a local perspective it is clear that more accurate evaluations, social impact assessments and public consultations are required before submitting bids to international event organizations if mega sport projects are to gain public support and become more democratically accountable ventures. In the future, public consultation forums can include community town hall meetings, perhaps through constituent representatives. A social impact panel should be established for every event to assess social impacts and to conduct consultations with special interest and stakeholders groups in the community.

7.3 OTHER RECOMMENDATIONS - EDUCATION

Providing quality services and events to the standards required by international tourists and international event organizations is a global challenge which can be exacerbated when there is little experience with special event production. In the case of Barbados there is little, if any, experience with golf event tourism. It has also been observed that those charged with the responsibility of delivering high quality events in Barbados have migrated from a variety of professions, including retail, insurance, business, economics and the civil service among others. Training will be necessary in order to combat deficiencies in the human resources pool. It was evident from this study that the success of any event requires a variety of skills and expertise. Individuals in the event industry will need to acquire knowledge in the areas of sports, event and tourism management and marketing, including knowledge of the principles of tourism planning and development. Skills will be required from individuals with experience in dealing with civic society and public relations.

The University of the West Indies currently runs a post graduate hospitality management degree with elective courses in sports management and event management. However, there is a need for more specialized degrees. A specialized degree in event management that can nurture and develop the necessary skills is advised. Education for future event managers needs to be developed from a multi-disciplinary perspective to equip managers with the necessary tools. In addition to the skills highlighted in the previous paragraph, those involved in the development of sport events will need to acquire skills and knowledge in sports tourism, social psychology and consumer behaviour. Courses in political science and the social history of the Caribbean would also enhance degree programmes. Socio-cultural history in particular can assist students in understanding the historical and cultural forces that help to shape sports consumption in the Caribbean and local residents' reactions to tourism development and tourists.

7.4 RECOMMENDATIONS FOR RESEARCH

This study raises a number of important issues that have consequences for the marketing and management of future events in Barbados. The findings have been meticulously documented; however, there is a need for a more coherent body of knowledge on event tourism in Barbados. The findings in this study demonstrate that Barbados needs to focus their inquiries on qualitative research rather than simply focussing on the collection of statistical data, which does not allow the tourists' or residents' voices to be heard. More qualitative research on international tourists should be complement by research that also explores the local dimensions.

This study needs to be repeated on a range of events in Barbados and other Caribbean islands to confirm if the same themes and issues are raised. The Barbadian tourism authorities need to have a better understanding of the international visitors' needs, expectations and the benefits that they seek from a Barbados holiday before the formulation of any event tourism policy. Thus, a considerable amount of work is required in order to target event visitors more effectively. This study has demonstrated the value of qualitative research through the rich descriptions and illuminating narratives presented by the participants and has uncovered many of the underlying issues associated with the management and marketing of event tourism in Barbados that could not be uncovered by quantitative methods. Whilst quantitative surveys can provide important data on the actual numbers of participants, and measure the strength and direction of perceptions, they are sometimes less able to uncover the reasons behind participation levels and perceptions and are therefore less able to provide clues for future marketing and management strategies. Understanding the less tangible, underlying, social and cultural issues can provide an added value, particularly in relation to future policy formulation. It is well recognized that perceptions influence customer purchase and expectations influence both product adoption and ultimate satisfaction. Future work needs to identify the different market segments of event tourism visitors and the expectations and perceptions of the various segments.

This study demonstrated the multi-disciplinary nature of event tourism in that it drew on theories derived from tourism, sports management and marketing, tourism marketing, history and consumer behavior in order to make sense of the emerging themes. Recently scholars have been advocating the need for a more multi-disciplinary perspective while Gibson (1998) suggested that theories from anthropology, social psychology and political science may be useful in helping scholars and practitioners to better understand event tourism. More collaborative research between scholars from these disciplines may provide the key to a more holistic understanding of the issues facing event tourism on the island of Barbados in particular.

7.5 PERSONAL REFLECTIONS AND LIMITATIONS

As with many other case studies, the findings in this investigation cannot be generalized to the wider population of mega events, host destinations or stakeholders. The investigation of perceptions and expectations in this case simply provided the researcher with a holistic gauge of the possible perceptions and expectations held by stakeholders with regards to golf events on the island. A further study can now be conducted on a similar event in another Caribbean island to see if the themes are consistent with the Barbados study.

It is acknowledged that a perception is a system of images and values that have their own cultural meaning and exist independent of individual experience. They represent a complex set of representations about a particular phenomenon that are formed within a social context (Fredline and Faulkner, 2000a). These representations are not inflexible but are dynamic processes that change over time. Thus, the representations expressed in this study can only be seen in context, relevant to the particular time, place and context within which this research took place. The views and opinions expressed are relevant only to those who took part in this study as seen through the eyes of this researcher. Likewise, it is acknowledged in the tourism literature that the expectations of tourists tend to change as they ascend the travel career ladder. The career ladder emphasizes that people have a range of motives for seeking out holiday experiences, but these change over time as individuals become more experienced travellers (Pearce, 1989). As with the perceptions of the stakeholders who contributed to this work, it is acknowledged that their expectations as well must be seen in this context.

This study, like other research, was not without methodological limitations. Limited access to the golf course at Sandy Lane meant that the researcher did not have access to the hospitality areas and as a result it was not possible to interview VIP's, high-ranking PGA officials and media personnel covering the event. Other constrains such as not being able to take pictures on the golf course or tape-record conversations and interviews contributed to its limitations. In such cases notes had to be taken manually and this was in part subjected to the researcher's memory. This qualitative researcher has reflected critically on who she is and acknowledges that this enquiry is sensitive to her own personal biography (see chapter two). Qualitative research is in that the researcher filters the data through a personal lens that is situated within a specific socio-cultural, political and historical context. This close personal involvement meant that it was necessary for this researcher to reflect upon her personal role as the collector and analyst of the data. To this end it was necessary to make visible all procedures engaged throughout the research process in chapter two so that others may judge the quality of the research (May, 1993). This is not to undermine the value of this work but rather it serves to highlight the fact that in research it is difficult to be totally objective and to separate the researcher's beliefs and assumptions from the issue under investigation (Lewis, 2002). As a result the researcher's background was revealed in chapter two, since the exposing of the researcher's values exposes the study to the critical analysis of the audience (Humberstone, 1997a). This reflection acknowledges the researcher's biases, values and personal interest. It also acknowledges the honesty and openness in which it was conducted.

7.6 CONTRIBUTION TO KNOWLEDGE

This investigation makes a contribution to the events industry literature. It also makes a valuable contribution to event management theory and methodology. It contributes to the literature by exploring

209

stakeholders' perspectives of a single event, at a specific place and at a specific period in time. The approach adopted explored a range of issues and provided 'rich' descriptions by allowing the stakeholders' 'voices to be heard' in their own words.

This study has provided a better understanding of the expectations and perceptions that the specific stakeholder groups hold of mega events in Barbados. The stakeholder approach adopted is a departure from other research strategies undertaken in Barbados, which tend to ignore the local stakeholders' views while placing more emphasis on international tourists. Furthermore, its qualitative nature provides a body of illuminating knowledge that provides insights into how these groups perceived the Golf World Cup. This is knowledge that can be applied to tourism development as a whole in small island states. In fact, its significance lies in the fact that it is interpretive bound and includes the perspectives of the local stakeholders who are hardly ever researched. Previous research into the impacts of events in Barbados has been directed towards economic impacts rather than focussing on stakeholders' perceptions and expectations. In this sense it is the first study of its kind to consider the views of a cross-section of individuals presenting a holistic picture of a single phenomenon.

The findings from this enquiry reveal the inextricable link between event tourism and the local environment. It illustrates the power that the stakeholders, particularly the international visitors and the local community, hold in the success and failure of a mega event. It clearly demonstrates that the success of any event requires the establishment of appropriate planning and management structures, market research, maximization of public participation, the development of appropriate facility design, and a choreography that reflects the destination theme and embraces local cultural traditions. Event organisers must ensure that there is an appropriate match between the event, international visitors and the host community, a point that is critical to the management of events on a small island like Barbados.

Researchers do not necessarily adopt a holistic approach to researching the perceptions of mega event; however this work illustrates the interdisciplinary nature of these perceptions. From a theoretical perspective, this work has highlighted the multiple conceptual issues associated with golf event tourism in Barbados.

The concepts identified can now be explored further with more research in order to determine the level of importance that they hold for event tourism in Barbados. Another significant contribution that this study makes to the knowledge of event tourism, particularly golf tourism, is that these concepts can be used by marketers and managers to guide future event marketing campaigns and event management strategies.

A significant concept which emerged from this research is that of social exclusion. As more events are designed in the Caribbean tourism authorities should certainly pay attention to the issue of social exclusion when marketing events to local consumers. Events in Barbados that are perceived to promote or cater to elitism will most likely fail to harness local support and participation. Social exclusion is not a concept that has held much weight in event tourism marketing or management and will therefore need to be conceptualised at a higher level through further research so that the roots of this phenomenon can be identified and annihilated. However, this work has certainly given this issue more saliency and highlights the need for more attention to be paid to this issue in the planning of future events. Significantly, the concept of atmospherics arises as an important concept to consider when designing a golf event. While this concept is more commonly used in the retail industry this research highlights the need for more attention to be given by event planners to the concept in the future. This work shows that perceptions of event enjoyment could be enhanced when the social and physical atmosphere is appealing to the event visitor. The atmosphere of the place is an integral part of the core product and it provokes emotions within the customer regarding perceptions of enjoyment and satisfaction levels. Research leading to a conceptual framework for accessing atmospherics at a golf event will be helpful in showing the event planner how to manipulate the environment where the event takes place in order to derived complete customer satisfaction.

Methodologically this work illustrates the usefulness and the importance of an eclectic approach to data collection for researching event tourism. While commentators have been advocating the need to use multiple methods of data collection when researching event tourism, normative discourses continue to pervade the tourism literature as researchers continue to employ the more traditional structured methods. This study is the first to demonstrate how semi-structured interviews, participant observation and the examination of documents can be successfully used to collect meaningful and illuminating data. It also demonstrates how participant observation and the examination of documents can be used to validate the information given by participants in semi-structured interviews, thereby bringing more credibility to the findings. The researcher was also able to use the data generated from the semi-structured interviews as a template for setting the observation agenda. In this case rather than the researcher determining the entire observation agenda solely based on prior knowledge or pre-conceived notions regarding what was important in this study, the participants themselves also made a worthwhile contribution to the observation agenda by demonstrating what was important in their interviews with the researcher. This research, thus, promotes the importance of unstructured or semi-structured techniques in the investigation of an otherwise unknown phenomenon.

The findings in this study can be used to provide useful information that would assist event organisers, destination managers, marketers, government officials and NGO's in developing strategies and setting policies regarding the staging of sport events and other hallmark events in the Caribbean islands and beyond. It demonstrates that more collaborative alliances need to be established between the agencies responsible for sport and tourism in Barbados. At the research level more multi-disciplinary research is needed to build on existing knowledge in sport and tourism.

BIBLIOGRAPHY

Aaker, D., A., Kumar, V., and Day, G., S., 1995, **Marketing Research**. New York: John Willey and Sons.

Agrusa, J., and Tanner, J., 2002, The economic significance of the 2000 Buy.Com golf tournament on the Lafayette, Louisiana area, **Journal of Sport and Tourism**, 7 (1), 6-24.

Alhemoud A., and Armstrong, E., 1996, Image of tourism attractions in Kuwait, **Journal of Travel Research** (Spring), 76-80.

Allan, G., 1991, Qualitative research, in Allan, G., and Skinner, C., (eds), **Handbook for Research Students in the Social Sciences**. London: The Palmer Press, 177-189.

Allen, J., O'Toole, W., Harris, R., and McDonnell, I., 2005, **Festival and Special Event Management.** Sydney: John Wiley and Sons Australia.

Allen, J., O'Toole, W., McDonnell, I., and Harris, R., 2002, **Festival and Special Event Management** (2nd ed.) Brisbane: John Wiley and Sons.

Altheide, D., and Johnson, J., 1994, Validity in qualitative research, in Denzin, N, K., and Lincoln, Y., S., (eds), **Handbook of Qualitative Research**. Thousand Oaks: Sage, 485-499.

Andersson, T., D., Rustad A., and Solberg, H., A., 2004, Local residents' monetary evaluation of sports events, **Managing Leisure**, 9 (July), 145-158.

Andranovich, G., Burbank, M., J., and Heying, C., H., 2001, Olympic cities: Lessons learned from mega-event politics, **Journal of Urban Affairs**, 23 (2), 113-131.

Andrews, D., L., and Jackson, S., J., 2001, Introduction: Sport celebrities, public culture, and private experience, in Andrews, D., L., and Jackson, S., J., (eds), **Sport Stars: The Cultural Politics of Sporting Celebrities.** London: Routledge, 1-19.

213

Arksey, H., and Knight, P., 1999, **Interviewing for Social Scientists.** London: Sage.

Assael, H., 1992, **Consumer Behaviour and Marketing Action**. Boston: PWS Kent Publishing Association, University of Technology Australia Ltd.

Babbie, E., 1998, **The Practice of Social Research** (8th ed.). Belmont, California: Wadsworth Publishing Co.

Baloglu, S., and Brinberg, D., 1997, Affective images of tourism destinations, **Journal of Travel Research,** 35 (4), 11-15.

Bannister, P., Burman, E., Parker, I., Taylor, M., and Tindall, C., 1994, **Qualitative Methods in Psychology: A Researchers Guide**. Buckingham: Open University Press.

Barbados Economic Report, 2006, **Central Bank of Barbados, Economic Report.** Unpublished.

Barbados Advocate, 2006, **Barbados facing challenges to tourist product.** [On-Line], Available: http://www.barbadosadvocate.com/NewViewNewsleft.cfm?Record=2 5389, accessed on May 30, 2006.

Barbados Government Information Service, 2006. [On-Line], Available: http://www.barbados.gov.bb/society.htm, accessed June 21, 2007

Barbados in a Nutshell, 2008, **Barbados Tourism Authority**, promotional brochure.

Barbados is Selected to Host the 2006 WGC-World Cup Next December, 2005. [On-Line], Available: http://www.seamless-golf.com/golf-news/Dec05feed/Barbados_is_selected_to_host_the_2006_WGCWorl d_Cup_next_December.rss.htm, accessed December 16, 2005.

Barbados Ministry of Tourism, 2003, **Annual Tourism Statistical Digest.** [On-Line], Available: http://www.barmot.gov.bb/reports/Statistical%20Digest2003_4.pdf, accessed on May 12, 2005.

Barbados Ministry of Tourism, 2006. [On-Line], Available: http://www.barmot.gov.bb/geninfo.htm, accessed May 29, 2006.

Barbados Private Sector Trade Team, 2004, **Sectoral Profile: The Tourism Sector in Barbados.** [On-Line], Available: http://www.tradeteam.bb/cms/pstt/files/sector/tourism/The_Tourism_S ector.PDF, accessed on June 29, 2006

Barbados set to host 2006 World Cup, 2005. [On-Line], Available: htpp://www.worldgolfchampionships.com/news/story/r169/9098838, accessed on 20 March, 2006.

Barbados Stay-Over Visitor Survey, 2005, **Caribbean Tourism Organization and Barbados Tourism Authority Statistical Survey.** Unpublished.

Barbados the heart of the World Cup, 2006, **Barbados Tourism Authority** brochure. Unpublished.

Bargeman, B., and Van der Poel, H., 2006, The role of routines in the vacation decision-making process of Dutch vacationers, **Tourism Management,** 27 (4), 707-720.

Basil, M., D., 1996, Identification as a mediator of celebrity effects, **Journal of Broadcasting and Electronic Media,** 40 (1996), 478-495.

Beall, J., and Piron, L., H., 2005, **DFID Social Exclusion Review,** London: Department for International Development, May 2005. [On-Line], Available: http://www.odi.org.uk/rights/Publications/BBeale&PironSocEx.pdf, accessed on July 10, 2007.

Becherel, L., 1999, Strategic analysis and strategy Formulation, in Vellas F., and Becherel L., (eds), **The International Marketing of Travel and Tourism: A Strategic Approach.** London: MacMillan Press Limited, 37-106.

215

Becken, S., 2005, The role of tourists icons for sustainable tourism. **Journal of Vacation Marketing,** 11 (1), 21-30.

Beckles, H., 1990, **A History of Barbados: From Amerindian Settlement to Nation State**. New York: Cambridge University Press.

Beeton, S., 2001, Smiling for the camera: the influence of film audiences on a budget tourism destination**, Tourism, Culture & Communication**, 3, 15-25.

Beeton, S., 2005, The case study in tourism research: a multi-method case study approach, in Ritchie, B., W., Burns, P., and Palmer, C., (eds), **Tourism Research Methods: Integrating Theory with Practice.** Massachusettes: CABI Publishing, 37-47.

Belch, G., and Belch, M., 1999, **Advertising and Promotion: An Integrated Marketing Communications Perspective.** Boston: Irwin.

Berg, B., L., 1989, **Qualitative Research Methods for the Social Sciences.** Boston: Allyn and Bacon.

Bigné, J., E., Sanchez, M., I., and Sanchez, J., 2001, Tourist image, evaluation variables and after purchase behaviour: inter-relationships, **Tourism Management**, 22, 607-616.

Bigne, L., E., and Andreu, l., 1999, Strategic marketing in the travel agency sector, in Vellas, F., and Becherel, L., (eds), **The International Marketing of Travel and Tourism**. London: Palgrave, 265-298.

Big gains from hosting world cup, 2006, **Nation News,** December 14, 2006, 11.

Blaikie, N., 1993, **Approaches to Social Enquiry**. Oxford: Blackwell Publishers Press.

Blythe, J., 1997, **The Essence of Consumer Behaviour**. London: Prentice Hall.

Bolsmann, C., and Parker, A., 2007, Soccer, South Africa and celebrity status: Mark Fish, popular culture and the post apartheid state, **Soccer and Society**, 8 (1), 109-124.

Bonn, M., A., Joseph-Mathews, M., S., Dai, M., Hayes, S., and Cave, J., 2007, Heritage/cultural attraction atmospherics: creating the right environment for the heritage/cultural visitor, **Journal of Travel Research,** 45 (3), 345-354.

Bowdin., G., McDonnell, I., Allen, J., and O'Toole, W., 1999, **Event Management**. Oxford: Butterworth Heinemann.

Bowen, D., 2002, Research through participant observation in tourism: a creative solution to the measurement of consumer satisfaction/dissatisfaction (CS/D) among tourists, **Journal of Travel Research**, 41, 4-14.

Bramwell, B., 1997, Strategic planning before and after a mega-event, **Tourism Management**, 18 (3), 167-176.

Branco, M., C., and Rodrigues, L., L., 2007, Positioning stakeholder theory within the debate on corporate social responsibility, **Electronic Journal of Business Ethics and Organisational Studies,** 12 (1), 5-15.

Brenner, M., Brown, J., and Canter, D., 1985, Introduction, in Brenner, M., Brown, J., and Canter, D., 1985 (eds), **The Research Interview: Uses and Approach**. London: Academic Press, 1-8.

Brewer, J., D., 2000, **Ethnography**. Philadelphia: Open University Press.

Briedenhann, J., 2004, **An Evaluation Framework For Rural Tourism Projects: A Respondent Perspective**. A PhD thesis, Buckinghamshire Chilterns University College, Brunel University. (Unpublished).

Brohman, J., 1996, New directions in tourism for third world development, **Annals of Tourism Research**, 23 (1), 48-90.

Brown, G., Chalip, L., Jago, L., and Mules, T., 2002, The Sydney Olympics and brand Australia, in Morgan, N., Pritchard, A., and Pride, R., (eds.), **Destination Branding: Creating the Unique Selling Proposition**. Oxford: Butterworth-Heinemann.

Browne, S., 2006, Barbados facing challenges to tourist product**, The Barbados Advocate**, May 30, 2006, 1.

Brokaw, A., Stone, G., W., and Jones, M., A., 2006, **A Model of the Factors Contributing to Fan Support at Small-College Athletic Events.** [On-Line], Available: http://www.thesportjournal.org/article/model-factors-contributing-fan-support-small-college-athletic-events, accessed August 3, 2008.

Bruguglio, L., Butler, R., Harrison, D and Filho, W., I., 1996, **Sustainable Tourism in Islands and Small States.** London: Cassell.

Brunt, P, 1997, **Market Research in Travel and Tourism**. Oxford: Butterworth-Heinemann.

Bryman, A., and Burgess, R., 1994, Developments in qualitative data analysis: an introduction, in Bryman, A., and Burgess, R., (eds.), **Analysing Qualitative Data**. New York: Routledge, 1-7.

Bryman, A., and Burgess, R., 1994, Reflections on qualitative data analysis, in Bryman, A., and Burgess, R (eds.), **Analysing Qualitative Data**. New York: Routledge, 220-226.

Bryman. A., 1988, **Quantity and Quality in Social Research**. London: Routledge.

Buhalis, D., 2000, Marketing the competitive destination of the future, **Tourism Management,** 21, 97-116.
Bull, C., and Weed, M., 1999, Niche markets and small island tourism: the development of sport tourism in Malta, **Managing Leisure,** 4, 142-155.

Burgan , B., and Mules, 1992, Economic impact of sporting events**, Annals of Tourism Research**, 19, 700-710.

Burgess, R., G., 1984, **In the Field. An Introduction to Field Research**. London: Urwin Hyman.

Burgess, R., G., 1987a, Early field experiences, in Burgess, R., G., (ed), **Field Research: A Sourcebook and Field Manual.** London: Allen and Unwin, 15-18.

Burgess, R., G., 1987b, Some role problems in the field, in Burgess, R., G., (ed). **Field Research: A Sourcebook and Field Manual.** London: Allen and Unwin, 45-49.

Burgess, R., G., 1987c, Elements of sampling in field research, in Burgess, R., G., (ed), **Field Research: A Sourcebook and Field Manual.** London: Allen and Unwin, 76-78.

Burman, E., 1994, Interviewing, in Bannister, P., Burman, E., Parker, I ., Taylor, M., and Tindall, C., (eds), **Qualitative Methods in Psychology**: A Research Guide Philadelphia: Open University Press, 49-71.

Burns, J., P., A., and Mules, T., J., 1989, An economic evaluation of the Adelaide Grand Prix, in Syme, G., J., Shaw, B., J., Fenton, D., M., and Mueller, W., S., (eds), **The Planning and Evaluation of Hallmark Events**. Aldershot: Avebury, 172-185.

Burns, R., B., 2000, **Introduction to Research Methods**. London: Sage.

Burroughs, A., 1999, Winning the Bid, in Cashman, R., and Hughes, A., (eds), **Staging the Olympics: the event and its impacts,** University of New South Wales Press Ltd, Australia, 35-45.

Busby, G., and Klug, J., 2001, Movie-induced tourism; the challenge of measurement and other issues, **Journal of Vacation Marketing**, 7 (4), 316-332.

Butler, R., 1980, The concept of a tourist area cycle of evolution, **Canadian Geographer,** 24, 5–12.

Butler, R., 1990, The influence of the media in shaping international tourists patterns, **Tourism Recreation Research**, 15 (2), 46-53.

Caribbean Tourism Organisation, 2003, **Statistical Report.** [On-Line], Available: http://www.onecaribbean.org/content/files/june4Lattab03.doc, accessed on April 12, 2006.

Caribbean Tourism Organisation, 2005, **Statistical Report.** [On-Line], Available: http://www.onecaribbean.org/content/files/may21Lattab05.doc, accessed on April 30, 2006.

Caribbean Tourism Organisation, 2006, **Statistical Report.** [On-Line], Available: http://www.onecaribbean.org/content/files/June12Lattab06.doc, accessed July 21, 2008.

Cashman, R., 2003, Impact of the Games on Olympic Host Cities. [On-Line],   Available: http://olympicstudies.uab.es/lec/pdf/cashman.pdf, accessed on May 1, 2005.

Cassidy, F., 2006, What motivates event tourists? **Conference Proceedings**, Business and Information, Academy of Taiwan Information Systems Research, International conference on business and information, 12-14 July 2006, Singapore,1-20.

Cegielski, M. and Mules, T., 2002, Aspects of residents' perceptions of the GMC400 – Canberra's V8 supercar race, **Current Issues in Tourism,** 5 (1), 54–70.

Chalip, L., 2002, **Using the Olympics to Optimise Tourism Benefits,** [On-Line], Available: www.blues.uab.es/iceoa/pdf/FL7_eng.pdf, accessed May 10, 2005.

Chalip, L., Green, B., C., and Vander Velden, L., 1998, Sources of interests in travel to the Olympic games, **Journal of Vacation Marketing,** 4 (1), 7-22.

Chalip, L., Green, C., and Hill, B., 2003, Effects of sport event media on destination image and intention to visit, **Journal of Sports Management**, 17, 214-234.

220

Chalip, L.1992, The construction and use of polysemic structures: Olympic lessons for sport marketing, **Journal of Sport Management,** 6, 87-98.

Chalip, L., and McGuirty, 2004, Bundling sport events with the host destination, **Journal of Sport and Tourism,** 9 (3), 267-282.

Chen, J., S., and Hsu, C., H., C., 2000, Measurement of Korean Tourists' perceived images of overseas destinations, **Journal of Travel Research**, 38 (May), 411-416.

Cheyne, J., Downes, M., and Legg, S., 2006, Travel agent vs internet: What influences travel consumer choices, **Journal of Vacation Marketing,** 12 (1), 41-57.

Chisnal, P., M., 1985, Marketing: **A Behavioural Analysis**. London: Mc Graw-Hill.

Chisnall, P., M., 1992, **Marketing Research**. Berkshire: McGraw-Hill.

Chon, K., S., 1992, Self-image/destination image congruity, **Annals of Tourism Research**, 19 (2), 360-363.

Chon, K., S., 1991, Tourism destination image modification process: Marketing implications, **Tourism Management**, 12 (1), 68-72.

Clark, J., and Causer, G., 1991, Introduction: Research strategies and decisions, in Allan, G., and Skinner, C., (eds), **Handbook for Research Students in the Social Sciences.** London: The Palmer Press, 163-176.

Clark, M.A., Riley, M. J., Wilkie, E., and Wood, R.C., 1998, **Researching and Writing Dissertations in Hospitality and Tourism**. London: International Thomson Business.

Clarke, J., 2000, Tourism brands: an exploratory study of the brands box model. **Journal of Vacation Marketing,** 6 (4), 329-345.

Coathup, D., 1999, Dominant actors in international tourism, **International Journal of Contemporary Hospitality Management**, 11 (2/3), 69-72.

Collins, M., F., and Kay, T., 2003, **Sport and Social Exclusion.** New York: Routledge.

Coltman, M., 1989, **Tourism Marketing**. New York: Van Nostrand Reinhold.

Conlin, M., V., 1995, Rejuvenation planning for island tourism: the Bermuda example, in Conlin, M., V., and Baum, T., (eds**), Island Tourism: Management Principles and Practice.** New York: John Wiley and Sons, 181– 202.

Conlin, M., V., and Baum, T., 1995, **Island Tourism: Management Principles and Practice. New York**: John Wiley and Sons.

Conway, D., 1993, The new tourism in the Caribbean: reappraising market segmentation, in Gayle, D., J., and Goodrich, J., N., (eds), **Tourism Marketing and Management in the Caribbean**. London: Routledge, 167-177.

Cooper, C., Fletcher, J., Gilbert, D., Wanhill, S., and Shepherd, R., 1998, **Tourism Principles and Practice** (2nd ed.). Essex: Addison Wesley Longman Limited.

Cooper, G., 1994, Product lifecycle, in Witt S., Moutinho, L., (eds), **Tourism Marketing and Management Handbook**. Hertfordshire: Prentice Hall, 341-345.

Cornelissen, S., and Swart, K., 2006, The 2010 Football World Cup as a political construct: the challenge of making good an African promise, in Horne, J., and Manzenreiter, W., (eds), **Sports Mega-Events: Social Scientists Analyses of a Global Phenomenon**: Oxford: Blackwell Publishing, 108-123.

Court, B., and Lupton, R., 1997, Customer portfolio development: Modelling destination adopters, inactives, and rejecters, **Journal of Travel Research**, 36 (1), 35-43.

Cresswell, J., W., 1994, **Research Design: Qualitative and Quantitative Approaches**. London, Sage.

Croes, R., 2006, A paradigm shift to a new strategy for small island economies embracing demand side economics for value enhancement and long term economic stability, **Tourism Management**, 27, 453-465.

Crompton, J., L., and Ankomah, P., K., 1993, Choice set propositions in destination decisions, **Annals of Tourism Research,** 20, 461-476.

Crompton, J., L., 1979, Motivations for pleasure, **Annals of Tourism Research**, (Oct/Dec/) 79, 408-424.

Crompton, J., L., 1996, The potential contributions of sports sponsorship in impacting the product adoption process, **Managing Leisure**, 1, 199-212.

Crompton, J., L., and McKay, S., L., 1997, Motives of visitors attending festival events, **Annals of Tourism Research**, 24 (2), 425-439.

Crompton, J., L., Lee, S., and Shuster, T., J., 2001, A guide for undertaking economic impact studies: the Springfest example, **Journal of Travel Research**, 40 (2001), 79-87.

Crotty, M., 1998, **The Foundations of Social Research: Meaning and Perspective in the Research Process.** California: Sage.

D'hauteserre, A., 2003, A response to 'misguided policy initiatives in small-island destinations: why do up market tourism policies fail?' By Dimitri Ioannides and Briavel Holcomb, **Tourism Geographies** 5 (1), 49-53.

Dann, G., 1977, Anomie, ego-enhancement and tourism, **Annals of Tourism Research**, 4 (4), 184-194.

Dann, G., 1992, Predispositions towards alternative forms of tourism among tourists visiting Barbados: some preliminary observations, in Smith, V., and Eadington, W., R., (eds), **Tourism Alternatives:**

Potentials and Problems in the Development of Tourism. Philadelphia: University of Philadelphia Press, 158-179.

Dann, G., M., S., and Potter, R., B., 1997, Tourism in Barbados: rejuvenation or decline? in Lockhart, D., and Drakakis-Smith, D., (eds), **Island Tourism: Trends and Prospects.** New York: Pinter, 205-228.

Davies, D., 2006, Everything that a golfer could want-and a world cup too, **The Times,** January 7, 2006, 18.

De Mooij, M., 2004, **Consumer Behaviour and Culture: Consequences for Global Marketing and Advertising**. London: Sage.

De Moragas Spa, M., Rivenburgh, N., K., Garcia, N., 1995, **Television and the Construction of Identity: Barcelona, Olympic Host.** [On-Line], Available: http://olympicstudies.uab.es/pdf/od005_eng.pdf, accessed May 20, 2005.

Deacon, J., 2006, Monkey business, **Canadian Business**, November 20-December 3, 2006, 2.

Dean, J., P., Eichhorn, R., L., and Dean, L., 1969, Limitations and advantages of unstructured methods, in McCall, G., J., and Simmons, J., L., **Issues in Participant Observation**. New York: Random House, 19-24.

Deccio, C., and Baloglu, S., 2002, Non-host community reactions to the 2002 winter olympics: the spill over impacts, **Journal of Travel Research**, 41, 46-56.

Decrop, A., 2000, Qualitative research methods for the study of tourist behaviour, in Pizam, A., and Mansfield, Y., (eds.), **Consumer Behaviour in Travel and Tourism.** New York: The Haworth Hospitality Press, 335-365.

Decrop, A., 2006, **Vacation Decision Making**. Belgium: CABI publishing.

Definitive Caribbean, 2006, The Travel Guide. [On-Line], Available: (http://www.definitivecaribbean.com/accommodation/SandyLane.aspx accessed December 12, 2006)

Della Bitta, A., J., Loudon, D., L., Booth, G., G., and Weeks, R., R., 1977, Estimating the economic impact of a short-term tourist event, **Journal of Travel Research,** 16 (2), 10-15.

Delphy, L., 1998, An overview of sport tourism: building towards a dimensional framework, **Journal of Vacation Marketing**, 4 (1), 23-38.

Denscombe, M., 1998, **The Good Research Guide for Small Scale Social Research Projects**. Buckingham: Open University Press.

Denzin, N., K., and Lincoln, Y., S., 2005, **The Sage Handbook of Qualitative Research**. London: Sage.

Dey, I., 1993, **Qualitative data Analysis: A User-Friendly Guide for Social Scientists**. London: Routledge.

Dibb., S., Simkin, L., Pride, W., M., and Ferrell, O., C., 1994, **Marketing: Concepts and Strategies**. Boston: Houghton Mifflin Company.

Dore, L., and Crouch, G., 2003, Promoting destinations: an exploratory study of publicity programs used by national tourism organisations, **Journal of Vacation Marketing**, 9 (2), 137-151.

Dovey, K., 1989, Old scabs, /new scars: The hallmark event and the everyday environment, in Syme, G., Shaw, B., and Mueller, W (eds.), **The Planning and Evaluation of Hallmark Events.** Aldershot, UK: Avebury, 73–80.

Doxey, G., V., 1975, A Causation Theory of Visitor Resident Irritants: Methodology and Research Inferences. **Conference Proceedings,** Travel and Tourism Research Association Sixth Annual Conference, 195-198.

Dunn, C., 1994, A perspective on the purpose and nature of tourism research methods, in Bannister, P., Burman, E., Parker, I., Taylor, M., and Tindall, C., (eds.), **Qualitative Methods in Psychology: A Researchers Guide**. Buckingham: Open University Press, 3-11.

Dunn, R., S., 1972, **Sugar and Slaves. The Rise of the Planter Class in the English West Indies, 1624-1713.** New York: Norton and Company.

Durkheim, E., 1964, **The Rules of Sociological Method**. New York: The Free Press.

Dyer, G., 1988, **Advertising as Communication.** London: Routledge.

Echtner, C., M., and Ritchie, B., 1993, The measurement of destination image: an empirical assessment, **Journal of Travel Research**, 2 (Spring), 3-13.

Elcock, Y., J., 2005, Sports tourism in Barbados: the development of sport facilities and special events, **Journal of Sport and Tourism,** 10 (2), 129-134.

Emery, P., R., 2002, Bidding to host a major sports event: the local organising committee perspective, **The International Journal of Public Sector Management**, 15 (4), 316-335.

Engel, J., Blackwell, R., D., and Miniard, P., 1995, **Consumer Behaviour**. Forth Worth: The Dryden Press.

Essex, S., and Chalkley, B., 1998, Olympic Games: catalyst for change, **Leisure Studies,** 17, 187-206.

Evans, N., and Elphick, S., 2005, Models of crisis management: an evaluation of their value for strategic planning in the international travel industry, **The International Journal of Tourism Research,** 7, 135-150.

Fagence, M., 1997, An uncertain future for tourism in microstates: the case of Nauru, **Tourism Management**, 18 (6), 385-392.

Fakeye, P., and Crompton, J., 1991, Image differences between prospective first-time and repeat visitors to Lower Rio Grand Valley, **Journal of Tourism Research**, 30 (2), 10-16.

Fan-tasy, 2007, **Nation News**, March 27, 2007, 1.

Farrell, K., A., Karels, G., V., Monfort, K., W., and McClatchey, C., A., 2000, Celebrity performance and endorsement value: The case of Tiger Woods, **Managerial Finance**, 26 (7), 1-15.

Faulkner, B., 1997, A model for the evaluation of national tourism destination marketing programs, **Journal of Travel Research**, 35 (3), 23-32.

Faulkner, B., and Tideswell, C., 1999, Leveraging tourism benefits from the Sydney 2000 Olympics, **Pacific Tourism Review**, 3, 227-238.

Fennell, D., A., 2001, A content analysis of eco-tourism definitions, **Central Issues in Tourism**, 4 (5), 403-421.

Font, X., 1997, Managing the tourist destination's image**, Journal of Vacation Marketing,** 3 (2), 123-131.

Fontana, A., and Frey, J., H., 2005, The interview: from neutral stance to political involvement, in Denzin, N., K., and Lincoln, Y., S., (eds.), **The Handbook of Qualitative Research** (3rd ed.). London: Sage, 695-727.

Foxall, G., Goldsmith, R., and Brown, S., 2003, **Consumer Psychology for Marketing** (2nd ed.). Surrey: Alden Press.

Frankenberg, R., 1987, Participant observation, in Burgess, R., G., (ed), **Field Research: A Sourcebook and Field Manual. London**: Allen and Unwin p. 25-52.

Fredline, E. and Faulkner, B., 2000a, Host community reactions: A cluster analysis. **Annals of Tourism Research**, 27 (3), 763–784
.

Fredline, E. and Faulkner, B., 2002a, Residents' reactions to the staging of major motorsportevents within their communities: A cluster analysis, **Event Management**, 7, 103–14.

Fredline, E. and Faulkner, B., 2002b, Variations in residents' reactions to major motorsport events: Why residents perceive the impacts of events differently, **Event Management** 7, 115–125.

Fredline, E., and Faulkner, B., 1998,. Resident reactions to a major tourist event: The Gold Coast Indy Car Race. **Festival Management & Event Tourism**, 5, 185-205.

Fredline, E., 2000, **Host Community Reactions to Major Sporting Events: The Gold Coast and the Australian Formula One Grand Prix in Melbourne**. A PhD thesis, Griffith University. Unpublished.

Fredline, E., and Faulkner, B., 2000b, Community perceptions of the impacts of events in Allen, J., Harris, R., Jago, L., K., and Veal, A., J., (eds), **Events Beyond 2000: Setting the agenda.** Sydney: University of Technology, 60-74.

Freeman, R., E., Wicks, A., C., and Parman, B., 2004, Stakeholder theory and corporate objective revisited, **Organisational Sciences**, 15 (3), 364-369.

Funk, D., C., Mahony, D., F., Nakazawa, M., Hirakawa, S., 2001, Development of the Sport Interest Inventory (SII): implications for measuring unique consumer motives at sport events, **International Journal of Sports Marketing and Sponsorship**, 3, 291-316.

Gans, H., J., 1987, The participant observer as a human being: Observations on the personal aspects of fieldwork, in Burgess, R., G., (ed), **Field Research: A Sourcebook and Field Manual**. London: Allen and Unwin, 53-61.

Garcia, B., 2001, Enhancing sport marketing through cultural and arts programs: Lessons from the Sydney 2000 Olympic arts festivals, **Sport Management Review,** 4, 193–219.

Gartner, W., C., 1989, Tourism image: attribute measurement of state tourism products using multidimensional scaling techniques, **Journal of Travel Research**, 28 (2), 16-20.

Gartner, W., C., 1993, Image formation process, **Journal of Travel and Tourism Marketing**, 2, 191-216.

Gauthier, R., and Hansen, 1993, Female spectators: marketing implications for professional golf events, **Sports Marketing Quarterly**, 2 (4), 21-28.

Gayle, D., J., and Goodrich, J., N., 1993, Caribbean tourism marketing, management and development strategies, in Gayle, D., J., and Goodrich, J., N., (eds), **Tourism Marketing and Management in the Caribbean**. London: Routledge, 1-19.

Gelen, A., 2003, Local Economic Impacts: The British Open, **Annals of Tourism Research**, 30 (2), 406-425.

Getz, D., 1991a, **Festivals, Special Events and Tourism**. Van Nostrand Reinhold, New York, NY.

Getz, D., 1991b, Special events, in Medlik, S., (ed), **Managing Tourism**. London: Butterworth-Heinemann, 115-130.

Getz, D., 1995, Island competitiveness through festivals and special events: the case of Newfoundland, in Conlin, M., and Baum, T., (eds), **Island Tourism: Management Principles and Practice**. Chichester: John Wiley and Sons, 149-165.

Getz, D., 1997, **Event Management and Event Tourism**. New York: Cognizant Communications.

Getz, D., 1998, Trends, strategies, and issues in sport-event tourism, **Sport Marketing Quarterly**, 7 (2), 8-13.

Getz, D., 2000a, Developing a research agenda for the event management field, in Allen, J., Harris, R., Jago, L., K., and Veal, A., J., (eds), **Events Beyond 2000: Setting the agenda.** Sydney: University of Technology, 10-21.

Getz, D., 2000b, Festivals and special events: life cycle and saturation issues, in Gartner, W., and Lime, D., W., (eds), **Trends in Outdoor Recreation, Leisure and Tourism.** Wallingford: CABI Publishing, 175-185.

Getz, D., 2003, Sports event tourism: Planning, development and marketing, in Hudson, S., (ed.), **Sports and Adventure Tourism.** New York: Hayworth Hospitality Press, Inc, 49-88.

Gibson, H., 1998, Sport tourism: A critical analysis of research, **Sports Management Review,** 1, 45-76.

Gibson, H., J., Willming, C., and Holdnak, A., 2003, Small-scale event sport tourism: fans as tourist, **Tourism Management**, 24, 181-190.

Giddens, A., 1990, **The Consequences of Modernity**. California: Polity Press.

Gill, H., 2005, Barbados aims high, **Nation News**, September 21, 2005, 43A.

Gill, J., and Johnson, P., 1991, **Research Methods for Managers**. London: Paul Chapman Publishing.

Gitelson, R., and Kerstetter, D., 1994, The influence of friends and relatives on the travel decision making process, **Journal of Travel and Tourism Marketing**, 3 (3), 59-68.

Gitelson, R., and Kerstetter, D., 2000, A new perspective on the decision-making process of arts festival visitors, in Allen, J., Harris, R., Jago, L., K., and Veal, A., J., (eds), **Events Beyond 2000: Setting the agenda.** Sydney: University of Technology, 179-185.

Glyptis, S., 1989, **Sport and Tourism in Western Europe**. London: British Travel Education

Glyptis, S., A., 1991, Sport and tourism, in Cooper, C., P., (ed.). **Progress in Tourism Recreation Hospitality Management**, Vol. 3, p. 165-183.

230

Gnoth, J., 1997, Tourism motivation and expectation formation, **Annals of Tourism Research**, (24), 283-304.

Godfrey K., 1998, Attitude towards "sustainable tourism" in the UK: a view from local government, **Tourism Management**, 19 (3), 213-224.

Gold, R., L., 1969, Roles in sociological field observations, in McCall, G., J., Simmons, J., L., 1969, **Issues in Participant Observation**. New York: Random House, pp, 30-39.

Goldbaltt, J., 1990, **Special Events** (3rd Ed.). New York: John Wiley and Sons.

Goldbaltt, J., 2002, **Special Events: Twenty-First Century Global Event Management** (3rd Ed.). New York: John Wiley and Sons.

Goldblatt, J., 2000, A future for event management: The analysis of major trends impacting the emerging profession, in Allen, J., Harris, R., Jago, L., K., and Veal, A., J., (eds) **Events Beyond 2000: Setting the agenda**. Sydney: University of Technology, 2-9.

Golf souvenirs way beyond one's pocket, 2006, **Nation News,** December 18, 2006, 18.

Gonzalez, A., A., and Bello, 2002, The construct 'lifestyle' in market segmentation: the behaviour of tourist/consumers, **European Journal of Marketing**, 36 (1/2), 51-85.

Gratton, C., and Dobson, N., 1999, The economic benefits of hosting major sport events, **Insights,** July (1999), 31- 36.

Gratton, C., Dobson N., and Shibli, S., 2000, The economic importance of major sports events: a case-study of six events, **Managing Leisure**, 5, 17-28.

Gratton, C., Shibli, S., and Coleman, R., 2006, The economic impact of major sports events: a review of ten events in the UK, in Horne, J., and Manzenreiter, W., (eds), **Sports Mega-Events: Social Scientists Analyses of a Global Phenomenon**: Oxford: Blackwell Publishing, 41-58.

231

Green, G., L., 2002, marketing the nation: Carnival and tourism in Trinidad and Tobago, **Critique of Antropology**, 22 (3), 283-304.

Green, B., C., 2001, Leveraging subculture and Identity to promote sport events, **Sport Management Review,** 4 (1), 1-19.

Green, B., C., and Chalip, L., 1998, Sport tourism as the celebration of sub-culture, **Annals of Tourism Research**, 25 (2), 275-291.

Gunn, C., 1988, **Vacationscape: Designing Tourist Regions** (2nd ed.). New York: Van Nostrand Reinhold.

Gwinner, K., 1997, A model of image creation and image transfer in event sponsorship,
International Marketing Review, 14 (3), 145-158.

Gwinner, K., and Eaton, J., 1999, Building brand image through event sponsorship: the role of image transfer, **Journal of Advertising**, 28 (4), 47-57.

Hakim, C., 1987, **Research Design: Strategies and Choices in the Design of Social Research**. London: Routledge.

Hall, C., M., 1989, Hallmark tourists events: analysis, definition, methodology and review, in Syme, G., J., Shaw., B., J., Fenton, D., M., Mueller, W., S., (eds), **The Planning and Evaluation of Hallmark Events. Aldershot:** Avebury, 3-19.

Hall, C. M., 1992a, **Hallmark Tourist Events: Impacts, Management and Planning.** London: Belhaven Press.

Hall, C., M., 1992b, Adventure, sport and health tourism, in Weiler, B., and Hall, C., M., (eds). **Special Interest Tourism**, New York: Belhaven Press, 141-158.

Hall, C. M., 1997, **Hallmark Tourist Events: Impacts, Management and Planning.** London: Belhaven Press.
Hall, C., M., 2006, Urban entrepreneurship, corporate interests and mega events: the thin policies of competitiveness with the hard outcomes of neo-liberalism, in Horne, J., and Manzenreiter, W., (eds),

Sports Mega-Events: Social Scientists Analyses of a Global Phenomenon: Oxford: Blackwell Publishing, 59-70.

Hall, C., M., and Selwood, J., 1989, America's Cup lost: paradise retained? The dynamics of a hallmark event, in Syme, G., J., Shaw., B., J., Fenton, D., M., and Mueller, W., S., (eds), **The Planning and Evaluation of Hallmark Events. Aldershot:** Avebury, 103-118.

Hammersley and Atkinson, 1995, **Ethnography. Principles in Practice** (2nd ed.). London: Routledge.

Hammersley, M., 1989, **The Dilemma of Qualitative Method: Herbert Blumer and the Chicago Tradition.** London: Routledge.

Handy, C., 1993, **Understanding organisations**. New York: Oxford University Press.

Hanefors, M., and Mossberg, L., 2002, TV travel shows-A pre-taste of the destination, **Journal of Vacation Marketing,** 8 (3), 235-246.

Hankinson, G., 2004, The brand images of tourism destinations: a study of the saliency of organic images, **Journal of Product and Brand Management,** 13 (1), 6-14.

Hansen, H., and Gauthier, R., 1993, Spectators Views of PGA golf Events. **Sports Marketing Quarterly**, 2 (1), 17-25.

Hansen, H., and Gauthier, R., 1994, Spectators views of PGA golf events, in Cochran, A., J., and Farrally, M., R., (eds), **Science and Golf 11 Proceedings of the 1994 World Scientific Congress of Golf**: London: E & FN SPON, 596-601.

Happy days ahead at The Oval, 2008, **Sporting Barbados,** Barbados: Hiltop Publications, 42-44.

Haralambus, M., and Holborn, M., 1995, **Sociology: Themes and Perspectives. London:** Unwin Hyman Ltd.

Hargreaves, J., 1986**, Sport, Power and Culture**. Cambridge: Polity Press

Hazlewood, S, 2005, Sandy Lane bids to be No.1, **Nation Newspaper December,** 21, 2005. [On-Line], Available: htpp://bararchive.bits.baseview.com/archive_detail.php?archiveFile=./ pubfiles/bar/arc, accessed, 23 June, 2006.

Hede, A., 2005, Sports-events, tourism and destination marketing strategies: an Australian case study of Athens 2004 and its media telecast, **Journal of Sport Tourism,** 10 (3), 187-200.

Hede, A., and Jago, L., 2005, Perceptions of the host destination as a result of attendance at a special event: a post-consumption analysis, **International Journal of Event Management Research,** 1 (1), 1-12.

Hede, A & Kellett, P. (2008): "Examining the Relationship Between Event Owners and Host Destinations": Paper Presented at The Cathe Conference, Hong Kong, China, 7-9 September, 2006.

Hennessey, J., 1992, **Global Marketing Strategies** (2nd ed). Boston: Houghton Mifflin Company.

Henwood, K., L., and Pidgeon, N., P., 1993, Qualitative research and Psychological Theorising, in Hammersley, M., (ed). **Social Research: Philosophy, Politics and Practice**. London: Sage.

Higham, J., 1999, Commentary – sport as an avenue of tourism development: an analysis of the positive and negative impacts of sport tourism, **Current Issues in Tourism,** 2 (1), 82-90.

Higham, J., and Hinch, T., 2002, Tourism, sport and seasons: the challenge and potential of overcoming seasonality in the sport and tourism sectors, **Tourism Management,** 23, 175-185.

Hiller, H., H., 1989, Impact and image: the convergence of urban factors in preparing for the 1988 Calgary Winter Olympics, in Syme, G., J., Shaw., B., J., Fenton, D., M., and Mueller, W., S., (eds), **The Planning and Evaluation of Hallmark Events**. Aldershot: Avebury, 119, 131.

Hiller, H., H., 1998, Assessing the impacts of mega events: a linkage model, **Current Issues in Tourism,** 1 (1), 47-57.

Hiller, H., H., (2000), Mega-events, urban boosterism and growth strategies: an analysis of the objectives and legitimisation of the Cape Town 2004 Olympic bid, **International Journal of Urban Regional Research,** 24 (2), 440-458.

Hinch, T., and Higham. J., 2004, **Aspects of Tourism: Sport Tourism Development**. Clevedon: Channel View Publications.

Hirschman, E.C., and Holbrook, M., B., 1992, **Postmodern Consumer Research: The Study of Consumption as Text.** Newbury Park, CA: Sage.

Hoek, J., Gendall, P., Jeffcoat, M., and Orsman, D., 1997, Sponsorship and advertising: a comparison of their effects, **Journal of Marketing Communications**, 3, 21-32.

Holbrook, E., C., and Hirshman, M., B., 1982, The experiential aspects of consumption: consumer fantasies, feelings and fun, **Journal of Consumer Research**, 9, 132-140.

Holder, J, 2003, **What is at stake for the Caribbean in hosting the Cricket World Cup 2007 event**, An address to the CTO Teachers Forum, July 2003 (Unpublished).

Holder, J., 1993, The CTO's role in Caribbean tourism development, in Gayle, D., J., and Goodrich, J., N., (eds), **Tourism Marketing and Management in the Caribbean.** London: Routledge, 206-219.

Holdtein, J., and Gubrium, J., 1997, Active interviewing, in Silverman, D., 1997 (ed). **Qualitative Research: Theory Method and Practice**. London: Sage, 113-129.

Honigmann, J., J., 1987, Sampling in ethnographic fieldwork, in Burgess, R., G., (ed), **Field Research: A Sourcebook and Field Manual**. London: Allen and Unwin, 79-90.

Hope, H., 2006, Barbados could be next venue for golf tour, **Nation News,** May 15, 2006. [On-line], Available: http://bararchive.bits.baseview.com/archive_detail.php?archiveFile=./pubfiles/bar/archive/2006/May/15/Business/19770.xml&start=0&numPer=20&keyword=Barbados+could+be+next+venue+for+golf+tour&sectionSearch=&begindate=1%2F1%2F1994&enddate=12%2F31%2F2008&authorSearch=&IncludeStories=1&pubsection=&page=&IncludePages=1&IncludeImages=1&mode=allwords&archive_pubname=Daily+Nation%0A%09%09%09, accessed, May 16, 2006.

Horne, J, D., and Manzenreiter, W., 2004, Accounting for mega-events. Forecast and actual impacts of the 2002 Football World Cup finals on the host countries Japan/Korea, **International Review for the Sociology of Sport**, 39 (2), 187-302.

Horne, J., and Manzenreiter, W., 2006, **Sports Mega-Events: Social Scientists Analyses of a Global Phenomenon**: Oxford: Blackwell Publishing.

Houlihan, B., 2003, **Sport and Society: A Student Introduction**. London: Sage Publications.

Hoyer, W., D., and Brown, S., P., 1990, Effect of brand awareness on choice for a common repeat- purchase product, **Journal of Consumer Research,** 17 (2), 141-148.

Hoyos, F., A., 1978, **Barbados: A History from Amerindian to Independence**. London: MacMillian.

Hudson, S., 2003, Sports **and Adventure Tourism**. New York: Hayworth Hospitality Press, Inc.

Hsu, C., Kang, S., and Lam, T., 2006, Reference Group Influences among Chinese Travellers, **Journal of Travel Research**, 44 (4), 474-484.

Hsu, C., H., C., and Powers, T., 2002, **Marketing Hospitality** (3rd ed.). New York: John Wiley and Sons.

236

Humberstone, B., 1997a, Perspectives on Research in outdoor education, values and ethics, **The Journal of Adventure and Outdoor leadership,** 14 (1), Spring, 7-9.

Humberstone, B., 1997b, Challenging dominant ideologies in the research process, in Clarke, G., and Humberstone, B., (eds), **Researching Women and Sport**. London: MacMillan Press Ltd., 199-213.

Hunt, K., A., Bristol, T., and Bashaw, R., E., 1999, A conceptual approach to classifying sports fans, **Journal of Services Marketing**, 13 (6), 439- 452.

Hunter-Jones, P., 2004, Young people, holiday taking and cancer, an exploratory analysis, **Tourism Management**, 25, 249-258.

Ingerson, L., and Westerbeek, H., M., 1999, Determining key success criteria for attracting hallmark sporting events, **Pacific Tourism Review**, 3, 239-253.

Ioannides, D., and Debbage, K., G., 1997, Post-Fordism and flexibility: the travel industry polyglot, **Tourism Management**, 18 (4), 229-241.

Ioannides, D., and Holcomb, B, 2003, Misguides policy initiatives in small-island destinations: why up-market tourism policies fail?, **Tourism Geographies**, 5 (1), 39-48.

Iso-Ahola, S., E., 1982, Towards a social psychological theory of tourism motivation:
A rejoinder, **Annals of Tourism Research**, 9, 256-262.

Issa, J., J., and Jayawardena , C., 2003, The 'all-inclusive' concept in the Caribbean, **International Journal of Contemporary Hospitality Management**, 15 (3), 167-171.

ITG Barbados, 2005, **Barbados Tourism Authority** promotional brochure.

Its Tee Time, 2006, **Sporting Barbados,** Barbados: Hiltop Publications Ltd, 80-89.

Janiskee, R., 1996, Historic houses and special events, **Annals of Tourism Research,** 23 (2), 398-414.

Jarvis, J., 1995, **The Tourism Impact of the Australian Open Tennis.** [On-Line], Available: http://www.arts.monash.edu.au/ncas/tourism/Austopen.htm, accessed on October 30, 2005.

Jawahar, I., M., and Mclaughlin, G., L., 2001, Towards a descriptive stakeholder theory: An organisational life cycle approach, **Academy of Management Review**, 26 (3), 397-414.

Jayawardena, C., 2002, Mastering Caribbean tourism, **International Journal of Contemporary Hospitality Management,** 14 (2), 88-93.

Jayawardena, C., 2003, Revolution to revolution: why is tourism booming in Cuba, **International Journal of Contemporary Hospitality Management**, 15 (1), 52-58.

Jennings, G., P., 2005, Interviewing: a focus on qualitative techniques, in Ritchie, B., W., Burns, P., and Palmer, C., (eds), **Tourism Research Methods: Integrating Theory with Practice**. Massachusettes: CABI Publishing, 99-117.

John, G., 2002, Stadia and tourism, in Gammon, S., and Kurtzman, J., (eds.), **Sport Tourism: Principles and Practice**, United Kingdom: Leisure Studies Association, p. 53-59.

Jones, C., 2001, Mega-events and host region-impacts: Determining the true worth of the 1999 Rugby World Cup, **International Journal of Tourism Research**, 3, 241-251.

Jones, M., and Stokes, T., 2003, The Commonwealth Games and urban regeneration: an investigation into training initiatives and partnerships and their effects on disadvantaged groups in East Manchester, **Managing Leisure**, 8 (October), 198-211.

Jorgensen, D., L., 1989, **Participant Observation: A Methodology for Human Studies**. London: Sage.

Kalakowski, L., 1993, An overall view of Positivism, in Hammersley, M., (ed), **Social Research: Philosophy, Politics and Practice**. London: Sage.

Kambitsis. C., Harahousou, Y., Theodorakis, N., and Chatzibeis, G., 2002, Sports advertising in print media: the case of the 2000 Olympic games, **Corporate Communications, an International Journal**, 7 (3), 155-161.

Kang, Y. S., and Perdue, R., 1994, Long-term impacts of a mega-event on international tourism to the host country: A conceptual model and the case of the 1988 Seoul Olympics, in Uysal, M., (ed), **Global Tourism Behaviour**. New York: International Business Press, 205-225.

Kasimati, E., 2003, Economic aspects and the summer olympics: a review of related research, **The International Journal of Tourism Research**, Nov/Dec (5:6), 433-444.

Kellehear, A., 1993, **The Unobtrusive Researcher. A Guide to Methods**. New South Wales: Allen and Urwin Pty, Ltd.

Kellner, D., 2003, **Media Spectacle**. London: Routledge.

Krohn, F., B., and Clarke, M., 1998, Psychological and sociological influences on attendance at small college sporting events, **College Student Journal,** 32 (2), 277-287.

Kim, H., and Richardson, S., 2003, Motion picture impacts on destination images, **Annals of Tourism Research,** 30 (1), 216-237.

Kim, N. and Chalip, L., 2004, Why travel to the FIFA World Cup? Effects of motives, background, interest, and constraints, **Tourism Management**, 25, 695-707.

Kim, S., S., and Morrison, A., M., 2005, Changes of images of South Korea among foreign tourists after the 2002 FIFA World Cup, **Tourism Management**, 26, 233-247.

Kim, S., S., and Petrick, J., F., 2005, Residents' perceptions on impacts of the FIFA 2002 World Cup: the case of Seoul as a host city, **Tourism Management**, 26, 25-38.

Kim, S., S., Chun, H., and Petrick, J., F., 2005, Positioning analysis of overseas golf tour destinations by Korean golf tourists, **Tourism Management**, 26, 905-917.

Kim, S., S., Lee, C., and Klenosky, D., B., 2003, The influence of push and pull factors at Korean national parks, **Tourism Management**, 24, 169-180.

Kinkead, N., 2002, **The Influence of Movies on Tourists' Travel Decision Making,** Masters Dissertation, University of Surrey. Unpublished.

Kinkema, K., M., and Harris, J., C., 1998, Media sport studies: Key research and emerging issues, in Wenner, L., (ed), **Media Sport**. New York: Routledge, 27-54.

Kirk, J., and Miller, M., 1986, **Reliability and Validity in Qualitative Research, Qualitative Research Methods Series No. 1**. London: Sage.

Kurtzman, J., and Zauhar, J., 1997, A wave in time –The sports tourism phenomena, **Journal of Sport Tourism**, 4, 5-10.

Knight, F., 1990, **The Caribbean. The Genesis of a Fragmented Nationalism.** New York: Oxford University Press.

Knowles, T., and Curtis, S., 1999, The market viability of European mass tourist destinations. A post-stagnation life cycle analysis, **The International Journal of Tourism Research**, 1, 87- 96.

Koh, K., Y., and Jackson, A., A., 2006, Special events marketing: An analysis of a country Fair, **Journal of Convention and Event Tourism**, 8 (2), 19-40.

Kotler, P., 1973, Atmospherics as a marketing tool, **Journal of Retailing**, 49 (4), 48-65.

Kotler, P., 2003, **A Framework for Marketing Management** (2nd Ed.). London: Pearsons.

Kotler, P., Armstrong, G., Saunders, J., and Wong, V., 2002, **Principles of Marketing.** Essex: Pearson Education Group.

Kotler, P., Asplund, C., Rein, I. and Haider, D, 1999, **Marketing Places Europe**. Harlow: Pearson Education Limited.

Kotler, P., Haider, D., H., and Rein, I., 1993, **Marketing Places**. New York: The Free Press.

Kozak, M., and Rimmington, M., 1999, Measuring tourist destination competitiveness: conceptual considerations and empirical findings, **International Journal of Hospitality Management**, 18, 273-283.

Laws, C., 1993, **Urban Tourism: Attracting Visitors to Large Cities**. New York: Mansell Publishing Limited.

Laws, E, 1995, **Tourists Destination Management**: Issues, Analysis and Policies. London: Routledge.

Laws, E., 1991, **Tourism Marketing: Service and Quality Management Perspectives**. Cheltenham: Stanley Thornes (Publishers) Ltd.

Laws, E., Scott, N., and Parfitt, N., 2002, Synergies in destination image management: a case study in conceptualization, **International Journal of Tourism Research**, 4, 39-55.

Lawson, F., and Baud-Bovy, M., 1977 *as cited in* Baloglu and McCleary (1999 p. 871).

Lawton, L., 2005, Resident perceptions of tourists attractions on the Gold Coast of Australia, **Journal of Travel Research**, 44, 188-200.

Lee, C., and Taylor, T., 2005, Critical reflection on the economic impact assessment of a mega-event: the case of 2002 FIFA World Cup, **Tourism Management**, 26, 595-603.

Legacy Barbados, 2006, **Barbados Legacy Document.** [On-Line], Available: www.totallybarbados.com/The_Legacy_Vision_For_Barbados.pdf, accessed on November 12, 2006.

Lehto, X., Y., O'Leary, J., T., and Morrison, A., M., 2002, Do psychographics influence vacation destination choices? A comparison of British travellers to North America, Asia and Oceania, **Journal of Vacation Marketing**, 8 (2), 109-125.

Lenskyj, H., 2000, **Inside the Olympic Industry: Power, Politics and Activism**. Albany: SUNY Press.

Lewis, A., 2002, **A Case Study of Tourism Curriculum Development in the Caribbean: A Stakeholder Perspective.** A PhD thesis, Buckinghamshire Chilterns University College, Brunel University. Unpublished.

Lewis, G., K., 1968, **The Growth of the Modern West Indies:** USA: Monthly Review Press.

Light, D., 1996, Characteristics of the audience for 'events' at a heritage site, **Tourism Management**, 17 (3), 183-190.

Lincoln, Y., S., and Guba, E., G., 1985, **Naturalistic Inquiry**. California: Sage.

Lockhart, G., G., 1997, Island and tourism: an overview, in Lockhart, D., and Drakakis-Smith, D., (eds), **Island Tourism: Trends and Prospects**. New York: Pinter, 3-20.

Loda, M., D., Norman, W., and Backman, K., 2007, Advertising and Publicity: suggested new applications for tourism marketers, **Journal of Tourism Research**, 45, 259-265.

Loury, G., C., 2000, Social exclusion and ethnic groups: The challenge to economics. **Conference Proceedings**, Annual World Bank Conference on Development Economics, 1999, 225-252. [On-Line], Available: http://www.bu.edu/irsd/files/socialethnic.pdf, accessed August, 3, 2008.

Loveridge, A., 2006, Heads up on a tough year for tourism, **Nation News**, May 8, 2006, 1.

Lowerson, J., R., 1994, Golf for all? The problem of municipal provision, in Cochran, A., J., and Farrally, M., R., (eds), **Science and Golf 11 Proceedings of the 1994 World Scientific Congress of Golf:** London: E & FN SPON, 602-610.

Lumsdon, L., 1997, **Tourism Marketing**. London: International Thomson Business Press.

Lundberg, D., E., 1971 *as cited in* Neirotti, Bosetti and Teed (2001: 327).

MacKay, K., J., and Fesenmaier, D., 1997, Pictorial element of destination image formation, **Annals of Tourism Research**, 24 (3), 537-565.

MacKay, K., J., and Fesenmaier, D., 2000, An exploration of cross-cultural destination image assessment, **Journal of Travel Research**, 38 (May), 417-423.

Mackellar, J., and Fenton, J., 2000, Hosting the international travel media-a review of the Australian tourists commission's visiting journalist programme, **Journal of Vacation Marketing,** 6 (3), 255-264.

Madden, J., R., 2002, The economic consequences of the Sydney Olympic Games: the CREA/Arthur Andersen Study, **Current Issues in Tourism**, 5 (1), 7-21.

Maguire, J., 1999, **Global Sport: Identities, Societies, and Civilizations. Cambridge**: Polity Press.

Malhotra, N., K., 1999, **Marketing Research: An Applied Orientation** (3rd ed). New Jersey: Prentice Hall.

Mansfield, Y., 1992, From motivation to actual travel, **Annals of Tourism Research,** 19, 399-419.

Marivoet, S., 2006, UEFA Euro 2004 Portugal: The social construction of a sports mega-events and spectacle, in Horne, J., and Manzenreiter, W., (eds), **Sports Mega-Events: Social Scientists Analyses of a Global Phenomenon:** Oxford: Blackwell Publishing, 127-143.

Markwick, M., C., 2000, Golf tourism development, stakeholders, differing discourses and alternative agendas: the case of Malta, **Tourism Management**, 21, 513-524.

Marris, T., 1987, The role and impact of mega events and attractions on regional and national tourism development. **Conference Proceedings**, AIEST, Calgary, Canada, 4-12.

Marshall, C., and Rossman, G., B., 1995, **Designing Qualitative Research** (2nd ed.). London: Sage.

Mason, D., S., 1999, What is the sports product and who buys it? The marketing of professional sports leagues, **European Journal of Marketing**, 33 (3/4), 402-418.

Mason, J., 1994, Linking qualitative and quantitative data analysis, in Bryman and Burgess (eds.), **Analysing Qualitative Data**. New York: Routledge.

Mason, J., 1996, **Qualitative Researching**. London: Sage.

Mason, P., Grapowski, P., and Du, W., 2005, Severe acute respiratory syndrome, tourism and the media, **International Journal of Tourism Research**, Jan/Feb, 7, 1.

Masterman, G., 2004, **Strategic Sport Event Management: An International Approach.** London: Elsevier.

Matheson, V., A., and Baade, R., A., 2003, **Mega-Sporting Events in Developing Nations:Playing the Way to Prosperity?** [On-Line], Available: http://www.holycross.edu/departments/economics/RePEc/Matheson_P rosperity.pdf accessed August 10, 2006.

244

Mathieson, A., and Wall, G., 1982, **Tourism: Economic, Physical and Social Impacts**. New York: Longman.

Matos, P., 2006, Hosting mega sport events: A brief assessment of their multidimentional Impacts. **Conference Proceedings**, The Copenhagen Conference on the Economic and Social Impact of Hosting Mega Sports Events, September 2006. [On-Line], Available: http://www.cbs.dk/layout/set/print/content/download/48306/694337/fil e/Pedro%20Matos%20Paper.pdf. accessed June 10, 2007.

Matzitelli, D., 1989, Major sports events in Australia–some economic tourism and sportsrelated effects, in Syme, G., J., Shaw, B., J., Fenton, D., W., and Mueller, W.,S., (eds.), **The Planning and Evaluation of Hallmark Events.** Aldershot, UK: Avebury, 195-202.

May, T., 1993, **Social Research: Issues, Methods and Processes**. Buckingham: Open University Press.

Maykut, P., and Morehouse, R., 1994, **Beginning Qualitative Research**: **A Philosophic and Practical Guide.** London: The Palmer Press.

Mayo, E., and Jarvis, L., 1981, **The psychology of Leisure Travel.** Boston: CBI Publishing.

McCall, G., J., and Simmons, J., L., 1969, **Issues in Participant Observation**. New York: Random House.

McCartney, G., J., 2004, Hosting a recurring mega-event; visitor raison d'être, **Journal of Sport Tourism**, 10 (2), 113-128.

McCracken, G., 1988, **Culture and Consumption: New Approaches to the Symbolic Character of Consumer Goods and Activities**. Bloomington, IN: Indiana University Press.

McCutcheon, L., E., Lange, R., and Houran, J., 2002, Conceptualization and measurement of celebrity worship, **British Journal of Psychology,** 93 (pt 1), 67-87

McDonnell, I., Allen, J., and O'Toole, W., 1999, **Festival and Special Event Management.** Brisbane: John Wiley and Sons.

245

McIntosh, R., and Goeldner, C., 1986, **Tourism Principles, Practices and Philosophies**. New York: John Wiley and Sons.

McIntosh, R., Goeldner, C., and Ritchie, J.,R.,B., 1995, **Tourism, principles, practices, philosophies** (7th ed.). New York: John Wiley and Sons.

McNeill, P., 1985, **Research Methods** (2nd ed.). London: Routledge.

Meenaghan, T., and Shipley, D., 1999, **Media effect in commercial sponsorship, European Journal of Marketing,** 33 (3/4), 328-347.

Melnick, M., 1993, Searching for sociability in the stand: A theory of sports spectating. **Journal of Sport Management**, 7, 44-60.

Mercille, J., 2005, Media effects on image: the case of Tibet, **Annals of Tourism Research**, 32 (4), 1039-1055.

Middleton, V. T. C., and Clarke J., 2001, **Marketing in Travel and Tourism** (3rd ed.), Oxford: Butterworth-Heinemann.

Mihalik, B., J., 2000, Host Population Perceptions of the 1996 Atlanta Olympics: Support, Benefits and Liabilities, in Harris, R. Jago, L. and Veal, A.J. (eds) **Events Beyond 2000: Setting the agenda**. Sydney: University of Technology, 134-140.

Miles, M., B., and Huberman, A., M., 1994, **Qualitative Data Analysis** (2nd ed.). London: Sage.

Miller, J., and Glassner, B., 1997, The 'inside' and the 'outside': finding realities in interviews, in Silverman, D., (ed), **Qualitative Research: Theory Method and Practice**. London: Sage, 99-111.

Miller, S., 1989, Heritage management for heritage tourism, **Tourism Management,** (March 1989), 9-14.

Millman, A., and Pizam, A, 1995, The role of awareness and familiarity with a destination: the central florida case, **Journal of Travel Research**, 33 (3), 21-27.

Milner, D., 1995, **Success in Advertising and Promotion.** London: John Murray.

Mintel, 2005, **Mintel Reports**. [On-Line], Available: www.http://Reports.mintel.com/sinatra/reports/search_results/show& &type=RCItem&page=... accessed 23/06/06.

Morgan, N., & Pritchard, A. , 1999, Contextualizing destination branding, in Morgan, N., Pritchard, A., and Pride, R., (eds.), **Destination Branding: Creating the Unique Destination Proposition**. Oxford: Butterworth-Heinemann, 11-42.

Morley, 1995, Theories of consumption in media studies, in Miller. D., (ed), **Acknowledging Consumption: A Review of New Studies**. London: Routledge.

Morse, J., 2001, The Sydney 2000 Olympic Games: How the Australian Tourist Commission leveraged the games for tourism, **Journal of Vacation Marketing,** 7 (2), 101-107.

Morton, A, 1977, **A Guide Through the Theory of Knowledge** (2nd ed.). Massachusetts: Blackwell Publishers.

Mossberg, L., L., and Hallberg, A., 1999, The presence of a mega-event: effects on destination image and product-country images, **Pacific Tourism Review,** 3, 213-225.

Moutinho, L., 1984, Vacation tourist decision process, **The Quarterly Review of Marketing,** (Spring), 8-17.

Moutinho, L., 1987, Consumer behaviour in tourism, **European Journal of marketing**, 21, (10), 5-44.

Moutinho, L., 2000, Trends in tourism, in Moutinho, L., (ed.), **Strategic Management in Tourism.** London: CABI Publishing, 1-16.

Mules, T., and Faulkner, B., 1996, An Economic Perspective on Special Events, **Tourism Economics**, 2 (2), 107-417.

Mullen, B., and Johnson, C., 1990, **The Psychology of Consumer Behaviour**. New York: Lawrence Erlbaum.

Murray, H., 1938, **Explorations in Personality**. New York: Oxford University Press.

National Strategic Plan of Barbados, 2005, **Government of Barbados National Strategic Plan of Barbados, 2005-2025.** [On-Line], Available: http://www.sice.oas.org/ctyindex/BRB/Plan2005-2025.pdf, accessed, December 12, 2006.

Nauright, J., 2004, Global games: culture, political economy and sport in the globalised world of the 21st century, **Third World Quarterly**, 25 (7), 1325-1336.

Neirotti, L., D., 2003, An introduction to sports and adventure tourism, in Hudson, S., (ed.), **Sports and Adventure Tourism.** New York: Hayworth Hospitality Press, Inc., 1-25.

Neirotti, L., D., Bosetti, H., A., Teed, K., C., 2001, Motivation to attend the 1996 summer Olympic games, **Journal of Travel Research,** 39, 327-331.

Nicholls, J., A., F., Roslow, S., and Dublish, S., 1999, Brand recall and brand preferences at sponsored golf and tennis tournaments, **European Journal of Marketing**, 33 (3/4), 365-387.

Nicholson, R. E., and Pearce, D., 2000, Who goes to events: a comparative analysis of the profile characteristics of visitors to four south island events in New Zealand, **Journal of Vacation Marketing** 6 (1), 237-253.

Nicholson, R. E., and Pearce, D., 2001, Why do people attend events: a comparative analysis of visitor motivations at four south island events, **Journal of Travel Research,** 39 (May), 449-460.

Nielsen, Christian, 2001, **Tourism and the Media**. Sydney: Hospitality Press, PTY.

Nogawa, H., Yamaguchi, Y., and Hagi., Y., 1996, An empirical research study on Japanese sport tourism in sport-for-all-events: Case studies of a single-night event and a multiple-night event, **Journal of Travel Research**, Fall (1996), 46-54.

Norris, C., E., Colman, A., M., and Aleixo, P., A., 2003, Selective exposure to television programmes and advertising effectiveness, **Applied Cognitive Psychology,** 17, 593-606.

O'Brien, T., Tapia, H., and Brown, T., 1997, The self-concept in buyer behaviour, **Business Horizons**, October, 65-71.

O'Donohoe, 1994, Advertising uses and gratifications**, Journal of European Marketing,** 28 (8/9) 52-75.

O'Brien, D., 2006, Event business leveraging: the Sydney 2000 Olympic Games, **Annals of Tourism Research,** 33(1), 240-261.

Olds, K., 1998, Urban mega-events, evictions and housing rights: the Canadian case, **Current Issues in Tourism**, 1(1), 2–46.

Oliver, P., 1997, **Teach Yourself Research for Business, Marketing and Education.** London: Hodder and Stoughton Ltd.

Olsen, M., D., and Connolly, D., J., 1998, Forces driving change in the Caribbean. A white Paper on the hospitality industry. **Conference Proceedings,** Caribbean Hotel Industry Conference, Bahamas, June 1998.

Oppenheim, A., N., 1992, **Questionnaire Design, Interviewing and Attitude Measurement.** London: Pinter Publishers.

Oppermann, M., 2000, Triangulation – A methodological discussion, **International Journal of Tourism Research**, 2, 141-146.

O'Toole, A., J., McDonnell, W., and Harris, I., 2002, **Festival and Special Event Management**. Queensland: John Wiley and Sons, Inc.

Otto, J., Ritchie, B., 1996, The service experience in tourism, **Tourism Management**, 17 (3), 165-174.

Palmer, R.W., 1993, Tourism and taxes: the case of Barbados, in Gayle, D., J., and Goodrich, J., N., (eds), **Tourism Marketing and Management in the Caribbean**. London: Routledge, 59-68.

249

Parasuraman, A., 1991, **Marketing Research** (2nd ed.). Massachusetts: Addison-Wesley Publishing Company.

Parker, I, 1994, Qualitative research, in Bannister, P., Burman, E., Parker, I., Taylor, M., and Tindall, C., (eds.)**, Qualitative Methods in Psychology: A Researchers Guide**. Buckingham: Open University Press, 1-16.

Par Ful Stuff, 2008, **Sporting Barbados**. Barbados: Hiltop Pubications Ltd., 97-100.

Past and Future World Golf Championships, 2006. [On-Line], Available, http://www.worldgolfchampionships.com/tournaments/history/r470/, accessed March 10, 2006.

Patton, M., Q., 1987, **How to Use Qualitative Methods in Evaluation**. California: Sage.
Patton, M., Q., 1990, **Qualitative Evaluation and Research Methods**. London: Sage.

Pattulo P., 1996, **Last Resorts. The Cost of Tourism in the Caribbean**. London: Cassell.

Pattulo P., 2005, **Last Resorts. The Cost of Tourism in the Caribbean**. London: Cassell.

Pearce, D., 1989, **Tourism Development** (2nd Ed.). Harlow: Longman Group, UK Ltd.

Perakyla, A., 1997, Reliability and validity in research based on tapes and transcripts, in Silverman, D., 1997, (ed.), **Qualitative Research: Theory Method and Practice**. London: Sage.

Persson, C., 2002, The Olympic games site decision, **Tourism Management,** 23, 27-36.

Peterson. K., I., 1994, Qualitative research methods for the travel and tourism industry, in Brent Ritchie, J., R., and Goeldner, C., R., (eds.), **Travel, Tourism and Hospitality Research: A Handbook for**

Managers and Researchers (2nd ed). New York: John Wiley & Sons, 487-492.

Petrick, J., 2002, Experience use history as a segmentation tool to examine golf travellers' satisfaction, perceived value and repurchase intentions, **Journal of Vacation Marketing,** 8 (4), 332-342.

Petrick, J., F., and Backman, S., J., 2002, An examination of the determinants of golf travellers' satisfaction, **Journal of Travel Research,** 40, 252-258.

Petrof, J., V., and Daghfous, N., 1996, Evoked set: Myth or Reality? **Business Horizons**, (May-June), 72-77.

Philips, M., and Magdalinski, 2003, Sport in Australia, in Houlihan, B.,(ed), **Sport and Society: A Student Introduction**. London: Sage, 312-344.

Pikkemaat, B., and Peters, M., 2004, **The Experience of Cities: On Perception of Cities' Attraction Points**. [On-Line], Available: www.uibk.ac.at/c/c4/c436/tourism/down/birgit/ttra2003.pdf, accessed on May 10, 2004.

Pizam, A., 1994, Planning a tourism research investigation, in Brent Ritchie, J., R., and Goeldner, C., R., (eds.), **Travel, Tourism and Hospitality Research: A Handbook for Managers and Researchers** (2nd ed). New York: John Wiley and Sons, 91-104.

Plog, S., 1974, Why destination areas rise and fall in popularity, **The Cornell Hotel and Restaurant Administration Quarterly**, 14, 55–58.

Plog, S., C., 1994, Developing and using psychographics in tourism research in Brent Ritchie, J., R., and Goeldner, C., R., (eds), **Travel, Tourism and Hospitality Research: A Handbook for Managers and Researchers** (2nd ed). New York: John Wiley and Sons, 209-218.

Poetschke, B., 1995, Key success factors for public/private-sector partnerships in island tourism planning, in Conlin and Baum (eds), **Island Tourism: Management Principles and Practice.** Sussex: John Wiley and Sons, 53-63.

Poon, A., 1988, Innovation and the future of Caribbean tourism, **Tourism Management,** (September), 213-220.

Poon, A., 1998, **Tourism Technology and Competitive Strategy**. Oxon: CABI Publishing.

Pratt, G., 2003, Terrorism and tourism: Bahamas and Jamaica fight back, **International Journal of Contemporary Hospitality Management,** 15 (3), 192-194.

Prentice, R., Witt, S., and Hamer, C., 1998, Tourism as experience: the case of heritage parks, **Annals of Tourism Research**, 25 (1), 1-24.

Preuss, H., 2003, The economics of the Olympic Games: Winners and losers, in Houlihan, B., **Sport and Society: A Student Introduction**. London: Sage, 253-271.

Priest, S., 1996, **Doing Media Research: An Introduction**. London: Sage.

Priestly, G., K., and Ashworth, G., J., 1995, **Sport Tourism: the Case of Golf, Tourism and Spatial Transformations.** Wallingford: CABI publishing.

Priestley, G., 1995, Sports tourism: The case of golf, in Ashworth, G., J., and Dietvorst, A., G., J., (eds), **Tourism and spatial transformations: Implications for policy and planning**. Wallingford: CAB I Publishing, 205-223.

Pringle, H., 2004, **Celebrity Sells**. Chichester: John Wiley and Sons, Ltd.

Punch, K., F., 1998, **Introduction to Social Research: Quantitative and Qualitative Approaches**. London: Sage.

Pyo, S., Cook, R., and Howell, R., L, 1991, Summer Olympic tourist market, in Medlik, S., (ed), **Managing Tourism**. London: Butterworth-Heinemann, 191-198.

Readman, M., 2003, Golf tourism, in Hudson, S., (ed), **Sports and Adventure Tourism**. New York: Hayworth Hospitality Press, 165-201.

Reid., S., D., and Reid, L., J., 1994, Tourism marketing management in small island nations: A tale of micro-destinations, in Uysal, M., (ed), **Global Tourism Behaviour.** New York: International Business Press, 39-60.

Richards, G., 2002, Tourism attraction systems: exploring cultural behaviour, **Annals of Tourism Research**, 29 (4), 1048-1064.

Riley J., and Riley, M.,W., 1959, Mass communication and the Social System, in Merton, R., Broom, L., and Cottrell, L, Jr., (eds), **Sociology Today, Volume 11, Problems and Prospects.** New York: Harper and Row Publishers, 537-578.

Riley, M., Wood, R., C., Clark, M., A., Wilkie, E., and Szivas, E., 2000, **Researching and Writing Dissertations in Business and Management**. Berkshire: Thomson Learning 2000.

Riley, R., Baker, D., and Van Doren, C., W., 1998, Movie Induced Tourism, **Annals of Tourism Research**, 25 (4), 919-935.

Riley, R., W., and Van Doren, C., W., 1992, Movies as tourism promotion, a 'pull' factor in a 'push' location, **Tourism Management**, 13 (3), 267-274.

Ritchie, B., 1984, Assessing the impacts of hallmark events: conceptual and research issues, **Journal of Tourism Research**, 1984, 2-1.1

Ritchie, J., and Lyons, M., 1990, Olympulse VI: A post-event assessment of resident reaction to the XV Olympic Winter Games, **Journal of Travel Research**, 28 (3), 14–23.

Ritchie, J., R., and Smith, B., H., 1991, The impact of a mega-event on host region awareness: A longitudinal study, **Journal of Travel Research**, 30 (1), 3-10.

Robson, C, 1993, **Real World Research: A Resource for Social Scientists and Practitioner-Researchers**. Oxford: Blackwell.

Roche, M., 1994, Mega-events and urban policy, **Annals of Tourism Research**, 21, 1-19.

Roche, M., 2001, Mega-events, Olympic games and the World Student Games 1991 - understanding the impacts and information needs of major sports events. **Conference Proceedings**, Major Sport Events-Learning from Experience, Spring Conference, UMIST Manchester, 1st May 2001. [On-Line], Available: http://http://www.sprig.org.uk/seminar2001/roche.pdf , accessed May 3, 2008.

Roche, M., 2002, The Olympics and 'global citizenship', **Citizenship Studies**, 6 (2), 165-181.

Roche, M., 2006, Mega events and modernity revisited: globalization and the case of the Olympics, in Horne, J., and Manzenreiter, W., (eds), **Sports Mega-Events: Social Scientists Analyses of a Global Phenomenon:** Oxford: Blackwell Publishing, 27-40.

Rooney, J., F., 1988, Mega-sports events as a tourist attraction: a geographical analysis. **Conference Proceedings**, Conference of Tourism Research: Expanding Boundaries. Travel and Tourism Research Association Nineteenth Annual Conference, Montreal, Quebec, Canada, June, 19-23, 93-99.

Ross, G., 1994, **The Psychology of Tourism.** Victoria: Hospitality Press.

Royal Westmoreland, 2006, **Royal Westmoreland**. Unpublished.

Ryan, C., 1991, **Recreational Tourism: A Social Science perspective**. London: Routledge.

Ryan, C., 1995a, Islands, beaches and life-stage marketing, in Conlin, M., V., and Baum, T., (eds), **Island Tourism: Management Principles and Practice**. New York: John Wiley and Sons, 79-93.

Ryan, C., 1995b, **Researching Tourists Satisfaction: Issues, concepts, problems.** London: Routledge.

Ryan, C., 1995c, Learning about tourists from conversations: the over 55s in Majorca, **Tourism Management**, 16 (3), 207-215.

Ryan, C., 1997, From motivation to assessment, in Ryan, C. (ed.), **The tourist experience: A new introduction**. London: Cassell, 59-77.

Ryan, C., and Cave, J., 2005, Structuring destination image: a qualitative approach, **Journal of Travel Research**, 44, 143-150.

Sack, A., and Johnson, A., 1996, Politics, economic development, and the Volvo International Tennis Tournament, **Journal of Sport Management,** 10, 1-14.

Sarantakos, S., 1988, **Social Research**. Hampshire: Palgrave.

Schofield, P., Cinematographic images of a city: alternative heritage tourism in Manchester, **Tourism Management**, 17 (5), 333-340.

Sealy, W. and Wickens, E., 2006, The potential impact of mega sport media on the travel decision-making process and destination choice. The case of Portugal and Euro, 2004. **Conference Proceedings**, The International Conference on the Impact of Movies and Television on Tourism, September 7- 9, 2006, Hong Kong, China, 246-258.

Sealy, W., and Wickens, E., 2008, The potential impact of mega sport media on the travel decision-making process and destination Choice. The case of Portugal and Euro, 2004, **Journal of Travel and Tourism Marketing**, 24 (2/3), 127-137. In Press.

Seaton, A., 1994, Tourism and the media, in Witt and Moutinho (eds.), **Tourism Marketing and Management Handbook** (2nd Ed). Hertfordshire: Prentice Hall International Limited, 135-144.

Seaton, A., V., 1997, Unobtrusive observational measures as a qualitative extension of visitor surveys at festivals and events: mass observation revisited, **Journal of Travel Research**, 35 (4), 25-30.

Sekeran, U., 2002, **Research Methods for Business: A Skill Building Approach (**4th ed.). Chichester: John Wiley and Sons.

Selby, M., and Morgan, N., 1996, Reconstructing place image: A case study of its role in destination market research, **Tourism Management**, 4, 287-294.

Shank, M., 1999, **Sports Marketing: A Strategic Perspective.** New Jersey: Prentice Hall.

Shilbury, D., Quick, S., and Westerbeek, H., 2003, **Strategic Sport Marketing.** Australia: Allen and Unwin.

Shone, A., and Parry, B., 2001, **Successful Event Management.** London: Continuum.

Shimp, T., 1997, **Advertising, Promotion and Supplemental Aspects of Integrated Marketing Communications** (4th ed). Fort Worth: The Dryden Press.

Silvera, D., H., and Austad, B., 2004, factors predicting the effectiveness of celebrity endorsement advertising, **European Journal of Marketing,** 38 (11/12), 1509-1526.

Silverman, D, 1993, **Interpreting Qualitative Data: Methods for Analysing Talk, Text and Interaction.** London: Sage

Silverman, R., 1997, **Qualitative Research: Theory, Method and Practice**. London: Sage.

Silverman, R., 2000, **Doing Qualitative Research.** California: Sage.

Silverstone, R., 1999, **Why Study the Media**. London: Sage.

Sinclair, D., 2005, Sports education - a priority for Caribbean sports tourism, **International Journal of Contemporary Hospitality management**, 17 (6), 536-548.

Sinclair, D., 2006, Golf tourism - World Cup Cricket 2007 - Guyana prospects, **International Journal of Contemporary Hospitality Management**, 18 (7), 583-592.

Sirgy, J., M., 1982, Self- concept in consumer behaviour, **Journal of Consumer Research**, 9, 287-300.

Smith, P., Berry, C., and Pulford, A., 1997, **Strategic Marketing Communications: New Ways to Build and Integrate Communications**. London: Kogan Page Limited.

Smith, S., L.J., 1995, **Tourism Analysis: A Handbook** (2nd Ed). London: Longman.

Solberg, H., 2003, Major sporting events; assessing the value of volunteers' work, **Managing Leisure** 8, 17-27.

Solomon, M., Bamossy, G., and Askegaard, S., 1999, **Consumer Behaviour: a European perspective.** New Jersey: Prentice Hall Europe.

Soutar, G., and McLeod, P., 1993, Residents' perceptions on impact of the America's Cup, **Annals of Tourism Research** 20 (3), 571–82.

Sparks, A., 1992, Writing and the textual construction of realities: some challenges for alternative paradigms in physical education, in Sparks, A, (ed), **Research in Physical Education and Sport: Exploring alternative visions.** London: The Palmer Press, 271-297.

Spencer, G., 1987, Methodological issues in the study of bureaucratic elites: A case study of West Point, in Burgess, R., G., (ed.), **Field Research: A Sourcebook and Field Manual. London**: Allen and Unwin, 23-30.

Spooner, P., 2005, Golf cup big plug for sport tourism, **Nation News**, December 28, 2005. [Online], Available: http://www.nationnews.com/342179411752387.php, accessed, June 10, 2006.

Spooner, P., 2006a, Barbados' golf drive, **Nation News**, May 5, 2006. [On-Line], Available: http://bararchive.bits.baseview.com/archive_detail.php?archiveFile=./p ubfiles/bar/archive/2006/May/05/Sports/19262.xml&start=0&numPer =20&keyword=Barbados%92+golf+drive%2C&sectionSearch=&begi ndate=1%2F1%2F1994&enddate=12%2F31%2F2008&authorSearch= &IncludeStories=1&pubsection=&page=&IncludePages=1&IncludeI mages=1&mode=allwords&archive_pubname=Daily+Nation%0A%09 %09%09, accessed August 10, 2006.

Spooner, P., 2006b, Barbados could be next venue for golf tour, **Nation News**, May 15, 2006. [On-Line], Available: http://bararchive.bits.baseview.com/archive_detail.php?archiveFile=./pubfiles/bar/archive/2006/May/15/Business/19770.xml&start=0&numPer=20&keyword=barbados+could+be+venue+for+next+golf+tour&sectionSearch=&begindate=1%2F1%2F1994&enddate=12%2F31%2F2008&authorSearch=&IncludeStories=1&pubsection=&page=&IncludePages=1&IncludeImages=1&mode=allwords&archive_pubname=Daily+Nation%0A%09%09%09, accessed July 10, 2006.

Spooner, P., 2006c, Tee time! US$4m World Cup gets going today, **Nation News**, December, 7, 2006, 1.

Spooner, P., 2006d, Tiger for cup, **Nation News,** September 21, 2006, 29A.

Spooner, P., 2006e, Full Monty Ahead, **Nation News,** December 7, 2006, 29.

Spooner, P., 2006f, Golf's top stars for Barbados tournament, **Nation News,** September 27, 2006, 43A.

Spooner, P., 2006g, Down to a tee: Barbados set for World Cup Golf, **Nation News**, December 5, 2006: 26A.

Spooner, P., 2006h, Golf Gift, **Nation News**, December, 9, 2006. [On-Line], Available: http://bararchive.bits.baseview.com/archive_detail.php?archiveFile=./pubfiles/bar/archive/2006/December/09/LocalNews/29969.xml&start=0&numPer=20&keyword=Golf+Gift&sectionSearch=&begindate=1%2F1%2F1994&enddate=12%2F31%2F2008&authorSearch=&IncludeStories=1&pubsection=&page=&IncludePages=1&IncludeImages=1&mode=allwords&archive_pubname=Daily+Nation%0A%09%09%09,accessed December, 20, 2006.

Sporting Barbados, 2007, **Barbados Tourism Authority**: Hilltop Publications.

Stacey, M., 1969, **Methods of Social Research**. Oxford: Pergamon Press

Standeven, J., and De Knop, P., 1999, **Sport Tourism**. Champaign: Human Kinetics.

Stead, D, 2003, Sport and the media in Houlihan, B (ed) **Sport and Society: A Student Introduction.** London: Sage.

Stoddart, B., 1990, Wide world of golf: A research note on the interdependence of sport, culture, and economy, **Sociology of Sport Journal,** 7, 378–388.

Storey, K., R.,1994, Targeting for success- the European golf market, in Cochran, A., J., and Farrally, M., R., (eds), **Science and Golf 11 Proceedings of the 1994 World Scientific Congress of Golf:** London: E & FN SPON, 589-601

Strachan, I., G., 2002, **Paradise and Plantation: Tourism and Culture in the Anglophone Caribbean**. Virginia: University of Virginia Press.

Strauss, A., 1987, **Qualitative Analysis for Social Scientists**. London: Cambridge University Press.

Strauss, A., Corbin, J., 1990, **Basics of Qualitative Research: Grounded Theory and Procedures and Techniques.** London: Sage.

Sullivan, M., 2004, Sport marketing, in Beech, J., and Chadwick., (eds), **The Business of Sport Management**. Essex: Prentice Hall, 128-153.

Sustainable Tourism Policy, 2002, Green Paper on the Sustainable Development of Tourism in Barbados - A Policy Framework. [On-Line], Available: http://www.barmot.gov.bb/Latest%20Tourism%20Policy%20Docume nt%20Revised%20May%2028%202001.pdf, accessed on March 26, 2006.

Swarbrooke, J., 1999, **Sustainable Tourism Management**. Oxford: CABI Publishing.

Swarbrooke, J., 2000, **Sustainable Tourism Management**. Oxford: CABI Publishing.

Swarbrooke, J., 2002, **The Development and Management of Visitor Attractions** (2nd ed.) Oxford: Butterworth-Heinemann.

Swarbrooke, J., and Horner, S., 2003, **Consumer Behaviour in Tourism** (2nd eds.). Oxford: Butterworth-Heinemann.

Tapachai, N., and Waryszak, R., 2000, An examination of the role of beneficial image in tourist destination selection, **Journal of Travel Research**, 39 (1), 37-44.

Teigland, J., 1999, Mega-events and impacts on tourism; the predictions and realities of the Lillehammer Olympics, **Impact Assessment and Project Appraisal**, 17 (4), 305 – 317.

The Legacy of Cricket World Cup, 2007, 2008, **Sporting Barbados**. Barbados: Hilltop Pubications, Ltd., 51-54.

Thompson, C., B., and Walker, B., L., 1998, Basics of research (Part 12): qualitative research, **Air Medical Journal**, 17 (2), 65-70.

Tindall, C., 1994, Issues of evaluation, in Bannister, P., Burman, E., Parker, I., Taylor, M., and Tindall, C., (eds), **Qualitative Methods in Psychology: A Researchers Guide**. Buckingham: Open University Press, 142-159.

Todd, S., 2001, Self-concept: a tourism application, **Journal of Consumer Behaviour**, 1 (2), 184-196.

Tomkovich, C, Yelkur, R., Christians, L., 2001, The USA's biggest marketing event keeps getting bigger: an in depth look at Super Bowl advertising in the 1990's, **Journal of Marketing Communications**, 7, 89-108.

Tooke, N., and Baker, M., 1996, Seeing is believing: the effect of film on visitor numbers to screened locations, **Tourism Management**, 17 (2), 87- 94.

Tooman, A., L., 1997, Applications of the lifecycle model to tourism, **Annals of Tourism Research**, 24 (1), 214-234.

Tourism industry vulnerable, **The Barbados Advocate**, May 30, 2006.

Tourism is Boss, **Nation News,** May 7, 2006. [Online], Available: http://bararchive.bits.baseview.com/archive_detail.php?archiveFile=./p ubfiles/bar/archive/2006/May/07/LocalNews/19317.xml&start=0&nu mPer=20&keyword=Tourism+is+Boss%2C&sectionSearch=&beginda te=1%2F1%2F1994&enddate=12%2F31%2F2008&authorSearch=&I ncludeStories=1&pubsection=&page=&IncludePages=1&IncludeImag es=1&mode=allwords&archive_pubname=Daily+Nation%0A%09%0 9%09

Travers. M., 2001, **Qualitative Research through Case Studies**. London: Sage.

Tribe, J., 2001, Research paradigms and the tourism curriculum, **Journal of Travel Research**, 39, 442-448.

Turco, D., M., Swart, K., Bob, U., Moodley, V., 2003, Socio-economic impacts of sport tourism in the Durban Unicity, South Africa, **Journal of Sport Tourism,** 8 (4), 223-239

Turner, L., J., 2004, The impact of pre-commercial break announcements on audience identification of official Olympic sponsors: a case study, **Journal of Marketing Communications**, 10, 255-265.

Turner, P., 2005, Identification of place emerging from the telecast of hallmark sporting events into Melbourne. [Online], Available: http://,www.parks-leisure.com.au/plasic/sport/keynotePapers/monday/PaulTurner_IDP.pd f#search='hallmark%20events%20melbourne, accessed October 28, 2005.

Twynam, G., D., and Johnston, M., 2004, Changes in host community reactions to a special sporting event, **Current issues in Tourism**, 7 (3), 242-261

Um, S. And Crompton, J., 1990, Attitude Determinants in Tourism Destination Choice, **Annals of Tourism Research**, 17 (3), 432-448.

Um., S., and Crompton, J., L., 1992, The roles of perceived inhibitors and facilitators in pleasure travel destination decisions, **Journal of Travel Research**, (Winter) 1992, 18-25.

Urry, J., 1995, **Consuming Places**. London: Taylor & Francis.

Van der Veen, R., 2006, Analysis of the implementation of celebrity endorsement as a destination marketing instrument. **Conference Proceedings**, The International Conference on the Impact of Movies and Television on Tourism, September 7- 9, 2006, Hong Kong, China, 18-30.

Vanegas, M., and Croes, R., 2003, Growth, development and tourism in a small economy: Evidence from Aruba, **International Journal of Tourism Research,** 5, 315-330.

Veal, A., J., 1997, **Research Methods for Leisure and Tourism: A Practical Guide** (2nd ed.). London: Pearson Education Limited.

Waitt, G., 2003, The social impacts of the Sydney Olympics, **Annals of Tourism Research**, 30 (1), 194-215.

Walle, A., H., 1997, Quantitative versus qualitative tourism research, **Annals of Tourism Research,** 24 (3), 524-536.

Wann, D., L., and Branscombe, N., 1993. Sport fans: Measuring degree of identification with their team, **International Journal of Sport Psychology**, 24, 1-17.

Wann, D.L., McGeorge, K.K., Dolan, T.J., and Allison, J.,A., 1994, Relationships between spectator identification and spectators' perceptions of influence, spectators' emotions, and competition outcome, **Journal of Sport and Exercise Psychology,** 16, 347-364.

Watts, D., 2006, Island sticks to high ground in quality market, **The Times London** (UK), January 7, 2.

Weed, M., and Bull, C., 2004, **Sports Tourism: Participants, Policy and Providers.** Oxford: Elseviser Butterworth-Heinemann.

Wells, W., D, and Prensky, D., 1996, **Consumer Behaviour.** New York: John Wiley & Sons, Inc.

Westerbeek, H.M., Turner, P., and Ingerson, L., 2002, Key success factors in bidding for hallmark sporting events, **International Marketing Review**, 19 (3), 303-322.

White, C., J., 2004, Destination image: to see or not to see?, **International Journal of Contemporary Hospitality Management**, 16 (5), 309-314.

Whitson, D., and Horne, J., 2006, Underestimated cost and overestimated benefits? Comparing the outcomes of sports mega events in Canada and Japan, in Horne, J., and Manzenreiter, W, (eds), **Sports Mega-Events: Social Scientists Analyses of a Global Phenomenon:** Oxford: Blackwell Publishing, 74-89.

Wickens, E., 1999, **Tourists' Voices. A Sociological Analysis of Tourists' Experiences in Chalkidiki, Northern Greece,** PhD thesis Oxford Brooks University. Unpublished.

Wickens, E., 2002, The Sacred and the Profane, **Annals of Tourism Researchers**, 29 (3), 834-851.

Wilkinson, P, 1989, Strategies for tourism in island microstates, **Annals of Tourism Research,** 16, 153-177.

Williams, A., 2006, Tourism and hospitality marketing: fantasy, feeling and fun, **International Journal of Contemporary Hospitality Management,** 18 (6), 482-495.

Wilmshurst, J., and McKay, A., 1999, **Fundamentals of Advertising** (2nd Ed.). New York: Butterworth-Heinemann.

Wilson, D, 1996, Glimpses of Caribbean tourism and the question of sustainability in Barbados and St. Lucia, in Bruguglio, L., Butler, R., Harrison, D and Filho, W., I., (eds), **Sustainable Tourism in Islands and Small States**. London: Cassell, 75-102.

Wing, P., 1995, Development and marketing of international tourism in small island states, in Conlin, M., V., and Baum, T., **Island Tourism: Management Principles and Practice.** New York: John Wiley and Sons, 95-103.

Witt, S., F., and Moutinho, 1989, **Tourism Marketing and Management Handbook** (2nd ed). New York: Prentice Hall.

Wood, R., C., 1999, Traditional and alternative responses to philosophies, in Brotherton, B., (ed.), **The Handbook of Contemporary Hospitality Management Research**. London: John Wiley and Sons, 3-8.

Woodfin, B., 1996, **An Examination of the Interface Between Sports Events and Tourism: the 1996 European Football Championship.** Masters Dissertation, University of Surrey. Unpublished.

Woodside, A., G., and Lysonski, S., 1989, A general model of travel destination choice, **Journal of Travel Research**, 27 (Spring), 8-14.

World Golf Championship, 2006 [Online], Available: www.worldgolfchampionship.com/tournaments/history/r169, accessed 20 March, 2006

World Class Society by 2025, says Arthur, 2005, **Nation News**, December 27, 2005, 1.

Yearwood, T., 2006, Barbados rolls out legacy vision, **Nation News**, May 30, 2006,

Yin, R., K., 1994, **Case Study Research** (2nd ed). London: Sage.